20-Minute

Learning

Connection

by Douglas B. Reeves, Ph.D.

Simon & Schuster
New York - London - Singapore - Sydney - Toronto

Kaplan Publishing
Published by Simon & Schuster, Inc.
1230 Avenue of the Americas
New York, NY 10020

For bulk sales to schools, colleges, and universities, please contact:
Order Department, Simon & Schuster, Inc.,
100 Front Street, Riverside, NJ 08075
Phone: (800) 223-2336 Fax: (800) 943-9831.

Kaplan® is a registered trademark of Kaplan, Inc.

Designed by Richard Oriolo

Manufactured in the United States of America

September 2001
10 9 8 7 6 5 4 3 2 1

Library of Congress Cataloging-in Publication-Data

ISBN: 0-7432-1176-6
ISSN:

Contents

Acknowledgements

In my discipline of statistics, we learn about *a priori* and *a posteriori* probabilities. There is a lesson in such study. My *a priori* obligations include a debt of thanks to the grandfather I never knew, Sherman Vester Reeves, but whose 1906 teaching license I found in my father's office. Teachers in Green Forest, Arkansas at the dawn of the 20th century had their test scores on their teaching licenses. If one were to search for the genesis of high academic standards, the search might profitably begin in Carroll County. My grandmother, Laura Anderson Johnson, was a teacher and superintendent of schools. My mother, Julie Reeves, taught as a volunteer for decades, with her only compensation being the love and admiration of her students. My father, J.B. Reeves, devoted his last years of his life to the professorate, but those who knew him would argue that from his time as a field artilleryman in World War II until his last breath, he was a teacher to generations.

My *a posteriori* obligations are to my children, whose enthusiasm, love, and kind words are the lights of my life. Having said those nice things, I offer this plea: If you see four children laughing uproariously in the education section of your local bookstore as they point at this book, their names are Brooks, Alexander, Julia, and James. Please tell them to behave themselves and return to the self-improvement aisle where they belong.

Between the past and future lies the present, in which I wrote this volume. Maureen McMahon of Simon & Schuster is walking evidence of Stephen King's maxim that, "to write is human; to edit, divine." Rudy Robles provided encyclopedic knowledge of state standards and synthesized his knowledge in a manner so clear and concise that he will never find employment in Washington, D.C. Lori Duggan Gold provided a steady stream of connections to reporters and policy analysts who helped me distinguish the rhetorical chaff from the intellectual wheat. Abby Remer's creative and thoughtful voice preserved an emphasis on art, music, beauty, and enjoyment in a world in which standards are stereotyped as sterile and dull.

Special thanks are due to the hundreds of parents, teachers, and school leaders who took the time to participate in focus groups and personal interviews as part of my research for this book. I am particularly indebted to Charles Sodergren, a retired principal and teacher, whose extensive comments and perspectives as a parent, grandparent, and career educator were very helpful.

For reassurance at just the right time, challenge when I needed it, and love when I least deserved it, I am always indebted to Shelley Sackett. This mother, lawyer, teacher, and wonderful spouse makes books worth writing and life worth living.

dr
Swampscott, Massachusetts

How to Get the Most Out of This Book

Here is the most important test question you will ever have:

A parent's best strategy to promote school success is to:

a) *Terrorize* children by threatening them with failure and loss of promotion to the next grade.

b) *Humiliate* children by comparing them to other kids with better scores.

c) *Exhaust* children by engaging in frantic last-minute test preparation.

d) *Build, nurture, and empower* children by giving them the skills to be confident and capable learners.

If the last choice appeals to you more than the first three alternatives, then this book is written for you. You will learn not only how to help your child meet academic standards and succeed on tests, but more importantly, you will learn how to help your child become a confident, capable, and empowered learner.

a busy parent

How Can You Make a Difference in Just 20 Minutes a Day?

Although we have not met, I believe I have a good idea of who you are and why you selected this book. You are a busy parent. Whether you work at home, at an office, or on the road, you manage multiple priorities and face many demands on your time. You want to be more involved in your children's education, but some days it seems as if the time required by your other responsibilities leaves little time for a focus on your child's schoolwork. You read the report cards and newsletters and often look at your child's schoolwork, some of which may be on your refrigerator door. You attend parent meetings and school events whenever you can. You read with your child, though not as much as you did during the preschool years. You have heard about academic standards and know that some of the tests required by the state and school district are very important, and you have a nagging feeling that your child should be better prepared. But at the end of a long day, you really don't feel like adding the role of substitute teacher to your long and growing list of duties. Am I getting close to your reality?

Practical Advice for Busy Parents

Your busy lifestyle is the norm, not the exception. Less than a third of children attending school today come from a home of the 1950s' television stereotype with a stay-at-home mother whose principal role is the management of family and nurturing of children. Far more typical is a case in which both parents are working outside the home or there is only one parent in the household, and that person must work to support the family. Even the parents who have chosen to stay at home and make the raising of children their primary goal have a far different routine than Donna Reed and her television counterparts. The caricature of the stay-at-home parent has given way to parents who are active in political, cultural, and social causes and for whom school activities are one of many other pursuits. The fact that these parents earn no money outside the home does not indicate that they are not working. These parents are subject to the same exhaustion, burn-out, and frustration as parents who rise at 5:30 every morning, get children ready for school, work a full day and more, and return home in the evening to potentially overwhelming demands for help from their children.

Here is the good news: If you can devote 20 minutes each day to helping your children succeed in school, you can make a profound difference in the intellectual development and emotional growth of your child. If you like the ideas put forth here, you may find that the amount of time you spend building confident, capable, and empowered children will be worth more than 20 minutes a day. But make no mistake: Twenty minutes a day, focused on the right questions and the most effective activities, can make a huge difference in the lives of your children and their success in school. We are not talking about aimless discussions and unproductive questions such as the exchange known to every parent:

"What did you do in school today?"
"Nothing."

Rather, we offer practical advice for kids and parents. Throughout this book you will find checklists, activities, even letters to school officials that have been written for you. While no one, least of all authors, can take the place of parents, we can save you some time and make your role in supporting school success somewhat less stressful and time consuming.

The path to student success is not without some challenges. Therefore, we will address the requirements for making some reasonable trade-offs and minor changes in family routine. Fair warning: This will involve a little less television and a little more reading. It will involve moving a few chairs and creating the space and time for an effective home learning environment. But our goal is joyful learning, not joyless boot camp. Even as an exceptionally busy parent, you can make 20 minutes into a powerful learning experience if you will commit to three principles:

First, be yourself. Find activities that you genuinely enjoy and with which you can model the creative energy that comes from intellectual engagement with your child. This book contains a wonderful variety of activities that directly support essential knowledge and skills for your child. Although the activities are arranged in the same order as the state standards, you need not go through them in that sequence. Find activities that are engaging, exciting, interesting, and fun for both you and your child.

The second principle that will make your 20 minutes most valuable is that you are supportive. Remember the last time you learned a new skill? Perhaps it was a computer program, a foreign language, or a musical instrument. No matter how talented and brilliant you are, learning new things takes some time and patience. No matter how motivated you are, learning requires some perseverance and emotional resilience. Some of the academic requirements for children in school today are as challenging for them as they were for you when you were struggling with and eventually acquiring complex skills. If you can recall the need for patience, understanding, and clarity during your own difficult learning experiences, then assume that those needs apply in exponentially large proportions for your child. An important part of your support is the clarity of your expectations. Two of the most important intellectual skills you will build with your child are reflection and self-evaluation. You will build those skills by regularly asking your child to revise and improve work, whether it is a letter to a relative or a recipe for dinner. Performing these activities will be most valuable if you encourage your child to take a moment to reflect and ask, "What did I learn and how can I do this better next time?"

Third, it is important that you are consistent. Find a regular time, perhaps immediately before or after your evening meal, for your 20-Minute Learning Connection. During this time, the television is off and the telephone answering machine is on. You are giving your children the gift that they need, indeed crave, more than anything else in the world: your undivided attention. The focus that you provide during these 20-minute activities will model the concentration and diligence that you associate with learning.

What Are Standards and Will They Last?

Academic standards have been the single most important movement in education in the last fifty years. Standards—simple statements of what students should know and be able to do—will continue long after every other contemporary educational fad has expired. While teachers and parents are weary of the "flavor of the month" educational reforms that come and go with the phases of the moon, standards have two qualities that guarantee their success: fairness and effectiveness.

Because so many educational movements have come and gone, it is reasonable to wonder whether standards will follow "new math" into oblivion. The enduring nature of standards rests with the fact that standards are the key to fairness, and fairness is a value that is timeless. Lots of trends come and go in education, but the simple requirement—that teachers, students, and parents should understand what students are expected to know and be able to do—is an enduring element of education both in the U.S. and abroad. Every state, and virtually every industrialized nation in the world, has some form of academic standards. The actual content of the standards varies, with some sets of standards emphasizing certain academic areas more than others. But the central idea of standards is consistent from Peoria to Paris, from Florida to Florence, from Los Angeles to London: School should not be an impenetrable mystery, and students have a right to know what is expected of them. Fairness will not go out of style.

Rather than exposing children to a demoralizing environment in which lucky students understand what makes the teacher happy and the unlucky just "don't get it," standards-based schools offer a clear set of expectations. With standards, students, teachers, and parents have the opportunity to know and understand what is expected of every student. Children have an innate sense of fairness. They understand that clarity is better than ambiguity and that consistency is superior to uncertainty.

The second essential quality of standards is that they are effective. When they are properly implemented, school standards have an impact on test designers, curriculum creators, teachers, and school leaders, as well as students. Far from transforming schools into joyless boot camps, effective school leaders use academic standards to make connections to the arts, extracurricular activities, and every other element of school life.

Thus standards are related not only to academic success but also to the emotional and intellectual welfare of children. Our desire is to help build confident, capable, and empowered learners. This means much more than drilling students in math and spelling facts (though that is still not a bad idea), and more than asking children to read aloud after dinner (though that is a wonderful family practice). Children become confident, capable, and empowered not only when they know the right answer on a test, but when they have the emotional resilience to persist in learning difficult concepts and when they persevere in the face of challenging, ambiguous, or seemingly impossible test items. Real student empowerment rests not in the futile effort to memorize the answer to every conceivable test question, but on the realistic prospect of developing strategies that can be used on every test in school, in college, and in the world of work and life beyond school.

empowered learners

Connections: Music, Art, Physical Education, and More

Although this book focuses on the most commonly tested academic standards—mathematics, language arts, social studies, and science—it is important to note that other areas of the school curriculum remain vitally important for your child's intellectual growth and development. Evidence from a number of research studies is consistent: Students who participate in the arts, physical education, and extracurricular activities consistently demonstrate superior academic and social skills. Thus, our focus on academic standards is not intended to diminish other athletic, artistic, and extracurricular activities that enrich the lives of children. In fact, many of the activities in this book combine academic and artistic, or academic and athletic skills.

Stress and Anxiety

Perhaps the most important message for parents is this: Stress and anxiety are communicable diseases. Children are not born with stress about school, homework, and tests; they *learn* that debilitating stress and anxiety are a part of school. Perhaps these destructive lessons are learned from schoolmates and teachers, but it is far more likely that such lessons are learned at home. No parent intentionally creates anxiety and stress for a child, but our conversations about school—particularly our discussions of tests—can have such an effect. This is very likely a reflection of the parents' own attitude toward school and testing. Take a few minutes to think about your own experiences and the stress and anxiety you experienced as a student. Most parents can objectively recognize that their school experiences had some good and bad elements. We are far more likely, however, to recall and transmit the parts of school that had the strongest emotional impact, and strong emotional impact in school is quite likely to be negative. The embarrassment over a failed exam, the humiliation as other students laughed, the feeling of despair and rejection when a teacher expressed disappointment—these memories linger far more than a hundred "smiley faces" that we routinely received on schoolwork. Thus, it is the parent, and no one but the parent, who adds balance and clarity to the school experience. The two essential ways in which effective parents add this balance include constructive and accurate discussions about school and the creation of learning opportunities that occur outside of school. The activities in this book are designed to support schoolwork and they will also develop students who are confident and capable. These activities have value not only because they are related to educational standards, but also because they will help to create a learning environment in your home. They will help you model the love of learning that every child must have and which every parent can nurture.

only a parent

The Most Important Teacher: You

The enormity of the task ahead can be daunting. After all, a parent might ask, "Shouldn't schools be doing this?" It's a fair question. In some cases, the schools can and should do more. But there is one thing that even the best schools with unlimited resources and brilliant teachers cannot do: They cannot be parents. Parents are the most important teachers any child can ever have. This doesn't mean that parents must be experts in every subject or masters of teaching techniques. But only a parent can give a child the ability to say words such as:

"I know that my mom and dad are proud of me."

"I mess up sometimes, but it's okay, because I know I can learn from my mistakes."

"I didn't do as well as I wanted to, but I know how to get better next time."

Only a parent can provide the emotional security and strength of character that build a child who is confident, capable, and empowered. Unfortunately, some parents substitute their own academic expertise for emotional resilience. Every time there is the "nuclear-powered science fair project" obviously done by a parent, the emotional consequence is not pride, but the absolute conviction by the child that "I'm not good enough to do this on my own." The activities in this book will show you how to create a learning environment in which you and your child learn together, make mistakes together, laugh together, and maintain a love of learning amidst all the chaos of daily life, as your child develops independence and confidence.

If You Don't Have Time for the Whole Book

A few readers are thinking, "I can't read the whole book—where do I start?" Although every page is here for a purpose, we recognize the limits of time and the need to focus on the essentials. Therefore, if your time is limited and you want the maximum value in the minimum time, we suggest that you focus on three areas. Start with Chapter 2 for the "why" of standards, then proceed to Chapter 5 for the "how" of standards. Then find an activity from the section starting on page 139 that you and your child will enjoy. Finish with a review of the appendices, where you can find additional resources that are directly relevant to your particular needs. Not every reader will be interested in the sections for students with special needs nor will everyone find the chapter on home schooling essential. We include those chapters because they represent significant and growing areas in education.

Learning Activities

At the end of this book you will find a variety of learning activities. You will find that these ideas have value, not only because they are directly related to the academic standards of your state, but also because they help to build the necessary thinking, reasoning, and communication skills your child needs in any school in any state. These activities will help you make family learning time a regular part of your routine.

A Special Note for Parents of Children with Special Needs

More than ten percent of students in school have a disability that influences their success in school. These disabilities range from differences in the way that they process information to profound physical and neurological challenges. These students are protected by a variety of federal and state statutes, the Individuals with Disabilities Education Act (IDEA) being the most significant legislation in this area. Parents of these students are often alarmed when a school official states that academic standards must apply to "all" students, sometimes adding sarcastically, "What is it about the word 'all' you don't understand?" Chapter 9 is devoted entirely to students with special needs. The bottom line, however, is the clear legal mandate that the individual needs of students must be taken into consideration in all matters involving standards, testing, and curriculum. Standards have great merit for schools, but there is danger in linking legitimate educational standards to the "standardization" of policies for students for whom the law clearly requires attention to individual needs.

It has been said that education is the "new civil right." This is true for students with special needs as well as disadvantaged families. The individualization of standards and testing requirements for students with special needs is not merely a nice thing to do; it is a legal requirement. Chapter 9 and the appendices provide sample letters and checklists for parents of students with special needs to ensure that you are empowered to protect the rights of your child and serve as an advocate on his behalf.

What about Changes in Standards and Tests?

Finally, the subject of standards and testing is changing on a daily basis. As this book goes to press, legislatures throughout the nation are being challenged to change tests and reformulate standards. The only thing that is certain is that tests and standards will continue to change. To help you keep up to date on the latest changes in standards and assessment for your state, we have created an Internet website with current information on the latest changes in standards and tests for your state. Just go to www.kaptest.com/crusadeintheclassroom and click on the name of your state for the latest updates on standards and assessment in your area. You will also find links to the state education department for your state where you can find the latest information on policy and procedures for education in your state.

The prospect of changes in standards, however, must not obscure this essential fact: While individual standards and particular testing policies may change, the fundamentals of standards are here to stay. Standards will endure because they are the most fair and effective way to educate children. While change may be a certainty in our world, it is also certain that the educational system will not retreat to the age of mystery in which a "standard" was whatever captured the interest of a teacher and "proficiency" varied from one classroom to another. Fads may come and go, but the imperatives of fairness and effectiveness will never vanish from the educational landscape.

communication

A Dose of Reality

My children are in public schools, including elementary, middle, and high school. My travels to schools throughout the world place me in contact with teachers, school leaders, and parents, hundreds of whom contributed ideas for this book. Each year I speak and listen to more than a hundred audiences, and thus far have worked in 49 states as well as Africa, Asia, and Europe. Whether these conversations take place in the United States or abroad, whether in an economically advantaged setting or a financially depressed area, there are remarkably common themes that I hear from parents, teachers, and school leaders. The number one issue is always communication. Parents want to hear more specific and more frequent information from the school; teachers want to have more immediate feedback from parents. Parents want to be welcomed into the classroom and insist that the individual needs and characteristics of their children be taken into account; educators and school leaders want parents to understand that today's schools are different from the classrooms of three decades ago. Most of all, parents do not wish to guess about the educational needs of their children. They want to know more than a list of subjects accompanied by a list of grades on a report card and demand to know what the expectations are and how their children can improve. This clarity and specificity is the essence of effective educational standards. I am also the beneficiary of a regular dose of blunt advice from Brooks, Alex, Julia, and James, children whose patience, love, and insight into educational matters are an unending source of inspiration and understanding. Thus, the following pages are not theoretical musings, but the result of daily contact with the real world of the reader.

Special Note to Academic and Professional Readers

Some teachers, school leaders, researchers, and professors may read the following pages and ask, "Where are the footnotes?" It is a fair question and it deserves a straight answer. This book is directed to a lay audience. In the interest of clarity, I have not provided the citations and footnotes that would normally accompany every allusion to research and each assertion of fact. For readers interested in my most recent writings directed toward a professional audience where the research is clearly cited, please consult the articles and book chapters that can be downloaded free of charge at www.edaccountability.org and www.makingstandardswork.com.

Chapter 1

Making the 20-Minute Learning Connection Work for You

The Power of 20 Minutes a Day

As important as the role of parent is, many parents have multiple roles, including spouse, worker, employer, neighbor, volunteer, and parent to other children. When asked to find 20 minutes a day for educational activities in an already crowded schedule, an exhausted parent might respond, "I've been up since 5:30 this morning and have four phone calls to make, dinner to cook, and after that comes Cub Scouts and choir practice. And you want me to do more to enrich my child's education? That's the school's responsibility. I'm doing the best I can!"

Both the fatigue and frustration are understandable, and the recommendations we offer to parents are not a retreat to the 1950s or an appeal only to parents with unlimited reserves of time and energy. There is great power in 20 minutes a day. This is not merely a convenient figure taken out of the air, but rather an amount of time that is both validated by research and supported by the practicalities of the busy lives of families. In one study of student achievement, those children who completed 20 minutes a day of independent reading outside of school were sixty percentile points higher than their counterparts who did no such reading. While reading an hour or more a day is wonderful, the greatest gain in achievement occurred from just 20 minutes a day.

What can you do in 20 minutes? This book is full of activities that are directly related to the academic standards of your state. But consider the routines that any family can create in just 20 minutes a day.

In 20 minutes you and your child can . . .

- **Read aloud for fifteen minutes, and then describe what the story or news article was about for another five minutes.**

- **Write a letter to a grandparent, friend, or relative.**

- **Measure the ingredients for dinner.**

- **Explore the factors affecting recent weather patterns and predict tomorrow's weather.**

- **Draft and revise step-by-step instructions for the use of adult-defying devices such as VCRs and electronic games.**

- **Plan an imaginary trip to an exotic location using maps, weather data, and transportation schedules.**

This chapter considers the practical details of creating the place and the time for your 20-Minute Learning Connection. The habits you develop and the time you invest in making a learning connection with your child can fundamentally change the way you talk about school and, more importantly, the way your child thinks about learning. You can move away from conversations that are unproductive and threatening to discussions that are focused on interesting and engaging activities. You can move away from an inspection of the backpack and the dreary march through the daily homework toward learning for the sheer joy of spending time together, developing new skills, and contemplating new ideas. Of course, the 20-Minute Learning Connection does not replace homework any more than it will avoid death and taxes. But these moments will give your child the skills, enthusiasm, and knowledge to make homework and other academic challenges more accessible.

opportunity for reflection

"What Did You Do in School Today?"

Most parents have had the following unproductive conversation:

"What did you do in school today?" Nothin.

"Why did you get that grade?" I dunno.

The antidote to this conversational dead-end is not browbeating the child until, after parental cross-examination, the child confesses some activity during the school day. Rather, we must re-frame the conversation about school. Let us begin by asking different questions. Here are some conversation starters that are quite different from "What did you do in school today?"

"What did you learn in school today?"

"What happened in school today that was scary?"

"What happened today that made you happy?"

"What happened today that made you sad?"

"What happened today that made you feel great?"

By shifting the conversation from a narrative of news events to a focus on the child's own feelings, there is the opportunity for reflection and personal engagement. Without asking these sorts of emotionally relevant questions, parents risk waiting until they read a bad report card or receive an alarming call from school before learning about significant problems.

The Power of Expectations

In a famous series of experiments in the early 1960s, two different groups of teachers were given students who were similar with regard to prior learning and demographic characteristics. One group, however, was described to their teachers as the "smart" group, while the other was described as "slow." A year later, both groups of students were measured on a variety of academic and intelligence tests. Despite the similarity of these two groups, the teachers and their widely varying expectations had an enormous impact on student performance, with the students living up to—and down to—the expectations of their teachers. Parental expectations are even more profound in their influence on student achievement. There is a fine line between parental pressure and expectations, and the difference is not always clear. We all know of the parents who "expect" their child to become a doctor or lawyer, and any professional or educational decision short of the mark leaves the child feeling like a failure in the eyes of the parent. Far more common, however, is the reluctance of parents to articulate clear expectations of academic success. While most parents are quite clear in their expectations of behavior and integrity, the same parents are less clear about the "house rules" regarding reading, homework, and learning.

The older children get, the more ambiguous the academic expectations of parents become. While every kindergartner has a world of potential ahead, the impulse to rate, rank, sort, and label children is in full flower by late elementary school. The child with brilliant potential in first grade has, by the sixth grade, been determined to be someone who "just isn't a reader" or "just isn't very good at math." While many sixth graders can express ambitions to be a jet pilot, opera singer, astronaut, or brain surgeon, parents none too subtly scoff at such ambitions just a few years later. The skepticism is not always obvious, but the message is clear. Even the well-intentioned, "If that's what you want to do, then you will have to do a lot better in school" becomes "You've got to be kidding! You—a brain surgeon? Forget it." This destructive disapproval is a long emotional distance from the cheering parent on the sidelines at a basketball game assuring the twelve-year-old who makes one basket out of fifty, "I know you can do it!"

How do parents express their expectations for student success? Here are some positive practices you may wish to consider. Parents who expect their children to do well in school and in life value learning and model that value, just as parents who expect their children to have integrity and compassion model those values. In order to model a love of learning, parents should consider the following steps toward the creation of learning time and learning space in their home.

learning together

Time and Space for Your 20-Minute Learning Connection

Set aside a "learning time" of 20 minutes every day. Many families devote the time after dinner to this purpose. Among my fondest memories of childhood are the times after dinner when someone would ask a question, and the family would discuss the idea, read about it, and learn something new. These were not extended multi-hour discussions, but they were clearly opportunities to learn that were not related to the school day. The discussions, readings, and questions were the result of a love of learning and a passion for inquiry. There is another critical element to such discussions: They provide adults with an opportunity to take the views of children seriously. A child's day is full of reminders of the impotence of children compared to the power of adults. When a parent or other significant adult takes the time to listen, question, and learn together with a child, there is more than merely the acquisition of new information taking place. There is the development of a sense of value, the ability of children to take themselves seriously, and in time, to expect others to take them seriously as well. The time consistently devoted to learning and exploration should be appropriate to your family's lifestyle and it should be consistent. Many families identify one night a week in which other activities are not allowed to intrude, and they play games, read, discuss, and enjoy one another's company. Other families take just 20 minutes after dinner. Still other families carve out time first thing in the morning before the busy day begins. Whatever time you establish, consistency will be important. It is important that you not allow the ideal to be the enemy of progress. In other words, even if ideally you would like to have a two-hour after-dinner discussion that is free of interruptions and unfettered by the activities of children and parents, such a vision should not stop you from making the best use of 20 minutes any time during the day.

Every home should have some "learning space" that is the family equivalent of a library. This space need not be a room devoted only to learning, for few family homes have libraries or studies. Rather, the learning space is instantly created by the way it is used. Your learning space might be the dinner table, a desk in the basement, or any place set aside that meets three conditions. First, it is relatively free of distractions. This means that when the learning space is being used, the television is turned off and a sibling is not practicing the trombone in the same area. Second, there is abundant light. Third, it is easily accessible. If the table in the kitchen or dining room is to be used as the learning place, then it becomes the learning place as soon as someone sits down and opens a book, begins to write, or otherwise starts learning. If it requires fifteen minutes of clearing and setting up before learning can begin, then it is not sufficiently accessible. The learning place need not be formal or expensive, but it does need to be quiet, well lit, and easy to use.

Parents' Checklist:

❑ Create a "learning space" in your home that is quiet, well lit, and easily accessible.

❑ Identify 20 minutes of "learning time" for your family to stop their other activities and learn together. This might involve reading alone or aloud, asking questions, or investigating a puzzling problem. To start your journey, we have suggested a number of learning activities that are specifically linked to the academic standards of your state. You will find the list of standards and activities starting on page 141.

---

a learning space

Chapter 2

What Are Academic Standards and Why Do We Have Them?

Academic standards give every parent essential information about what children are expected to know and be able to do in school. Parents need not guess or speculate about the idiosyncratic preferences of teachers. More importantly, children need not worry about what it takes to succeed in school. With the proper implementation of academic standards, guesswork is replaced with clarity.

The Importance of Knowing the Rules

Any parent who has observed children playing games in the park or on the playground knows the following scenario well. Children are playing a game and a new child joins the fun. Within minutes, however, it is clear that something is wrong. Cries of "That's not fair!" fill the air. The sounds of playground glee are replaced by tears, anger, and the indignant wail, "I'm never playing this game again!" When the mess is sorted out, there are no villains, no cheaters, no schemers determined to deny the aggrieved party his due. Rather, the tears, anger, and resolution to play no more all stem from ambiguity about the rules. All parties to the dispute thought that they knew how the game was played, and all had strikingly different understandings of what the rules of the game were supposed to be. Our children know that it is impossible to play any game without knowing the rules. Without clear rules, our determined efforts are reduced to random guessing, and the errors that we make do not provide useful feedback to improve our performance, but only greater frustration, more anger, and a river of tears. Whether the game is a seemingly inconsequential contest in the park or a high-stakes test with important consequences for a child's future, it is impossible to play the game without knowing the rules.

Standards: The Rules of the Game

Any discussion of games in the context of education invites cynicism. The careless use of this analogy might indicate that education, standards, and testing are nothing more than trivial games where strategy is elevated above moral, ethical, and educational issues. Nothing could be further from the truth. In fact, there are a number of elements of games that reflect not merely strategic considerations, but fundamental values, such as fairness. Thus, my reference to games in the context of educational standards is designed to force us to confront the fact that, while clarity and fairness are routine requirements in games ranging from the playground to professional sports, the necessity for clarity and fairness applies no less to every important endeavor, including education. While these values may have trivial implications in a game, they are at the very heart of understanding why standards are so essential. Standards provide students with clear, unambiguous statements of what is required of them. In other words, standards are the rules of the game in school.

As I stated before, academic standards are statements of what students should know and be able to do. Although there are, to be sure, numerous examples of standards that are poorly worded, vague, over-reaching, unrealistic, and otherwise unhelpful, we must consider the alternative. Without standards, what would students have? They would be left with the mystery, guesswork, and ambiguity that prevail in the absence of rules.

Whenever I ask grandparents and experienced parents to tell me about the lessons they have learned about effective parenting, I find a theme in their advice. "You have to be consistent," they counsel. "Don't confuse sympathy and understanding with weakness. You have to be clear." For added emphasis, they warn, "You won't always make the right decisions, but children must know that they can count on you, and that requires consistency and dependability." There is wisdom in the words of these elders. Because perfection in parenting is not an option available to most of us, we are left with making the best of our imperfection. One way to reduce the risk of the mistakes that we inevitably make is clarity and consistency. This certainly does not guarantee the popularity or even the rectitude of our decisions about parental discipline, but clarity and consistency certainly will increase the probability that our children perceive us as fair, predictable, and dependable.

In contexts as diverse as child discipline and playground games, the role of standards is clear. Rules are necessary for motivation and fairness. Why is the role of standards so controversial in education? The value of clarity, consistency, and fairness is clear in the context of discipline and games. When the third-grade soccer championship or the sixth-grade music competition is on the line, few people doubt the necessity of standards, for the rules are the guarantor of fairness. Why does a football field always have 100 yards or a chessboard always have sixty-four squares? The answer is obvious: Without such clear and consistent rules, few people would be willing to play the game. Clarity and consistency are essential if people of any age are to be motivated sufficiently to engage in an activity. These standards are necessary in order for contests of any type, from the trivial to the most serious, to be regarded as fair. The fundamental rationale for educational standards is the same: a commitment to fairness.

The Old Way: Grading "On the Curve"

There are some people who are very upset with the standards movement and who have led angry demands for the abandonment of educational standards. They see standards as a device by which schools are rendered joyless boot camps and the needs of children are sacrificed to the needs of corporate employers. We should, therefore, consider where classrooms and schools would be if we had no standards. Recent history (and, unfortunately, many present-day schools) provides the answer. Without standards, we have the bell curve. You know that your child's school does not have a commitment to standards when you overhear the following conversation among children:

"How did you do on that assignment?"

"I didn't get the question right, but I was better than Steve!"

It is untrue that this school lacks standards. The standard is Steve, or any other child to whom another student can be favorably compared. No one knows what is really expected, because no one knows what Steve can do from one day to the next. But they do know this: If they can just beat Steve, then the teacher will have someone else on whom negative attention can be focused. Am I overstating the case? Consider the following authentic conversation from teachers in the schools I routinely visit:

"How do you evaluate students?"

"The best paper gets an A, the worst paper gets an F."

"How do you know what student work is acceptable?"

"I can't really tell you, but I know it when I see it."

Astonishingly, some parents embrace grading on the curve because it appears to foster the competitive spirit. After all, they reason, the cream rises to the top. It's a tough world out there, so my kids must get used to the competition. Ironically, grading on the curve does not produce the superior results and competitive spirit desired by parents. Rather, it creates the worst of both worlds because it discourages the competent student and fosters complacency in the incompetent student. The

"Steve Standard" provides justification to students who produce schoolwork that is incomplete, inaccurate, and disorganized but that is not quite as wretched as Steve's scrawl. With equally bad logic, the "Steve Standard" demoralizes the student who worked exceptionally hard to complete a wonderful assignment, but despite its exemplary quality, it was one footnote shy of the work submitted by Steve. Whether Steve is a wonderful student or a terrible student, the "Steve Standard" represents the shifting standards of grading on the curve. It is an inherently unfair and inaccurate way to evaluate students.

Some parents have a ready rejoinder: "But I don't want my child to be just 'good enough,' I want her to be the best. Only by comparing my child to other children can I be sure that she is meeting high standards." The subtext of this reasoning is the unrelenting counsel of successful business leaders of the past few decades who have insisted that business managers must be graded on the curve. This logic receives reinforcement from the sports world where there can be, after all, only a single champion. Because grading on the curve has proponents in business and athletics, it might be useful to use terminology that more accurately distinguishes a standards-based system from the alternative. Rather than call the competitive system "grading on the curve," we shall label it more accurately: mystery grading.

changing rules

The Worst Evaluation System: Mystery Grading

Imagine two children playing in the park. Lois challenges Robert to a ball game. With pleasure, Robert accepts the challenge, confident that he has played ball games successfully in the past. Lois then takes the ball and runs past an imaginary line and exclaims, "That's one point for me—I'm ahead!" Robert catches on quickly, takes the ball, and runs past the line happily. "You ran the wrong way!" Lois shouts. "That's another point for me—it's two to zero, my favor." Robert starts to pick up the ball, but Lois provides a quick elbow to his solar plexus, takes the ball, and runs past the line. "Three to zero," she says with a smile. Robert is upset, but under control. Confident that he now understands the game a bit better, he delivers a retaliatory blow to Lois and takes the ball, crossing the line with a smile of victory. "Foul!" Lois cries. "That's an automatic point for me—it's four to zero!" Robert is a bright child. How long do you think he will continue to play this game? It is a testimony to Robert's good grace and self-control that he has not been dispatched to the principal's office after having let his aggravation with Lois get the better of him. But despite his chivalry, this much is certain: Robert will not play this game again.

When the awarding of points is a mystery and when the rules of the game appear to shift with the winds, then children will not continue to play the game. When victory involves guessing and no amount of skill or prior information is of any value, then the game becomes an idle pursuit and not a purposeful enterprise.

Is this analogy exaggerated? Ask students why they received the grade they did. Sometimes you will receive a well-reasoned and clear answer. One student might say,

"The requirements of the assignment were this, but I actually did that. Therefore, I failed to meet the requirements and received a low grade. Having received this valuable feedback and recognizing the error of my ways, I shall return to my desk forthwith, revise this assignment, and resubmit it to my teacher."

If your child provides such a response, please return this book for a refund, proceed to the nearest radio station, and host a call-in show for perfect parents with perfect children in perfect schools. For most of us and for our children, grading remains mysterious. Even teachers who take the time to create clear and precise grading systems find that precision is an illusion, far clearer to the designer of the system than to the students who must perform under its mandates.

For the vast majority of students, grading remains a mystery dominated by the largely unknown personal preferences of the teacher. The student is placed in the role of the sorcerer's apprentice, weakly emulating the acts of the master, hoping that some of the magic will rub off. Systematic learning is impossible because teaching comes only from the inscrutable wisdom of the master teacher, and learning is a matter of fortunate insight rather than diligent work. It is no wonder that such a system is discouraging to the student who finds luck more important than skill. There is a better way. We can replace mystery with clarity. Students can replace guesswork with hard work. Parents can replace aimless searching with careful direction. In brief, we can have standards.

The Best Way: Know the Rules Before You Play the Game

The game played by Lois and Robert was unfair. The failure of fairness was not a result of the scheming of Lois, but rather the absence of rules. The fundamental requirement of fairness is the existence of clear and consistent rules—standards, if you will—that let the participants know what conduct is acceptable and what is not. We can only play the game when we know the rules.

This is hardly an alien notion to schools. During the first few hours of the first day of classes in most schools in the country, teachers discuss the importance of behavior, respect, and decorum in the classroom. Teachers do not display elaborate posters on classroom walls that contain the precise words of the Board of Education's disciplinary policy or the state criminal statutes. Rather, each teacher has a single piece of paper labelled "class rules," which lays out in simple and clear language the requirements of conduct for students. "Respect yourself and others," the rules typically begin. "Do not talk while others are speaking." "Raise your hand before speaking." "Be kind and help others." There is a long tradition of identifying the standards of behavior in classrooms with clarity and precision. These same qualities must be the goal of those desiring academic excellence.

clarity

What Standards Mean for Students

While the word "standards" conveys to some parents a threat of failure and an association with difficult academic tests, the actual implications of school standards are quite positive. In a standards-based school, students know what is expected and they routinely receive constructive feedback on how to improve their performance. The typical parent-child conversation after report cards are issued in a school without standards begins with the question, "How did you get that grade?" followed by the plaintive response, "I don't know." With standards, this unproductive conversation is replaced by these confident statements:

"I know what the teacher wants me to do."

"I know when I'm successful and when I am not."

"I know how to get better and I can do so tomorrow."

"I know what it takes to win and I know that I can be a winner."

"I can help someone else and still be a winner—I don't have to beat Steve to be a great student."

real achievement

What Standards Mean for Parents

It is stunning for me to hear some parents bemoan the standards movement as a new educational fad when the requirement for fair and reasonable relationships among teaching, learning, curriculum, and assessment are as old as Socrates. Although our children may think their parents went to school in the Lyceum, we need not recall ancient Greece to consider our own examples of standards. Think of your favorite teacher or coach. Did that person patronize you with constant pats on the head or make your success a matter of mystery and luck? Or did that favorite coach or teacher let you know that whatever else had happened in your life, you would be a success if only you worked hard, followed the rules, and met the standards that the teacher clearly identified? These favorite teachers did not make learning easy, nor did they make learning impossible. Rather, our favorite teachers and coaches made learning challenging, fair, reasonable, and rewarding. This is the essence of standards-based teaching and learning.

Now that they are vividly called to mind, these influential teachers and coaches offer another interesting quality. Your success was not accomplished when you simply defeated another student, but when you met the standard articulated by the coach. Chances are, that standard included not only personal excellence, but also a willingness to help your teammates. While rivalries within teams are natural, the team that is beset by constant competition within the team is seldom able to deal with competition against other teams. In fact, your success was elevated by your willingness to help your colleagues. When you helped other students, you discovered an important truth: Not only did their performance improve, but your understanding of the same subject soared when you had the opportunity to help others master the subject. You found that helping other students was not an entirely altruistic act, but rather was the result of a collaborative process in which you both gave and received valuable lessons.

Academic standards imply a very different environment in school than many parents may have experienced. If your educational experience involved grading on the curve, frantic efforts to please a teacher, and a certain degree of mystery about the nature of your performance, then it is only natural that you might expect your own children to have a similar experience in school. If you have been successful in school and in life, you might initially prefer that your children attend a school that closely matches your own experiences when you were a student. Nevertheless, the case we have made for standards is based not upon personal history or popularity, but upon the fact that standards are fair and effective. Even if a standards-based approach to student achievement is not what you experienced as a child, please give it a chance. Your children will thrive in an environment in which the rules of the game are clear and their performance is rewarded based on real achievement rather than merely on a victory over a classmate.

What Standards Mean for Teachers and Schools

Standards offer clarity, fairness, and effectiveness, so teachers should universally rave about the use of academic standards. After all, if the case for standards is so overwhelming, why would any educational professional object? In fact, the reaction to standards by teachers and school administrators has been varied. Some teachers enthusiastically endorse the idea of standards and emphasize that it is hardly new. "What you call standards," they remark, "is what I have called 'good teaching' for about twenty-five years now."

But many other educators are wary. They have seen a number of educational fads come and go, and they reasonably wonder if this is just one more trend that will evaporate when something more popular comes along. In addition, some teachers resent the fact that standards were oversold when they were first introduced. Some proponents of standards let their enthusiasm surpass their judgment when they gushed, "Standards will make teaching easy!" Of course, nothing makes the difficult and complex job of teaching easy. Most of the objections to standards come from the failure of those who wrote the initial drafts of state standards to express their expectations with precision. Many standards swing from one extreme to the other, either describing curriculum content in excessive detail, or describing expectations of student performance in such broad generalities that teachers are left with little constructive guidance. Some teachers object that the standards are too difficult and too numerous. Considering all the other subjects that traditionally have been in the school curriculum, the additional layers of academic content seem to be too burdensome given the limited amount of time students spend in school. Finally, there are teachers who sincerely object to any outside interference in their classroom. Their rejoinder to standards or other intrusions is, "Just leave me alone and let me teach!" In their judgment, standards easily could become standardization, and such an approach to teaching fails to recognize the unique qualities of each individual student. Only the teacher, they argue, can make the subtle judgments required to identify what is appropriate for each child, and standards designed at the state or school district level fail to take into account the individual needs that are known only to the teacher.

Many parents have heard these arguments and have interpreted them as arguments against all academic standards. Every argument but the last one, however, is actually a persuasive case against poor standards, and the logical response is not the abandonment of standards, but the continuous improvement of them. Those people who make the final argument characterized as, "Just leave me alone and let me teach," will object to any standard. Improvements would not be sufficient, for even the most clear and constructive standard would represent an intrusion into their classroom and their curriculum.

Parents naturally appreciate a teacher who wishes to take into account the individual needs of their children. Moreover, most parents would object to any policy that appears to "standardize" their unique children. A balanced approach to standards might look something like this: The freedom and discretion of teachers are honored, respected, and encouraged, provided that this discretion takes place within a framework. That framework is one of academic excellence and equity in which all students have clear and fair guidelines and expectations. Educators have broad discretion to consider alternative strategies for teaching reading to a student who appears to be slow to catch on to phonics; the teacher does not have the discretion to say, "Considering his difficult upbringing and poor neighborhood, we really can't expect him to learn to read this year." Teachers can be creative and have wide latitude to collaborate with their colleagues to determine the best ways to improve mathematics skills, but they do not have the discretion to say (as I have actually heard a teacher and administrator claim),

"Well, those kids don't need algebra anyway." In a balanced approach to standards, there is neither micromanagement by school administrators, nor aimless anarchy among teachers. Standards need not dictate the day-to-day, minute-to-minute agenda for the classroom, but standards do establish the expectations of what all students should know and be able to do. When teachers have creative supplementary strategies to help students meet those expectations, that creativity is respected and rewarded. When, however, teachers make decisions that take students outside of the framework at the expense of meeting standards, then they have supplanted the needs of the child with the personal preferences of the teacher. That, in a school committed to excellence and equity, is not acceptable.

an effective classroom

What Standards Mean for Daily Life in School

The best way for students and teachers to succeed in school and to meet academic standards is a consistent emphasis on the thinking, reasoning, analysis, communication, and love of learning that characterizes any effective classroom. The frequent claim that the path to meeting standards lies in mindless drills, rather than analysis and thinking, is wrong. In extensive research from organizations as diverse as the Education Trust, the Center for Performance Assessment, and the National Science Foundation, the evidence is clear: Higher test scores on standards-based assessments are more likely to occur when students and teachers engage in critical thinking, extensive analysis, and frequent writing. The appropriate application of academic standards encourages an increase in thinking, reasoning, and communication by students.

To be sure, standards are the cause of some changes in schools, and those changes can be uncomfortable for the critics of standards. There are elementary classes that devote many hours of prime reading time to craft projects and preparation for performances, few of which are related to the improvement of student achievement. Some secondary teachers announce that next quarter will be devoted to current events "rather than standards," as if the possibility of relating contemporary political events to the study of history and government is impossible. There are many traditional projects that consume large chunks of time and the only thing that sustains these activities is their popularity, not their contribution to student learning. What is lost by the establishment of standards? Surely not thinking, reasoning, or even the fun of interactive and engaging activities in the classroom. What must be abandoned or modified, however, are the projects that have persisted year after year based only on the personal preference of the teacher and popularity with students and parents. Perhaps the least attractive feature of the standards movement is that it displaces popularity with effectiveness.

Does this mean that the kids can no longer carve pumpkins in October or dress up like Pilgrims in November? Certainly not. We know that hands-on activities and dramatic reenactments are splendid ways for students to learn. But some of these activities require close reexamination and detailed modification. If pumpkins are to be the theme for a few days, then much more than carving and candy must be the order of the day. There are wonderful classrooms in which students read about pumpkins, write about them, measure them, weigh them, compare them, and explore them. The traditional Thanksgiving drama, in which two students speak and many others look on in silence, can be replaced by an activity in which many students participate in writing the play based on their own reading and research. The speaking parts can be widely shared among all students, and the predominant feature of the activity is student learning rather than parent entertainment.

reasonable preparation

Won't Standards Result in Teaching to the Test?

Some teachers and parents have linked standards and testing to the point that any suggestion that standards are the basis of classroom instruction leads to the allegation that schools are "teaching to the test." It is true that there are examples around the nation in which some misguided administrators have encouraged a regimen of test drills and memorization rather than deep study, analysis, and reflection. It is also true that there are some schools that have curtailed traditional classroom activities and field trips, and a few people have blamed standards as the culprit that turned their schools into grim, academic factories.

The very phrase "teaching to the test" implies something unethical, as if teachers had sneaked into the State Department of Testing, secretly copied the test, and then conducted drills in class in which students memorized the answers by chanting, "Number 1 is C, number 2 is A, number 3 is B…" In fact, what most teachers have done is to use the freely available models of the practice tests to let students look at sample items in order to become more familiar with the format of the test. Moreover, thoughtful teachers also have reviewed their own curriculum and made appropriate revisions. "If my students need to know about graphs and tables for a test in March, and I was not going to address those skills until April, then it would be much more fair to my students if I changed my schedule to give them those skills before they take the test."

The contention that ethical teaching requires that testing must be a mystery must be challenged as absurd and unfair. Can you imagine students in a musical performance sitting down to discover that the music before them is completely unfamiliar? Can you imagine the football coach who refuses to use a football in practice or take students near an actual football field because practicing under such conditions would be "teaching to the test?"

The most appropriate way to discuss the relationship of classroom teaching to the tests students take is not "teaching to the test," but "teaching to the standard." Teachers cannot anticipate every single item on the test, but they can provide students with a fair opportunity to do well on any test. The opportunity for fairness is best provided when students have received curriculum and instruction based on the standards, and when the test designers have used those same standards as the basis for creating the tests. When the context is driving, music, or football, this would be called common sense. When the context is academic performance, it is not only common sense, but also fair and effective.

The Most Important Teacher Your Child Will Ever Have

When I was discussing this book with a teacher and grandparent in a border community where Spanish was the predominant language, she suggested a title for the Spanish-language edition of the book. "There's no doubt about it," she said. "Your title must be *Los Primeros Maestros.*" This is a play on words, indicating that parents are not only the first teachers, but also the most important teachers that children will ever have. Her insight speaks volumes to parents of every culture, because we are all the first and most important teachers for our children.

Parents teach children so many things that they will never learn in school, including integrity, values, and respect for oneself and others. Parents also teach children about their interest in learning. This is not the same as their interest in school. Our children see through the ruse of the parent who berates a child over a poor grade in reading but never picks up a book for pleasure. Our children notice our inconsistency when we exclaim our disappointment in their writing abilities but fail ever to take pen in hand ourselves to write a letter. The most important lessons we teach are those with our actions and values, not our lectures.

Parents' Checklist:

❑ Read the standards appropriate to your child's grade.

❑ Find one activity that you can complete in 20 minutes that will help your child achieve standards.

❑ Talk with your child's teacher about standards. If the teacher's attitude is negative, ask if the problem is the specific wording of the standards, or if the problem is any effort by the state to influence classroom activities. It is important for you to understand the teacher's commitment or aversion to standards.

❑ Find the exact dates of state tests for your child. Mark them on the calendar so that you can limit distractions and interruptions during that week.

❑ Ask your child about standards. "What do you think you have to do this year to be a great student?" Then listen carefully for the response. Standards only have meaning when children understand them. The response you receive will be your guide to future activities and discussions with teachers, school leaders, and your child.

ask your child

Chapter 3

What Tests Tell You—and What They Don't

Tests are part of life. Babies take the Apgar test within moments of birth in the delivery room, and the results of that test can lead to essential and immediate medical intervention for the newborn child. Before formal schooling has begun, children routinely explore the world around them by experimenting with language and behavior. They "test" the world dominated by adults and older children and make instant observations about effective and ineffective strategies to meet their needs. When the young child is the one doing the testing and when the results of the test are immediately used to benefit the child, it is a remarkably effective way to learn about the world. In a few short years, however, the word "test" gains a very different meaning. It is no longer a way of learning and exploring, no longer a mechanism for gaining new knowledge and meeting the child's needs. Tests are soon associated with anxiety, demands for performance, and the prospect of failure. Three-year-old children take admissions tests for preschool and their older siblings are subjected to tests that will determine their acceptance or rejection by special programs in kindergarten. Within the minutes or hours that it takes to administer these tests, the path is set. Perhaps the child will bear the label of "gifted and talented" or "special needs" or, heaven forbid, "normal."

Because the tests purport to have scientific properties, the labels bestowed on children are rarely challenged. The purpose of this chapter is to confront the common acceptance of these labels by providing some background on what tests can and cannot tell parents about their children. Once you know that tests are merely snapshots of knowledge rather than definitive pronouncements about student ability, both you and your child can examine test results for what they are—a momentary record of achievement, not a certain prediction of future failure or success. Whether the test in question affects the labeling of a child, the acceptance into or rejection from a special program, or simply the awarding of a grade on a report card, the way that parents talk with children about tests reflects a philosophy that can be either discouraging or encouraging. Only through a deliberate effort to change the talk between parents and children into learning conversations will we make the transition away from test terror.

conquering anxiety

From Test Terror to Testing for Learning

Parents who have witnessed the transformation of testing from innocent exploration to childhood terror may express their dismay at how much inappropriate pressure is placed on children, not knowing that their own comments have already signaled the parents' anxieties to their children about the importance of tests. There are few more powerful psychological forces than the fear of disappointing a parent. Perhaps you can recall a time in which you would have preferred physical punishment to that look of dissatisfaction from a parent who sent the message, "I am disappointed in you." Few spankings could have been as painful. While no parent ever intends to send debilitating and terrorizing messages to children, we sometimes cannot help it. The stress and anxiety of every examination we have ever taken can subtly and unintentionally become the test terror we transmit to our children.

Constructive Skepticism for Tests

Fortunately, history is not destiny. Parents can fundamentally change their children's perceptions of testing. This cannot be accomplished by casually dismissing tests as unimportant. Our children see through that ruse, knowing that tests are indeed important, but that we are seeking to protect them. As surely as children know if they won or lost the soccer match in the supposedly "fun and scoreless" games that masquerade as noncompetitive exercises, children also know when tests are important, but their parents don't want to talk about them. If we are to liberate our children from test terror, we will do so not with patronizing tales about the irrelevance of tests, but with a philosophy toward testing that can best be described as "constructive skepticism."

Perhaps the best way to understand constructive skepticism for tests is to consider the opposite. Rather than engaging in rational analysis of the test, some students fall prey to analytical paralysis, when the test taker is convinced that failure, inadequacy, and stupidity are the inescapable diagnoses from an unsuccessful test attempt. "After all," these children reason, "either you know it or you don't, and I guess I just don't know it." The results of such analytical paralysis are predictable: anger, fear, and the studied avoidance of test taking opportunities in the future.

Constructive skepticism for tests is strikingly different. The child with constructive skepticism understands that every test is a game. Most of the rules of the game are clear, but the moves of the other side are not always obvious. Therefore, some strategy, some knowledge, and yes, some luck is involved in the successful completion of the game. Supplied with constructive skepticism for tests, children know that their success on a test is not necessarily the mark of genius, but of capable gamesmanship. When confronted with a test question that is unclear and ambiguous, the child with constructive skepticism does not conclude, "I'm a failure and I can't do this." Rather, this empowered test taker says, "I'm as smart as the person who wrote this test, but the right answer isn't very clear. Now I know that "B" is dumb and "D" is impossible, so I guess it's "A" or "C." I'm going to make a smart guess and move on, because this game is just about over..."

Constructive skepticism does not involve anger or the presumption of failure as the inescapable result when the right answer is not immediately clear. Rather, constructive skepticism provides students with the emotional resilience to persist even in the face of ambiguity and uncertainty. It is not just the intellectual ability to narrow the range of possible answers to a test question; it is the emotional ability to remain engaged in the game of test taking long after other students have given up on that test question and perhaps on the entire test. When students feel a sense of failure, they tend to generalize it: "I'm not only a failure on the soccer team; I can't do *anything* right! I can't read, I can't do math, and I can't kick the darn ball into the darn goal..." By contrast, the child with healthy skepticism for the test at hand possesses the emotional resilience to say, "Okay, so I can't remember what a rhombus is. Big deal. This question is asking about sides of a polygon, so that means that the answer has to have sides. So it can't be a circle and it can't be an ellipse—it must be either a trapezoid or a rhombus. I'll guess that it's a rhombus and move on to the next question."

At this point, the student with constructive skepticism is still in the game, engaged in the next question, convinced that thinking, reasoning, and skill are the keys to success. The student without this sort of resilience has given up, with pencil held limply in hand while the head rests on the desk waiting for the torture of this test to end. Whatever tests the future holds for your child, among the many valuable gifts you can provide is the gift of resilience—the ability for your child to remain engaged in a test or other difficult challenge, even when the questions are ambiguous and the answers are elusive.

Some readers may be uncomfortable referring to tests as games, especially when discussing tests with their children. "This is serious," they reason, "and references to gamesmanship trivialize tests, school, and education in general." This is a legitimate concern and it deserves a serious answer. The references to games in this chapter have three purposes, none of which trivializes tests or education. First, references to games help children recall experiences that have been successful and enjoyable. This is a more constructive basis for a conversation between parents and children than a stern lecture about the life-changing importance of a test and the associated risk of parental disappointment should the child not score sufficiently well. Feelings of trust, confidence, competence, and fun are the foundations of happy children and successful students, and parents do better when they nurture those feelings. Second, references to games involve strategy that both children and parents understand. Because tests are never perfect and answers are not always free of ambiguity, knowledge alone is insufficient. Strategy—thinking about the point of view of the test writer, eliminating wrong answers, and dealing with the uncertainty and ambiguity present in every test—is not only a great thinking skill for children, it is also the key to emotional resilience. Strategy—gamesmanship, if you will—is the bridge from "I don't know the answer so

I must be stupid" to "The right answer may not be obvious, but if I work on this I think I can figure it out." Third, I have observed that parents (with the exception of the stereotype of the abusive "Little League Dad") usually approach the performance of their children in games in a constructive and encouraging manner that builds confidence, success, and emotional resilience. When children play games, parents applaud, encourage, laugh, and console—all qualities sadly lacking in many discussions between parents and children when the subject is testing, homework, and school. In the final analysis, the references in this book to games have one central theme: Our children are more than the sum of their test scores, and the role of parents is not to cram every conceivable answer into the heads of their children, but to build healthy, happy, confident, capable, and empowered kids who know that they are loved and accepted by their parents.

emotional resilience

Tests Are Important, But . . .

It is national sport to ridicule school tests. After all, many people believe it is common knowledge that children are over-tested, that tests are irrelevant, that tests are political tools misused by critics of public education, and that tests fail to tell the complete and accurate story of student achievement. While each of these allegations may contain an element of truth, a fundamental fact remains: tests are an important and continuing part of life both during the early years of school and continuing into college, technical education, and the world of work. Moreover, students who have the intellectual and emotional ability to perform well on tests will find more open doors for educational and professional success. No doubt about it: Tests are important.

Success in test taking involves not only knowing the material, but also understanding the emotional foundations for successful test performance. Many readers can recall an instance in which they were intellectually prepared for a test and, as soon as the test administrator uttered the words "you may begin," their minds went blank. Terror replaced confidence and mystery replaced the clear organization of facts and concepts that the student possessed only moments before the test began. To make matters worse, we knew of students who had scarcely prepared for the same test, but who appeared to breeze through the examination. Our recollections of the power of panic make a profound case in favor of recognizing the importance of emotions in test success.

The Power of Emotions

encouragement

While the prevalence of emotions over intellect may be perplexing to students, it is great news for parents. Although we may not always be able to provide the right answer on math or geography homework, every parent can provide extraordinarily powerful support for the emotional resilience and psychological endurance of their children. The power of emotions in test preparation is an essential element of parent support. This is why "Let me help you with your homework" is far less powerful than "You're a smart kid and I believe in you; I *know* that you can do this!" As parents, we want to help our children. It is only natural. It hurts to see them struggle. It would be instructive, however, to recall the first steps of our toddler. The parent cannot walk for the child, but can only hold out loving arms and offer earnest encouragement. "Come on, *you can do it!*" And they do. Our praise is genuine, enthusiastic, and encouraging. That praise, confidence, and encouragement set a standard in the minds of our children that is a difficult bar to reach in later years. "You can do it!" gives way to "Turn off the darn television and finish your homework!" "I believe in you" is replaced by "I just don't understand how you messed this up so badly." The emotional connection of parent and child has been replaced with one more layer of anxiety and stress.

Building Confident, Capable, and Empowered Children

Although few children enjoy tests, most children love games. They particularly enjoy games they can win. Think about it: Children's games, from Crazy Eights to Monopoly to a host of board and card games are typically a combination of knowledge, skill, strategy, and luck. Clever game designers know that part of maintaining the interest of children is the reasonable prospect of success. Parents help to build confident, capable, and empowered children every time they participate in an activity in which it is possible for children to succeed. This does not mean that parents deliberately lose and children win every time. Such games, children quickly learn, are boring and unrewarding. They know that the rewards that come too easily have little value. Part of building emotional resilience and persistence in the face of difficulty is the habit of trying again after a failure, full of confidence that success is a function of endurance, skill, and a little luck.

My youngest child, James, is on a basketball team. A ten-foot basketball hoop appears to be an insurmountable goal for a group of six- and seven-year-olds. During practice, the balls fly everywhere, it seems, but into the net. But once in a while—perhaps once every five to ten minutes—there is a "swish" of the ball through the net that keeps the enthusiasm of everyone in the room at a high level. There is a lesson here: We do not build capable, confident, and empowered children through the contrivance of easy tasks and low expectations. Whether the challenge is the ten-foot basket or two-digit subtraction, the prospect of success is what keeps the players engaged. They do not need the certainty of success every time, but they need to know precisely what the rules of the game are so that, when success comes, the delicious moment of victory can be savored for a moment before the players return to the game.

The game scenario has practical applications for how parents interact with children about homework and tests. Many parents tend to one of two extremes, in which one parent demands, "Go to your room and don't come out until all the homework is done!" and another parent hovers over the nervous student, correcting every error and focusing exclusively on every misstep. Can you imagine the same parents exploding with disappointment at every missed basket? Can you imagine these parents saying, after the ball goes into the basket, "Well, he made the shot, but he's no Michael Jordan!" On the contrary, these parents wait and wait, offering encouragement and perhaps a few sympathetic groans, and then they roar with approval and applause when a child—any child—makes a basket. When was the last time we roared with approval and applause for a homework assignment well done, a test question answered correctly, or a project completed on time? In some arenas, parental feedback is immediate, positive, and relevant to success. In other cases, parental feedback is infrequent, negative, and related to vague expectations of perfection that seem unreachable by the student.

The Confusion of Self-Esteem and Self-Confidence

Much has been written and said about self-esteem, with most of these words substituting rhetoric for evidence. The facts are clear: Self-esteem is important. When students, or for that matter, adults, feel a sense of self-worth, they tend to perform at higher levels. The issue is not whether self-esteem is important, but how this elusive quality is best achieved. Some parents believe that we build self-esteem through challenge and rigor, in the way that the movie stereotype of the Marine drill sergeants "build men" in boot camp through a mix of ridicule, shouting, and demands. Other parents, and an astonishing number of teachers, believe that we build self-esteem through constant affirmation of children, including reassurances that children are always great, wonderful, and terrific even when the children know that they are not always great, wonderful, and terrific. Both extremes are wrong. Parents must balance affirmation with honesty. We cannot tell a child that she made the basket when her own observation is to the contrary. It is equally unwise to tell a child that his performance is inadequate when the child just scored a point for his team.

Let us move the context from the playground to schoolwork. We should not tell the child that her paper is wonderful when she knows and we know that it is careless and inaccurate. We should not tell the child of her shortcomings because her paragraph of sixth-grade work falls short of Hemingway. Honesty, rather than excessively high or low expectations, best serves children. We build self-esteem with clear, honest feedback, not with impossible challenges or improbable reassurances. "This was great and I'm really proud of you!" is as appropriate as "You are really getting good at this! With a little more work you're going to be even better. I know you can do it!"

While the distinction may appear subtle, the difference between self-esteem and self-efficacy is an important one. Esteem alone is not sufficient. Humans must not only feel a sense of worth, but they must also have the bone-deep conviction that their efforts make a difference. In other words, their self-esteem is the result of their genuine worth and effort, not merely awarded by someone out of sympathy for an incompetent child. Anyone who has listened attentively to the conversations of children about the important adults in their lives knows that children have a profound and insightful understanding of the difference between sympathy and confidence. The patronizing compliments of adults can be withdrawn, but the capacity that children have to make a difference in their own lives is enduring. Thus, it is not merely esteem that our children must develop and maintain, but efficacy. In the words of Dr. Jeff Howard, president of the Efficacy Institute, "Smart is something you get, not just something you are." When students believe that they have the capacity for improvement, they are far more resilient and persistent than when they depend on another person for compliments, assurances, and affirmation.

The Limits of Tests

As important as tests are, it is essential that parents and children understand what tests tell us and what they don't. The best any test can do is to report the performance of a student on a particular set of questions on a particular day. Just as a blood pressure test does not represent a complete physical and just as blood pressure is subject to change from one reading to the next, so also test results do not represent a complete analysis of student ability, and those results can change radically depending on testing conditions and student preparation.

The most meaningful tests report not only a score, but also how to get better. This is one of the most significant advantages of student self-evaluation. Rather than submitting work to an all-knowing teacher who then awards a grade, the student who engages in self-evaluation must understand the difference between acceptable and unacceptable work. Rather than communicating only a letter or numerical grade, the most effective tests challenge the complacent student and encourage the discouraged child. On letter-graded tests, the complacent student might receive an A or a B and receive the message, "I'm doing pretty well, so there isn't much else to learn." The discouraged student might receive a low grade and receive the message, "That's as well as I can do, so I guess I'm just not a very good student." The best tests not only evaluate, but educate students. These tests communicate to parents about the performance of their children and also provide specific information about what students know and where they need to improve. Supplied with these insights, parents can help their children improve. Of course, these ideal tests are rare in most schools. Parents receive a score, and that's it. Rather than attempt to draw conclusions from a score alone, parents need to be advocates for tests that educate. In addition, parents must be careful to avoid "over-interpreting" a test score or grade.

Consider the case of the child who brings home a "C" on a test. One parent's frame of reference might be that a C is acceptable, if not great work, so perhaps it's best not to make a big deal out of it, and another parent might exclaim, "You obviously didn't do your best work on this test—what went wrong?" Both conclusions are unhelpful and probably inaccurate. The focus of the parent-child conversation should not be on the evaluation, but rather on the learning that did and did not take place. Rather than begin the conversation with evaluative statements, we should reframe every discussion as a learning conversation. It is always wise to begin with something positive, such as, "You did a great job on number 17—I didn't know you knew all of that! Tell me more about it." Then we must do what is one of the most essential, and rare, activities of parents: We must listen. Parents and teachers routinely engage in the fantasy that because they are talking, children are learning. While there is value to talk from parents and teachers, conversations are far more constructive when they are informed by the child's point of view. Thus, we begin with what the child does know and the places on the test where the performance was satisfactory. After giving the child an opportunity to elaborate on the good parts of his performance, we can then ask, "What do you wish you had done differently on this test?" This opens the door to a discussion of the questions that were blank or answered incorrectly. You might learn that the child ran out of time. You might learn that the child had failed to study. You might learn that the child does not understand fundamental concepts necessary to performance on this test. But my experience suggests that it is far more likely that you will learn that the child knew the material, but failed to understand the instructions. You might learn, for example, that the child was so confident that the haste to display her knowledge got in the way of taking time to read the instructions. You might also learn that the instructions were unclear and that many reasonable test takers, including you, might have had the same misunderstanding as your child. And it is possible that you will learn that the response was correct after all and that the scoring of the test was wrong. None of these learning conversations will occur, however, if we respond to the grade on the test rather than the content of the test.

focus on learning

Report Cards and Learning Conversations

Just as learning conversations should prevail in our discussions of tests and homework, so should the communication between parent and child about report cards focus on learning rather than evaluation. This is difficult. As I write these words, I reflect on the times I have reacted in haste to report cards, with joy at the "A" and with disappointment at lower grades, and in neither case conducting a learning conversation with my children. Taking a deliberate break from our natural reactions toward evaluation rather than education requires intellectual and emotional discipline, and those qualities can be in short supply when any parent, including a professional educator, first sees a report card. But the skill can be learned. Consider the physician who looks at your test results and exclaims, "Oh boy, are *you* in trouble!" And with those words, orders you to "work harder in the future" and then quickly leaves the room. The bewilderment, fear, and rage that might be our natural reactions to such a confrontation with a preoccupied physician are not unlike the reactions of children to typical discussions of report cards with their parents. We expect the physician to stop, think, reflect, and then not only to offer the results of medical tests, but to engage in a conversation about how we can improve. If there is ambiguity or if the results indicate a problem, the wise physician might order additional tests or conduct additional examinations before coming to a hasty and potentially inaccurate conclusion. Even a physician who reports that a patient is in perfect health might be expected to offer analysis, insight, and discussion of how such excellent health can be maintained. We owe our children no less than the wise physicians owe their patients.

Inappropriate Uses of Test Scores

Just as we expect the wise physician to have a sound basis for drawing a conclusion, so must the wise parent and teacher have a reasonable body of evidence for the determinations they make about children. Incredibly, single tests are used inappropriately to make instant decisions on a routine basis. When this occurs, parents must become advocates not only for their children, but for the cause of accuracy in tests and the analysis of test results. By far the most common error made in the use of test scores is the overgeneralization about children, teachers, and schools. Based on a single test, a child can be denied promotion, a teacher's effectiveness can be questioned, or a school can be labeled as a failing institution. Worse yet are the life-changing decisions made based on a single test. Such decisions are typically associated with "high stakes" tests such as high school graduation examinations, but in fact many tests with significant consequences for children occur on a regular basis and do not have the label or the publicity associated with high stakes tests. Such important tests in which a few hours can make an enormous difference in the education and life of a child include the assessments used to label children as gifted or learning disabled, tests that grant or deny admission to special learning opportunities, and tests that claim to predict the ability, aptitude, or interests of children.

Parents should be deeply suspicious of tests that claim to draw conclusions about children, particularly when those conclusions are linked to words such as "intelligence" or "ability" or "aptitude." There is a sorry history of such tests stemming back to the early years of the twentieth century when the test results were appropriated by the eugenics movement to support their racist conclusions. With the jargon, statistics, and confidence of testing experts, the nation was assured of the scientific "proof" of the genetic inferiority of people of Irish, Italian, and Jewish descent, particularly if they came from southern or eastern Europe. These absurd conclusions were based on the low scores of recent immigrants taking the "Army Alpha" tests during the early days of World War I. Interestingly, the same populations displayed much higher scores a generation later as their language skills and familiarity with cultural references in the tests improved. Such changes prove that those tests did not measure anything like "intelligence" or "aptitude" because such qualities theoretically are not subject to change. If, however, the tests provide only a snapshot of the present knowledge of the test taker, then the results can change with the active decision of the test taker to improve. While the reader may find the racism of the test advocates of 1917 to be shocking and unacceptable, there is no logical distinction between the inappropriate conclusions based on a single test then and the overgeneralizations based on a single test for children in the early years of the twenty-first century.

Defenders of the use of tests for important decisions frequently refer to the objectivity, reliability, and validity that experts have claimed for these tests. Although this is not the forum for a professional discourse on the attributes of testing, there is one concept with which all parents should be familiar: validity. In lay terms, a test is valid when we test what we think we are testing. While this may seem simple on the face of it, the element of validity in testing is quite inconsistent. Consider the driving test we require in every state. Success on a multiple-choice test would not be a valid representation of driving ability. That is why every prospective driver must also get behind the wheel and demonstrate to the examiner some degree of proficiency in driving. Similarly, pilots do more than pass a multiple-choice exam; they must complete their flight examinations with an equal number of take-offs and landings. If the driving and pilot examinations result in the granting of licenses to unqualified applicants, the public safety is at risk. Conversely, if these examinations result in the denial of licenses to qualified applicants, it is not only inconvenient, but probably will result in litigation by the person to whom a license is denied. Such a reaction is possible because the test taker knows the impact of each test and is aware of the link between the test and an adverse decision.

While the requirement for validity is the same in every test, whether the subject is driving or kindergarten placement, the quality of testing is very different. We routinely make decisions about the educational opportunities for children based on test results, and in many cases the link between the test and the adverse decision is unclear or even secret. Counselors, teachers, and administrators give or deny students a variety of opportunities such as special reading groups or enrichment programs based on their performance on a single test. Worse yet, sometimes the decisions are based on tests that were taken during the prior school year.

The defenders of such decisions sometimes maintain that the students in special programs do better than the "average" and thus such tests must have been valid. In this context, validity becomes a self-fulfilling prophecy. A student does well on a test and then receives extra instruction from teachers who have high expectations. They come home to parents who have been told that their child is superior. If there is a challenge in school for such children, they assume that they can work harder, ask for help, and ultimately succeed. That is, after all, what smart kids, gifted kids, successful kids such as themselves would be expected to do. Of course, this combination of strategy, encouragement, expectations, persistence, and self-confidence would serve any student well. The converse is true. When a test indicates that a student has a poor math aptitude or is unlikely to become a good writer, then the subsequent expectations of teachers, parents, and the students themselves will assure that the negative prediction is accurate.

Does this mean that we should abandon all tests? Of course not. It is the use of the tests and the inappropriate interpretation of their results that should be reformed. The distinction that must be drawn is between tests as information and tests as prediction. Tarot cards provide information because the names of the cards are clear to any observer; few people outside of the Psychic Friends Network, however, would argue that the interpretation of the tarot cards can become transformed into accurate predictions. Consider other measurements in life. The bathroom scale may be mathematically accurate, but the next step—interpretation and prediction—can take one of two markedly different paths. A reading of 180 pounds can result in the inference, "I'd feel better if I lost ten pounds and I know just how to do it," or "I'm fat and stupid and ugly and can never change." The test was the same and the numbers were the same. The difference in the two responses involves interpretation and prediction.

Although parents may not always be able to influence the content or results of tests, we can make a profound impact on the interpretation of those tests and can fight the predictions that might be inaccurately made based upon those tests. The first challenge is in our own conversations about tests, focusing on learning and information rather than on evaluation, interpretation, and prediction. If parents fail to model learning conversations with children, they cannot influence the self-talk by children that inevitably occurs when parents are absent. Self-talk is powerful and, in the absence of strong logical challenges, can seem persuasive to anyone, particularly a child. Cognitive therapists challenge the illogical conclusions of their patients by helping them to identify the logical errors and destructive consequences of their self-talk. We do not need a therapist, however, to help our children think through why they believe as they do about their own successes and failures in school. If we listen, we might find thought patterns revealed in such self-talk as "I'm no good at math!" The source of such self-talk is rarely a scientific examination in which the algebra gene was found to be missing. Rather, there was some test, some conversation, some announcement of student proficiency in mathematics, and on that tenuous basis, an inappropriate conclusion was drawn. Sometimes the parent's first response is to offer assurances to the doubtful child such as, "Sure, you're good at math," or worse yet, "You think you were bad? I had trouble in math as well." It would be more constructive if we ask, "Why do you think that?" And then complete the conversation in a way that children can challenge their own conclusions. This might require some gentle inquiry and lots of listening by the parent. While the encouragement, love, and high expectations of parents are undeniably important, we must also develop the self-confidence of our children by giving them the skills to challenge their own negative images that stem from inappropriate interpretation and predictions of their past performance on tests.

fair tests

Standards: The Path Toward More Fair and Meaningful Tests

Because the words "standards" and "testing" are frequently used in the same sentence, some people have associated bad tests and inappropriate usage of test information with the standards movement. In fact, the proper application of academic standards leads to tests that are more fair and educational than traditional tests that are shrouded in mystery. Standards-based tests are fundamentally different from traditional tests in that student performance is compared to a standard rather than to the performance of other students. An academic standard is a simple statement of what students are expected to know and be able to do. Because the standards are public documents, students need not guess about the expectations of teachers. Thus, with standards, tests are not a game of *Jeopardy* in which the student with the most encyclopedic memory of many disconnected facts is the winner. Rather, any student who meets the standard can be a winner. Student success in a standards-based environment is a matter of what you know, not who you beat.

Because standards-based tests reject the notion of comparing one student to another, the traditional bell-shaped curve is rejected as a method of analyzing student performance. When schools use the bell curve, they assume that there are a few students who perform significantly above the average, a few students who are significantly below the average, and the vast majority of students who are in the middle. The last group forms the "bell"—the large hump in the middle of the curve. Although the bell curve is widely used in statistics and has been a staple of educational evaluation for more than a century, there is just one thing wrong with it: It is an inaccurate way to describe student achievement. When educational evaluation is based on a comparison to the average—the middle of the bell curve—then we have another self-fulfilling prophecy. If the instrument used to evaluate children only allows for a few students who are very much above average, then the use of that instrument—not the nature of children being tested—establishes the proof of the bell curve.

Test designers have a clever way of avoiding any evidence that does not fit their theory. If, for example, all children get a particular question right, then some observers might be delighted at the obvious result of diligent work by teachers and students. But in a test dedicated to the bell curve, such a question is simply discarded. The "good" questions are those that clearly differentiate one student from another. Ironically, the technical term for such differentiation is "discrimination," a term whose connotation of unfairness might be more accurate than the statistical meaning of identifying differences among students.

There are some instances in which a bell curve approach to testing might make some sense. If there are scarce resources to be allocated—such as admission to a selective college or selection for a high-paying job—then some people argue that only a bell curve test can rank students from best to worst. This sounds great in theory. After all, isn't the ninety-eighth percentile always better than the ninety-sixth percentile? The answer is, not necessarily. In fact, on many tests, the difference between those two rankings might be the response on a very small number of questions and student mastery of the those questions may or may not be related to success in the college or job under consideration. In fact, the difference between those two might be random or, at the very least, not relevant to the decision at hand. Consider other examinations, such as those for firefighter or jet pilot. In both cases, it is not sufficient for one candidate to beat another candidate. Any successful candidate applying for these positions must meet demanding physical and mental requirements. If no one meets those standards, the examiners do not say, "You can't carry someone out of a flaming building, but you're above the average of the other candidates, so we will accept you." Moreover, if there are several qualified candidates, the examiners do not say, "You are both highly qualified candidates, but Mary knew a little more about particle physics than Joe did, and therefore we will select Mary for the job." The candidates meet the standards or they don't, and if more people meet a standard than are needed to fill a vacancy, then the appropriate decision is not to resort to irrelevant information. In the context of education, the ultimate objectives should be accuracy and fairness. When schools use standards, teachers are liberated from the ancient and inaccurate practice of grading "on the curve" and instead can speak the truth: The student is proficient or not proficient compared to a standard, and a comparison to the work of other students is not relevant to my decision.

Standards are hardly a revolutionary approach to education. In fields as diverse as music and athletics, educators have long used standards. When a student wishes to play in the orchestra or participate on the basketball team, the requirement is not merely to beat other students, but rather to play scales, shoot baskets, or otherwise meet a standard that the conductor or coach has prescribed. The rules of the game are clear, and students need not guess about the height of the basket or the number of strings on a violin. Chapter 2 provides more detailed information about academic standards and what they mean for your child.

What about Talent and Intelligence?

Some readers are thinking, "Wait a minute! In the real world, everybody can't be a winner. Besides, there are some things that just can't be taught, and those things include talent and intelligence. You can't teach a golfer to be a Tiger Woods or a violinist to be Joshua Bell." This controversy about the relative impact of "born" traits versus taught skills has been at the center of educational debates since Plato. The Greek philosopher believed that there were "men of gold" who ruled over the "men of bronze." Not much has changed in the more than two thousand intervening years, as many people assume that "some kids have it and some don't."

Consider the example of musical talent, a quality many people assume is "born, not made." The Suzuki method of musical instruction has influenced literally millions of students and parents on every continent on the globe. As a result of the influence of Suzuki training, students without obvious genetic heritage of musicianship have found places in symphony orchestras throughout the world. Although the debate over talent and intelligence continues, those who discount the primacy of teaching and learning over inborn traits are deliberately indifferent to the evidence. There are surely cases of the most exceptional musicians, mathematicians, and athletes who may have some genetic predisposition toward their chosen careers. Nevertheless, the experience of the legions of students who have benefited from the Suzuki method make clear that the existence of exceptional talent and intelligence in a very few cases does not negate the general principle that talent and intelligence of the many can be nurtured, encouraged, and expanded. As Dr. Howard said, "Smart is something you get, not just something you are."

constructive conversations

Talking with Your Child about Standards and Tests

Children attribute an unusually high degree of credibility to what they hear at school, and thus the potentially negative conversations surrounding tests and standards that your child may encounter must be the subject of serious home discussion. Parents, not the local rumor mill, must determine the appropriate way for each child to react to standards and testing. This is not an issue on which the final parental word is, "Because I said so!" In our discussions with children, we must seek to equip them to stand on their own in the conflicts of the classroom and hallway. Thus, the following "point/counterpoint" dialogues are designed to suggest ways for you to talk constructively with your child about standards and tests.

"Those tests tell you how smart you are. If you don't do well, it means you're a dummy."

"Tests don't tell how smart you are, but tests do tell you a couple of things. They tell you what you have learned and they also tell you how good you are at figuring things out even when the right answer isn't very clear. That's why it's a good idea to pay attention and study,

and it's also a good idea to sit down with me and look at some of your old tests. If there is ever a test where you don't do well, we'll just work on it a little more. You're smart—and if you don't do well on a test, it just means we need to think through what happened and figure out how to do better. I know you can do it."

repeat positive

"If I don't do well on this test I'll be ruined! I won't get to go to the next grade with my friends. I just know I'm going to blow it!"

experiences

"It sounds as if you're pretty nervous about this test. Tell me how you're feeling about it right now. (Pause.) It's pretty scary, isn't it? Now, tell me how you felt when you did a great job in school. Remember that time when you got a perfect score on the math test and when you were so happy about your geography test? Tell me how you felt then. (Pause.) When you feel smart and good and happy, what did you do to make yourself feel that way? Let's make a list. Maybe we can discover the things that you have done when you felt smart and good and happy and we'll figure out how to do those things again now. If you do those same things, I know that you'll do a great job. And you know what? Even if your pencil breaks, the wind blows your test paper away, and the teacher turns into a green-eyed dragon and breathes fire on everybody's test, I'm going to love you anyway. Do we have a deal? Let's start making that list. . ."

"I can't possibly memorize all these things. My teacher said that the standards were impossible anyway and that no kids our age could do them. Mrs. Johnson said the same thing in the car on the way to school today. There's just nothing I can do. I give up!"

"I don't know. I've heard a lot of people say that kids can't do things, like play soccer or go on the Internet or create plays and make up songs, and then the kids do a great job anyway. When you said that the standards were impossible, which standards were you talking about? (Pause.) Well, I haven't read them either, so do you want to look them up and see if they are really impossible or if you can do most of them after all? What's your best subject? Let's start there . . ."*

*The state standards for grades 6 through 8 are reprinted in the second part of this book.

"I don't want to meet the standards—I want to be me! All my teachers have said I was a great writer ever since first grade. Now they tell me that I can only write the same way, every time, with a beginning, middle, and end. I used to write funny stories with crazy characters and goofy conversations, but now they say I have to be more serious. I hate standards, and so does everybody else. I have a dumb assignment because the dumb standard says that I have to compare two different dumb things. It's just stupid, and I don't want to do it. I want to write my stories!"

"I love your creative stories, too. I've saved some of the ones that you've written in the past. They show me that you are an intelligent, creative, and passionate person. You really care about what you write. Did you know that there are other people, aside from me, who could be moved by your writing? Tell me about something that really makes you angry. It might be people hurting animals or each other. It might be about the environment. It might be something at school or in our community. It might even be something about me or that happens at our house. Take a minute and think about it, and tell me something that makes you angry and that you want to change. (Pause, and let the child think of several options—you might get a fairly long list from a middle school student.) That's great! This is something that makes you really angry and that you want to change. Now, here's what we're going to do. You're a great writer, and writers can change things with their ideas and words. Write a letter about this. You might write it to me, to the President, to your teacher, to the principal, to the newspaper, or to anyone who can make a difference on this matter that makes you so angry. Let's agree that your letter should be your very best work. That means that you'll probably need to make an outline first. Then you'll write a draft, then edit it for errors in spelling, grammar, and punctuation. Finally, you will write your final copy. Of course, if you want to write persuasively, you will have both passion and evidence, so make sure that you support your arguments with research and examples. Because this is your very best work, your letter will have a clear beginning, middle, and end. If your letter is to me, I promise that I'll write a personal response to you. If your letter is to anyone else, I promise that I'll mail it to the recipient. I'm really proud of you for caring so much about this. I can't wait to see your letter!"

Your Right to Know about Tests in Your Child's School

Testing need not be mysterious or filled with terror. In fact, federal law establishes a parent's right to know what tests their children are taking and what the tests are about. This right includes everything from the weekly spelling tests to psychological tests to diagnostic tests to high-stakes graduation tests. If tests are mysterious, it is because parents do not ask the right questions. A sample letter from a parent to school officials requesting access to test information appears on page 92.

Parents' Checklist:

☐ Ask questions about your child's day based on his feelings and emotions, rather than events.

☐ Find out what tests are given in your child's school and how they are used to make any decisions about your child. Enter each of these test dates on your family calendar so that you can help to provide encouragement and reduce anxiety for your child.

☐ Celebrate your child's school accomplishments with the same enthusiasm you found in her first steps or her latest victory in a game.

---

celebrate
accomplishments

Chapter 4

Parents' Questions about Standards and Tests

This chapter is the result of hundreds of encounters with parents in focus groups, interviews, casual conversations, and letters. My research included parents from a wide variety of economic, educational, and cultural backgrounds. Although the parents with whom I spoke frequently expressed the conviction that their concerns were unique, the themes of these conversations were remarkably consistent. Parents have heard many rumors about academic standards, and much of what they have heard is the cause of significant fear and apprehension. The most consistent and significant desire expressed by parents is for specific communication from teachers about what children need to know and be able to do. Parents want more than a report card and annual parent-teacher conference. Parents want to play a role beyond working at a table at the school carnival or operating the copy machine in the school office. Parents, in brief, want information that is accurate and relevant to their children.

Despite the differences among the parents interviewed for this chapter, all of them have one thing in common: They care deeply about the educational opportunities for their children. Whether the parent was a Harvard-educated attorney or a high school dropout, the message was the same: Parents want their children to have more opportunities than they had and they are willing to support schools that provide such opportunities. They also insist on fairness for their children and clear communication from schools. Parents detest jargon, slogans, patronizing speeches, memos, and notes that appear to diminish the importance of the family. At the same time, parents are leery of the implication that they are primarily responsible for the education of their children. Whether the subject of discussion was math homework, test preparation, or summer reading, many parents bristled at the notion that they were responsible for doing a job that the school was supposed to do. Finally, the parents with whom I spoke were deeply concerned about the impact of a single test on their child, and most parents saw more threats than opportunities in the high-stakes testing movement.

The questions and responses that follow are hardly exhaustive, but they represent a synthesis of the attitudes, feelings, beliefs, and concerns of parents throughout the nation. You might recognize some of your own questions in the dialogue that follows.

What Is the Fundamental Purpose of School in the Middle Grades—That Is, the Grades Between Elementary School and High School?"

Many parents are confused about the fundamental purpose of middle school. Is it to explore different subjects, or to build the self-esteem of adolescents during a particularly difficult time of life? Many professional educators and state policymakers have strong disagreements about the purpose of middle school. Over the past 30 years, considerable research has been devoted to the unique needs of adolescents and pre-adolescents. While reasonable people disagree on many of these points, my response to this question is as follows: First, the fundamental purpose of education in the middle years between elementary school and high school is to prepare students to enter high school with confidence and success. High school teachers are nearly unanimous in the belief that incoming students must have strong skills in reading, writing, mathematics, time management, organization, and personal discipline. Second, the desire for exploration of many different subjects is understandable, as adolescence is an inquisitive time of life. Nevertheless, if parents and educators must choose between exploration and the development of basic skills in reading, the latter should take precedence over the former. Third and most important, educational researchers and parents of more than one child are unanimous on one point: Children acquire information at different rates. Therefore, the curriculum of the middle grades should assume differentiation, not uniformity. Some students require one period a day to master seventh-grade reading skills, while other students need two or three periods. Students are not widgets in a factory to be moved about in a uniform manner, but individuals with needs that are variable. Effective schools provide a different schedule to meet the individual learning needs of different students, and parents should support the recognition, analysis, and curriculum changes that result from a recognition of different student needs.

reduce anxiety

What Should I Say to My Child about Standards and Tests?

This is a great opportunity to move your children away from test terror toward becoming confident and capable students. Start with a clear definition: *Standards are the things that you should know and be able to do.* Then identify some of the standards that your children are already meeting. Review just a few of the standards in this book and tell your child, "You are already doing this. You see, standards aren't always something new and extra that you must learn; you already know many of these things right now!"

It is difficult to have a discussion with your child about academic standards without also discussing the tests based on your state's standards. This conversation is about emotions, not just about facts. Some parents are tempted to say something like, "You'd better study hard or you'll flunk the test!" In fact, the primary emotion of fear is already overwhelming, and the role of the parent is not to add to that anxiety, but to reduce it. How can you reduce your child's anxiety? Avoid false reassurances such as, "It's no big deal!" or "I'm sure you'll do just fine, so don't worry about it." When, in the life of parents, has the statement "Don't worry about it" served as a useful reassurance? What children most need to know is that their parent has heard and understood their fears. It is better to say, "Yes, tests can be pretty scary. When you fear something, it's always better to talk about it than to pretend that it's no big deal. What is there on this list of standards, or what have you heard about the test that is the most scary for you?" The parent finally has the information that can take the conversation from a dialogue filled with fear to the realm of the confident and empowered child. You will know that you have succeeded in these conversations—don't expect the matter to be resolved with a single discussion—when your child starts saying things such as:

"I know what I'm supposed to do in school."

"If I don't know how to do something, I know that I can figure it out or I know where I can get some help."

"I may not get a perfect score on the test, but I know most of the things on there. And if I miss a few questions, it doesn't mean I'm stupid. I'll just continue to learn all I can and do my best."

These are the words of a confident and empowered child. Parents need not give their children illusions, as if the Test Fairy will come to their aid in time of need. Rather, parents must give their children facts: what the standards are, what the tests mean, and how children's own efforts will improve their ability to achieve standards and do well on tests.

Is This Just Another Fad?

fairness

Yஸou have probably heard of educational terms that sounded like fads, from "new math" to "whole language" to "learning styles" to "brain research" and a host of other labels that seem to dominate the discussion of educational matters from one year to the next. How do you know that the term "standards" is not just another passing fad? First, let's remember what standards are all about. The label is not important, but the essence of standards is vital. Standards are just about fairness. Because standards express what students should know and be able to do, and because standards-based schools expect teachers to give children the opportunity to meet those standards, there is nothing new or fancy at work here other than a simple commitment to fairness. Standards will not go "out of style" unless the desire of parents and teachers for fairness becomes a passing fad.

Who Sets the Standards?

In every state except Iowa, academic content standards are established by the state. In Iowa, every school district sets its own standards. Thus, some form of academic standards exists in every public school in the nation. Indeed, whether or not the term "standard" is used, most private and parochial schools also have a clear set of academic expectations for students.

One frequent misunderstanding is that "national standards" govern the content of the academic disciplines. In fact, a few groups such as the National Council for Teachers of Mathematics, National Council for Teachers of English, and other academic and professional organizations have offered suggested standards that frequently are used as resources by state departments of education and local school districts. There is not, however, a "Federal Department of Standards" in Washington, D.C. where busy bureaucrats wake up every morning plotting new ways to remove the local authority of school boards. There are no federally established academic standards imposed on schools. Although the federal government has broad authority with respect to protecting individual civil rights in school—particularly with regard to discrimination on the basis of ethnicity, gender, or disability—the federal role in curriculum is strictly advisory.

The evidence of state and local control over the curriculum is best revealed in the wide variation in the academic content standards of the states. Some states, such as New York and California, have very specific academic expectations, and those academic requirements are linked to curriculum documents and test objectives. Other states, by contrast, have academic requirements that are much more vague, leaving the discretion to select specific curriculum and test objectives to local school districts.

Despite the differences among state standards, there are some important commonalities. The most important distinguishing characteristic of standards-based schools is the comparison of students to a standard rather than to the average of other students. Many states blur this distinction in their testing policies. Rather than refer to the percentage of students who meet a standard, some state documents continue to make reference to "percentile" or other methods of ranking students. It will take some time before every state policy maker and administrator applies standards carefully and accurately.

Do Standards Place Too Much Emphasis on Academics?

Many parents expressed the concern that standards emphasize academic subjects to the exclusion of extracurricular activities, the arts, and simple fun in school. Some of these parents have heard alarming news stories (and more than a few unsubstantiated rumors) about schools that have been transformed into academic boot camps. In these dreary places, students do nothing except prepare for tests all day long. Work sheets and mock tests have replaced music and art. A number of popular writers have fanned the flames of this hysteria, fueled more by anecdote than by evidence.

It is true that when standards have been established with care, some traditional activities have been replaced by lessons with a greater academic orientation. This does not, however, imply the elimination of holiday celebrations and the systematic removal of fun from the school day. Students in standards-based schools will, for example, probably continue to discuss current events, enjoy physical activities, and participate in performing arts. It does not hurt the cause of student enjoyment, however, when students learn more about measurement and biology in their physical education classes, improve their mastery of fractions in their music classes, and otherwise incorporate academic relevance into fun activities. Indeed, the activities in this book make it clear that fun, engagement, and academic standards are not mutually exclusive.

Why Can't School Just Be Fun?

One of the frequent concerns expressed by parents I interviewed was the lament that school is no longer fun. Parents have heard tales of multi-hour homework assignments and children who complained that "Monday is the worst day of the week" because school was so terrifying. Some of these parents assumed that the appropriate reaction to the state of affairs must be a reduction of the academic expectations for their children. Parents should consider that it is entirely possible that the difficulties the students are facing arise because previous teachers did not have sufficiently high expectations of them. When everyone is focused on making school fun, the teacher who insists that students learn something is accused of being demanding and mean. This reinforces the notion that learning is burdensome and that school is dreadfully dull. The problem compounds itself in middle school, high school, and even in college, when the expectation of rigor is abandoned and students are viewed as "customers" who must be satisfied by credits that are easy, fun, and worthless.

What about the Basics—Reading, Writing, and Arithmetic?

Some parents are concerned that an emphasis on the higher order thinking skills included in many academic standards will reduce an emphasis on the "basics"—that is, skills in reading, writing, and arithmetic. In fact, there is not a contradiction between the requirement for higher order thinking and basic skills. Students cannot learn to master the challenge of mathematical problem solving if they do not have arithmetic skills. Moreover, students cannot respond to the challenge of critical thinking in social studies and science if they are unable to read their social studies and science textbooks or write a lab report.

The controversy over basic education has been particularly acute in mathematics. Partisans of pure "problem-solving" believe that an emphasis on mathematical concepts is essential, and that the dreary "drill and kill" of traditional worksheets must be discarded in favor of an emphasis on thinking. Of course, most mathematics teachers and parents recognize the intuitively obvious proposition that problem-solving and math skills are inseparable. Even in an age of calculators and computers, students must have "number sense." This means that students not only must be able to compute that $9 \times 9 = 81$ but they must also be able to understand that the number 81 is comprised of nine groups of nine and comprehend the notion that there are many other ways to achieve a product of 81. For example, consider these three levels of mathematical understanding, using the same example that begins with the question, "What is 9×9?"

The lowest level of understanding is expressed by the student who grabs the calculator and punches the buttons: $9 \times 9 =$ receives the answer 81. The next level of understanding is the student who recalled from memory that the product was 81 and did not need the calculator for assistance. But neither of these levels of understanding approaches the sophistication of the student who not only understands that $9 \times 9 = 81$, but also understands that since $3 \times 3 = 9$, then 81 is also the product of $3 \times 3 \times 3 \times 3$. For this student, the study of exponents in a future grade will be intuitive and easy. He will immediately grasp that $3^4 = 81$ rather than perceive exponents as a new and foreign mathematical concept that must be memorized without understanding. In other words, students need both the basics and thinking skills. The two are complementary, not competitive concepts.

Similarly, we expect students to have a deep understanding of causes and effects in history and science. But these deep understandings will elude students who do not have the ability to read and understand the paragraph before them. Moreover, the thinking skills involved in understanding the interplay of politics, geography, economics and conflict will elude students who did not study the factual details of those subjects. Thus, anyone who contends that an emphasis on standards excludes a commitment to basic skills has not carefully read the standards. I have met with angry parent groups whose concerns about standards were allayed when presented with the actual words of the standards. The academic standards make clear that students must not only master thinking, reasoning, and analysis, but also must understand how to read, write, and compute, as well as know the content associated with the foundational academic subjects.

understanding

Will Standards Mean the Elimination of Music, Art, and Physical Education?

There is a legitimate concern expressed by many parents that the overwhelming emphasis in state tests and standards on mathematics and language arts will exclude music, art, and physical education in some schools. In most successful schools I have studied, mathematics, social studies, science, music, art, and physical education are an integral part of the academic life of the school. For example, students in music class routinely use melody, rhythm, and song lyrics as a bridge to better understand history, learn new vocabulary, and master fractions. Students in art class use the visual images of art to expand their vocabulary and enhance their ability to compare and contrast different images. Moreover, students in effective art classes are able to master the art of scale and ratio, measurement, and the relationship between different geometric figures. There are wonderful physical education classes in which students acquire a better understanding of measurement. When the coach has given students the choice to run a millimeter or a kilometer, and the students make the wrong choice, the lesson on metric measurement tends to remain with them for a long time. Moreover, I have seen effective physical education teachers conduct vocabulary relays and math relays in which students must not only run fast but also must understand vocabulary and mathematical information in order to continue the race. This is the ideal intersection of the academic, the aesthetic, and the athletic.

Many middle schools and junior high schools have attempted to offer so much to so many different students that they have forgotten their fundamental mission: helping students to enter high school with confidence and success. It is clear from my interviews with high school teachers that the most important skills middle school students need are reading, writing, time management, and organization. Because classes in physical education, art, and music all can help to build these skills, they are not frills, but essential to the preparation of students for high school. The essential nature of these classes, of course, depends on teachers who understand that every class contains an academic component and that they are not a "teacher of music, art, and physical education," but rather a teacher of children.

the ideal intersection

Does My Child Really Have to Meet All of the Standards?

One of the weaknesses of standards as they have been articulated in most states is the failure of prioritization. In fact, not every standard is of equal value. Some standards recognize the need of basic skills, including reading, writing, and arithmetic. Moreover, the standards recognize the need of students to analyze and understand a relatively narrow set of facts. But neither every fact nor every skill has equal value for the student. Thus, it is not accurate to say that children have to meet every single standard elaborated by the state. One method of distinguishing the more important standards from those that are interesting but less valuable is the concept of "power standards." Chapter 5 provides more detailed elaboration on this concept.

What Happens If My Child Doesn't Meet the Standards?

When children do not meet academic content standards, the most immediate response should be the opportunity for additional learning. In other words, the immediate consequence for the failure to achieve a standard should be neither a low grade nor the repetition of an entire year of school. Rather, the initial consequence should be the opportunity for additional learning. This recognizes what all parents know to be true: Students learn at different rates. Many states have implemented high-stakes tests that are associated with academic content standards and some of these tests have dramatic consequences. For example, in some states, students must pass a reading proficiency test in order to enter the fourth grade. In other states, students must pass middle school proficiency tests in order to enter high school. A growing number of states—twenty-six at this writing—have established high school graduation examinations, which must be successfully completed by students in order to receive a high school diploma.

In the best school districts, the student performance on these examinations is rarely a surprise. In fact, students have multiple opportunities to prepare for important tests. Parents also have many opportunities to know well in advance of the test whether their children need additional help. Unfortunately, many school districts have a reactive response to high-stakes tests. Remediation and opportunities for additional learning only take place after a student has failed a test. Worst of all is the fallacy of remediation in high school for problems that have their roots in elementary and middle school.

If you are concerned about the performance of your child on a high-stakes test, then the use the letter format on page 92 to inquire of your school administration what specific testing policies will affect your child. Once you have this information, identify the particular knowledge and skills that your child will be required to have. Then you will be able to identify the gap between what your child knows at this time, and what your child will need to know and be able to do when the test is administered.

Parents frequently make the same mistake as schools, becoming involved in a child's academic challenges only after a student is experiencing difficulty in school. The most successful parental involvement occurs long before a child has experienced academic difficulty. Therefore, if you are concerned about the performance of your child in an upcoming test, the time to become involved is now, not after you receive your child's score.

My Child Just Doesn't Get It. What Do I Do?

Lots of frustrated parents share your concern. Most of us attempt to teach our children in the same way that we learned. In other words, if we learned by having someone read to us or speak to us, we assume that our children learn the same way. If we learned by having instructions written out for us, then we assume that our children will benefit from our own written instructions. Fortunately, children have a way of emulating some but not all of our characteristics. One of the things that they may not inherit is your learning style. As a result, please do not assume that your child "just doesn't get it" simply because the child is not learning the same way that you did.

You can discover your child's learning style by identifying the circumstances in which your child performs at a very high level. For example, perhaps your child plays a game exceptionally well. Perhaps your child enjoys a particular story, chapter, or book so much that she is able to recall it with astonishing detail. Perhaps your child enjoys writing to a relative or receiving mail. These will give you clues about the ways in which your child acquires information, processes that information, and applies information to the task at hand. Of course, just because a person prefers one learning style does not mean that the rest of the world will always accommodate that need. Therefore, children need to be able to process information from written text, oral instructions, and the context of the world around them. By finding your child's preferred method of learning, you can capitalize on that strength and also be more attentive to building skills in those learning methods that do not come so easily to your child.

When you become frustrated with your child's performance, one of the most important things that you can do is to stop the common practice of giving your child a single set of instructions involving the performance of multiple tasks. The most common example is, "Clean up your room!" For some children, this instruction is clear. For others, we must be more clear by breaking down the tasks: "Take the clothes off the floor and put them in the hamper." Then, after the successful completion of that task, "Empty the trash." Then, "Let your brother out of the closet," and so on, until the task of cleaning the room is completed. The breaking down of complex instructions into individual tasks is essential in the academic context as well. The only way you can isolate the difficulty your child is having is by providing clear instructions in a step-by-step manner. You may find that the problem is neither an inability to comprehend your instructions, nor an unwillingness to act on them. The difficulty, rather, may be that your child, like all of us, prefers some types of instructions to others. It is also quite likely that there is a difference in understanding when your child hears instructions compared to when the same instructions are printed on a page and your child must independently read and respond to them. The difference between oral and visual strengths is not the only learning style you should consider. Some children who do not respond well to oral or written instructions can perform the same tasks well if they see a physical model of the expected result, watch a demonstration, or engage in trial and error. The point is not that one of these learning styles is "right," but rather that every person learns in different ways, yet all of us occasionally are compelled to acquire information in a manner that does not correspond to our strengths. By understanding the need to listen, read, or observe demonstrations, a parent can support a child's strengths and offer encouragement and practice to deal with learning styles that are less familiar and, in the past, less successful.

Another common reason for children having difficulties in school is the disconnection between previous learning and current expectations. For example, students are bound to have difficulty with seventh-grade math requirements, such as finding the area of a circle by multiplying the square of the radius of the circle by pi, if they failed to master multiplication and exponents in earlier grades. Students are not going to be able to create a three-paragraph essay in eighth grade if they were unable to write coherent sentences in earlier grades. One of the principal benefits of the standards movement has been the requirement that teachers communicate with one another so that, in the best standards-based schools, there is a seamless transition from one grade to the next. An eighth-grade teacher has confidence about what students learned in the seventh grade because the seventh-grade curriculum was not based on the personal preferences of the teacher, but rather on a coherent curriculum that led directly to the instructional needs of the eighth-grade classroom. This process of building from one grade to the next must begin in elementary school. Students are not going to be able to create a satisfactory paragraph in fifth grade if they did not learn how to construct a proper sentence in earlier grades, and these same students will be lost in eighth grade when faced with the challenge of writing a persuasive or expository essay. The curriculum of each grade should be designed to equip students with the skills and knowledge required to master the curriculum of the next grade. It is fair to say, however, that this ideal, seamless transition from one grade to the next is the exception rather than the rule in most American schools. Moreover, many schools have high rates of student and teacher mobility so that it is impossible to assume that every child in every class had a common foundation of learning.

The final consideration with respect to children who are having difficulty in school should be evaluation for learning disabilities. When you have tried to analyze a child's learning style with few results, and when you have attempted to help your child fill in the gaps from previous grade levels, it may be that your child continues to have immense difficulties in school. In these cases, it is appropriate to request an evaluation of your child for a variety of learning disabilities. Some parents fear that if they request an evaluation of their child, a label with negative connotations such as "special education" may be applied to their child. It is essential to note that both federal laws and public perceptions have changed markedly in the past several years on this issue. If your child is among the 11 percent of students nationwide with an identified learning disability, it does not mean that your child is "stupid" or otherwise incapable of great performance. The fields of law, medicine, music, and governmental leadership include many men and women who have learning disabilities. Indeed, identification of and compensation for a learning disability are the keys to their success. It is also very likely that children who are evaluated will not have a learning disability, and that work by those children, along with parents and teachers, on academic and behavioral issues will help them reach their full potential.

request an evaluation

What If My Child Has a Learning Disability?

More than eleven percent of students across the United States have some sort of learning disability. We have made great strides in this country in diagnosing, understanding, and even valuing the diversity of learning styles that different students bring to class, and this includes learning disabilities. The notion of "valuing" a learning disability is not merely a politically correct posture designed to make students and parents feel good about a bad situation. Marcus Buckingham and Donald Clifton of the Gallup Organization, one of the leading polling and management consulting firms in the world, provide examples of how even the profoundly challenging reading disability, dyslexia, can result in positive effects for students and adults who recognize the disability and carefully plot strategies for dealing with it. Students with learning disabilities have clear legal rights expressed in the

Individuals with Disabilities Education Act (IDEA). Moreover, the students frequently have rights that are protected by local district policy and state law.

Foremost among the rights of learning disabled students is the right to have the "least restrictive environment" for learning. This typically means that learning disabled students are sitting next to students in regular education classes with regular teachers. The students, therefore, must have accommodations and adaptations made for them, particularly when it is time for a test. The most frequent accommodations and adaptations include time, environment, reading, and writing. The adaptation of time is provided to students who process information slowly, but accurately, and thus taking more time on a test allows them to accurately express what they know. The adaptation of environment provides for a quiet and secluded test-taking environment for students whose learning disability limits their concentration. The adaptation of reading allows students who understand words, but cannot process words in printed form, to have tests read aloud to them. Finally, the adaptation of writing allows a student who can speak words, but cannot write them, to dictate test responses to an adult for the writing portion of the test. Of course, these are only some of the many adaptations that are available to students with disabilities.

It is absolutely vital that parents and teachers distinguish between appropriate accommodation and the reduction of rigor for a test. Many professions include members who are extraordinarily gifted and intelligent, and yet suffer from some learning disability. The gifts of these professionals would never have been recognized had their teachers and parents reduced rigor rather than sought the most appropriate adaptation for the needs of the students. There are instances in which parents and teachers harbor grave misconceptions about the distinction between appropriate accommodation and an inappropriate reduction in rigor. Such misunderstandings are usually revealed in the form of a statement such as, "She's in special education so I had to give her a B," or, "He has a learning disability, so even though he didn't take the test or complete the project, I had to give him a C." Such statements are at odds with both federal law and the best interests of the child. The focus of IDEA is appropriate consideration of individual needs. There is not a single sentence in the law or accompanying regulations that requires teachers to lie to parents about the nature of student performance. Indeed, the requirements for individual considerations in curriculum and assessments are not a prescription for "dumbing down" requirements, but rather a requirement for appropriate accommodations and adaptations. When those adaptations are offered to students, it is typical that the report card will indicate that the student "achieved standards with appropriate adaptations and accommodations." Moreover, when a student does not meet an academic standard, the appropriate and accurate report should reflect that "the student met these objectives in the educational plan and did not meet the other objectives in the educational plan." The path to improved performance by all students, including students with learning disabilities, is accuracy and honesty in assessment.

For more information on students with learning disabilities, please consult Chapter 9.

accuracy and honesty

What If I Disagree with the State and Local Standards?

Standards are political documents. They represent the efforts of a group of people who have endeavored to identify what students should know and be able to do. Nevertheless, as with any product of any committee, the documents are typically flawed. One can accept the obvious notion that some standards are too broad, some are too narrow, and most remain "works in progress," and nevertheless grasp that standards are superior to the poorly described curriculum or pedagogical anarchy that preceded them. It is entirely reasonable, and even likely, that thoughtful parents may disagree with some of the standards. Perhaps you disagree with the quantity of standards, with their specificity, with their vagueness, or even with their content. For example, I have heard a parent exclaim, "I don't care if my children can write, as long as they can read!" This was in direct response to the requirement of the state academic standards that children must be able to write coherent paragraphs. While this parent has a legitimate right to express such a point of view and, ultimately, to remove the children from the state school system, the parent should not have the right to require teachers to have a different set of standards for those children than for other children.

In many districts, parents have an extraordinary degree of influence on what the expectations are for their children. Unfortunately, these expectations are often used to reduce expectations and rigor and, as a result, dumb down the curriculum. In the example cited above, I confess to a prejudice. The research is clear and unambiguous: Writing is an effective way for students to think, reason, and learn. The fact that some parents may wish that their children did not have to write is not a sufficient justification for the absence of the requirement. I have worked in other schools where parents have asked the rhetorical question, "Why do these kids need algebra anyway? They will never use it." These parents, too, deserve a thoughtful hearing, but do not deserve to have their advice govern the curriculum standards for the school, district, or state that must serve all children.

There are other circumstances, however, in which the standards genuinely have deep flaws that contradict the philosophical, moral, or religious beliefs of parents. In these cases, parents have an opportunity to make their concerns known. Parents can exclude their students from tests and from subjects of study that they find objectionable on religious or moral grounds. Most schools ask parents specifically for permission to discuss issues involving human sexuality, birth control, religion, and other sensitive subjects. Schools routinely offer an alternative area of study and alternative literature to respond to parent wishes.

How Can I Deal with Stress and Anxiety about Tests?

Stress and anxiety are undeniably important parts of test performance. Most readers of this book can recall an instance in which they were well-prepared for an examination, or other challenge, and nevertheless performed below their ability. The reason for their poor performance was the stress and anxiety associated with a circumstance under which they had to perform. Although parents cannot completely eliminate childhood stress and anxiety, they can mitigate the negative impact by giving students healthy coping skills. These skills include the "second look" view of any situation in which children feel unprepared or uncomfortable. If the first look at a test question or other challenge reveals the student does not immediately know the answer, some students will simply assume that the challenge is impossible, emotionally shut down, succumb to the pressure at hand, and give up not only on the question before them but on the entire test. Other students, by contrast, have the ability to take a second look at a question or challenging circumstance. The second look of the student is comparable to the runner's second wind. This boost of energy occurs when students are able to use strategy, rather than mere recall, to address the question or challenge at hand.

Although parents need not conduct a test preparation academy from their home, they can give their students the ability to maintain and expand their repertoire of second look skills. Examples of second look skills include the following:

Two-pass technique—This technique suggests that students focus first on the questions to which they know the answer. Because every question typically has the same point value, students can generate the greatest yield on their investment of time when they focus first on those questions to which they immediately know the answer. After they have made the first pass going through all questions on a test, students can return to the beginning of the examination and devote additional energy to those questions that are ambiguous or more difficult. In most cases, students are well served to eliminate one or two obviously wrong answers, then guess the answer to these questions and quickly move along to the next challenge.

Outlining—Whenever students are faced with an essay question, there is a direct relationship between the amount of time spent outlining an answer and the time saved in creating the final answer. When students immediately launch into writing the final answer, they frequently produce an aimless and disorganized essay. When, on the other hand, students take the time to outline an answer first, they have the ability to produce a crisp and well-organized essay. Moreover, the very presence of the outline makes it clear to the teacher that the student understands the question and has taken the time to provide a detailed and well-organized response.

Process of elimination—In some cases, the right answer is not clear. Sometimes this is due to the difficulty of the test item. In many cases, however, this is due to the deliberate ambiguity of the test items. This is particularly true in the case of national standardized tests in which the test writers have determined that there must be a wide variation in the "difficulty value" of the test items. That is, some items are constructed in a manner so that many students will get them correct, and other items are constructed so that very few students will get the correct response. In the latter category, the cause for such a few number of students finding the correct answer is as likely the ambiguity as it is the difficulty of the question. In such cases, the students with the ability to persevere and take a second look at the question will find that, despite the difficulty or ambiguity of the question, they can at least eliminate one wrong answer and therefore have a higher probability of guessing the correct response. There is a great deal of mythology with respect to guessing on tests. In most cases, however, guessing strategies need not be mysterious at all. On many examinations, there is no "guessing correction factor" and therefore students should always guess if they do not know the right answer. On other tests, students are penalized for every wrong answer. In those cases, it only makes sense to guess if the student can eliminate one or two wrong answers. Consider these examples:

Mary is taking a test without any guessing correction factor. It is a multiple-choice test with four possible answers: A, B, C, and D. After reviewing her work, there are still eight questions that she just can't understand. Should Mary guess? Absolutely yes. If she just marks "A" for each of those eight questions, she has a one-in-four chance that "A" is correct, and thus she is likely to get two out of the eight questions correct. That is an extra two correct answers that she otherwise would have missed if she just left them blank.

In our second example, however, the rules are a little different. Bob is taking a similar test, with four possible answers. But for each question Bob misses, he will be penalized $\frac{1}{3}$ point. Bob also has the same chance of guessing correctly that Mary had, and indeed, he answered two out of eight questions correctly. But what about the other six questions? Because Bob lost $\frac{1}{3}$ point for each of those six, he was penalized two points ($\frac{1}{3} \times 6$), and thus he gained no advantage guessing.

What if Bob was able to eliminate two possible wrong answers? In other words, he is not guessing among choices A, B, C, and D, but only among choices A and B, because he determined that C and D were not possible right answers. Now Bob has a 50/50 chance—it's either A or B—of guessing correctly. With eight questions, he probably will get four correct. He will be penalized $\frac{1}{3}$ point on the other four, for a total of $1\frac{1}{3}$ points ($4 \times \frac{1}{3}$). Because Bob could eliminate two possible wrong answers, it was a good strategy for him to guess.

The suggestions offered here are essential elements of educational and psychological strategy. One of the most powerful forces operating in the life of the empowered child is emotional resilience. Children with the ability and willingness to persevere in the face of seemingly great odds have the gift of emotional resilience. This lifelong ability has importance that extends far beyond test taking and academic pursuits. We routinely see parents encourage the skill of perseverance and emotional resilience in athletic competition. "You can do it!" the proud parents exclaim. The same level of perseverance can be encouraged through parent support for the resubmission of student work after the first draft did not meet the standard, encouraging more than one attempt at an essay, and encouraging one additional try for success at the mathematics homework. This encouragement is the source of emotional resilience that will be as valuable in algebra class as it is on the soccer field. In the future, this sense of empowerment, perseverance, and resilience will serve your child well in college, in relationships, and in any professional endeavor.

What If My Child Is Not Ready for a Test?

It is relatively uncommon for children to say with confidence, "I'm ready for this test and I'm going to ace it!" More often than not, we have created a sense of fear and loathing for tests, including those tests for which students are reasonably well-prepared. Parents have an important role to play here. First, parents have an obligation to help students be prepared for tests. The first step is simple: Mark test dates on the family calendar. When it is clear that Thursday is a test day, then Wednesday is not the ideal evening for a movie or an appeal for a later than usual bedtime. Most teachers—particularly at the secondary level—confirm that the difference between the superior students and the vast majority of their students is more a matter of time management and organizational skills than intellect. While parents cannot take tests for their children, nor should they, parents can give students the gift of organization and that includes a calendar, appropriate focus on test preparation, and a consistent theme that performance on tests is improved with preparation and hard work. Parents must obliterate the notion that prevails among many children that, "either you've got it or you don't—studying doesn't make much difference." In fact, the harder they work, the better they will perform in school and most other areas of life.

Consider the typical exchange between parent and child: "Do you have any homework tonight?" When the response is in the negative, parents need to ask a few more questions. The absence of homework might be genuine. On the other hand, the absence of homework, particularly in middle school and in upper elementary school, might be due to the fact that there is a test the next day. Students of every age should maintain a calendar with important dates on it. This is one of the key lifelong time management skills that everyone must master. The skill and discipline of maintaining an accurate and up-to-date calendar and task list not only separates successful students from unsuccessful students, but also distinguishes people in the professional and business world from one another. When there is a test the next day, the result need not be endless anxiety, trepidation, and fear. Rather, there must be a systematic approach to test preparation.

The systematic approach to test preparation includes the following steps. First, students must outline exactly what the test entails. Sometimes it is clear, such as all the traditional spelling tests in elementary school. At other times, a chapter test in a book will provide a clear and accurate preview of the test that students must face in the classroom. At other times, however, the content of the test may not be so clear, and some questions must be asked. If this inquiry takes place at half past nine o'clock the evening before the test, there are few alternatives other than an investigation into the mysteries of the backpack and notebook. If, by contrast, this inquiry takes place several days before the test, there is an opportunity to give the student responsibility for asking the teacher for help and for seeking additional guidance from other sources.

Second, students should prepare a sample test. One of the most effective learning exercises is for students to create a test. For younger students, acting as a teacher is a fun and engaging way to learn. For older students, such an activity may lack pure enjoyment, but the intellectual advantage is nevertheless very significant. In addition, when students practice creating and taking a test, they have not only provided themselves with a cognitive edge over their peers, but they also have provided themselves with an emotional safety net. By facing the unknown in friendly circumstances—the family room or bedroom—the student has the opportunity to endure natural test jitters in an environment that is far less consequential than in the classroom the following day. Moreover, it is my experience that students generally ask themselves far more difficult questions than those posed by the teacher.

In a Technological Age, Why Should Kids Take Paper and Pencil Tests?

It is a common parlor game for people to fantasize about the future. For years we have contemplated a world in which pencils and paper would become obsolete. The "paperless office" has been a concept considered by business people for years. Alas, the reality of our daily lives flies in the face of our fantasies. In fact, both students and people in the world of work must be able to create visual images, words, sentences, and paragraphs using pencil and paper, white boards, chalkboards, and a host of other media. In addition, the use of pencil and paper to slowly and carefully express ideas offers students the ability to think through problems without necessarily resorting to the guesswork involved in a multiple-choice question.

It is true that twenty-first century students must achieve a degree of technological literacy. Nevertheless, we also expect students to achieve a high degree of thinking, reasoning, and analysis. Those skills are best reinforced when students must take pen or pencil in hand, express an idea, communicate their thinking, and subject their reasoning to the critical review of others. Although computers clearly will play a role in the classroom and the future of today's students, technology does not replace the need for students to communicate clearly, accurately, analytically, and yes, legibly, in written form.

How Can I Help My Child with Homework and Projects Without Doing the Work Myself?

The subtext of this question is quite revealing. Every parent has observed instances in which the work presented to the teacher is clearly the product of a parent rather than the student. Such projects reveal far more about parental ambition than they do about student ability. The problem is that parents do not like to see their children become frustrated, angry, and ultimately disengaged from school. So how much "help" is appropriate and when do we cross the line from appropriate coaching and assistance to the inappropriate substitution of our own efforts for those of our children?

Parents are best served when teachers provide clear expectations for student performance. Some teachers are also clear about the nature of acceptable help and the instructions will clearly say, "Ask a parent or friend for help on this part," or, "Do this part all alone—don't get help from anyone else." Unfortunately, this level of clarity and specificity is the exception rather than the rule. One method that is particularly helpful when students are doing projects is the use of a scoring guide (sometimes called a "rubric" in educational jargon). When there is a clear set of teacher expectations, parents are able to help students not by doing work for them, but by asking students this critical question: If you were the teacher and you were grading this assignment using the scoring guide or rubric that the teacher provided, what grade would you give?

The cognitive scientist Benjamin Bloom made a tremendous contribution to the field of education when he recognized that the abilities to synthesize and evaluate information were essential for the intellectual development of children. When parents ask students to evaluate their own work, they are challenging students to engage in the advanced skill of evaluation, something too frequently left only to the teacher. If the teacher has provided a clear scoring guide or rubric—particularly a scoring guide that is expressed in student accessible language—then students can place themselves in the role of the teacher-evaluator and ask themselves how they would evaluate their own performance.

Too frequently, however, students merely do their best work, or do the work in the minimum amount of time given the exigencies of an upcoming television program, and assume that the teacher will evaluate the work in his or her own mysterious wisdom. This common practice of reserving evaluation responsibilities exclusively for the teacher denies students the opportunity to evaluate and learn. Make no mistake: This is not an exercise in making children feel good about themselves or engaging in unwarranted self-congratulatory smiling faces affixed to non-proficient work. Rather, the practice of evaluation and reflection requires thoughtful criticism, evaluation, and in many cases, rewriting, correction of errors, and the improvement of the quality of work. When parents insist that students engage in evaluation, they are doing far more than helping students on an individual homework assignment. These parents are giving their children the lifelong skills of reflection and evaluation.

a sense of accomplishment

How Much Homework Is Reasonable?
How Much Is Too Much?

In the early elementary grades, students revel in sharing school work, stories, and projects with parents. It hardly seems like "homework," but rather is a chance to share a daily sense of accomplishment. Some practice and reinforcement on basic skills, as well as a review and revision of school work, might require fifteen to twenty minutes each school night. As students enter the fourth and fifth grades, teachers are mindful of the need to prepare students for the homework demands of middle school. Most upper elementary teachers require about thirty minutes of homework each evening. In the middle grades (usually sixth through eighth grade), students should expect about ninety minutes of homework each evening. It is important to note that these are averages. Before you conclude that your child has too much homework because of a project that requires four hours to complete, it might be useful to note whether the project was assigned three weeks ago. If that is the case, don't be surprised if, the night before the project is due, you hear the claim that "My teacher gave me five hours of homework!"

If the averages noted above are consistently exceeded, then it might be reasonable to have a conversation with the teacher about how the student can better use classroom time to finish work and how the homework burden can be made more reasonable.

In addition to the quantity of homework, parents should attend to the quality of homework assigned by teachers. Are students building skills, conducting independent research, reading for understanding, and building confidence? These are the characteristics of effective homework assignments. If, on the other hand, students are bewildered, unfocused, bored, or completing worksheets on skills they have already mastered, then the value of the homework assignment is subject to question. The best way to approach the teacher is not with a complaint about "too much homework" but rather with the request that homework be challenging and meaningful. "I understand your desire to instill discipline through daily work," you might say, "and I want to be supportive of those habits as well. Perhaps we could work together to find assignments that will be best suited to my child's needs."

The most important contribution that parents can make on the homework front is to make it a priority, with a consistent place and time for the completion of daily work. When no homework has been assigned, the place and time remain available for learning activities in this book as well as those that you and your child create. In this way, you have a regular commitment to learning at home that will sustain your child whether or not homework has been assigned by the teacher.

What If I Can't Help My Child with a Subject in School?

I have a confession to make. I studied and taught mathematics, and yet sometimes I find my own children's homework in that subject baffling. Even more embarrassing, I have given my children the wrong answers when I violated my own rules and helped them too much with their homework. If these mistakes can be committed by a former teacher and professor, how much more likely is every parent to make them? If you have ever felt intimidated by your children's homework, you certainly are not alone.

Even if you can provide the answer, this is rarely the most appropriate way for you to help children. When your children ask for your help, here are some steps that will produce better results than insisting they do everything themselves, or doing their homework for them.

First, ask the child to make an attempt. In some cases, this means breaking the problem down into steps. For example, if there is a multi-step story problem in mathematics, and the child does not know how to frame the answer to the problem, an appropriate step toward solving the problem might be creating a picture that accurately describes the problem. This is particularly effective coaching because many children understand visual images of a problem better than they do the words of the story problem. This also makes the point that the key to answering a problem successfully is the accurate understanding of the problem, not merely asking the parent for help.

Second, ask the child to solve a single part of the problem. If, for example, the problem involves a complex series of geography questions, and the child does not have all the answers, encourage the child to answer only one or two of the possible problems. Every time we break a large and complex problem down into its component parts, the problem becomes more approachable. This gives your child not only excellent task and time management skills, but also reduces the anxiety associated with the majority of complex and difficult problems.

Third, it is entirely legitimate for the child to write down these words: "I don't know the complete answer—I tried, but this is as far as I got." The child then makes a good faith attempt to respond to the challenge at hand. This demonstrates to the teacher that the child considered the problem, thought about the problem, and genuinely did not know the answer. This is far more important information for a teacher than when a child merely leaves a piece of paper blank or turns in nothing at all. In such cases, the teacher is unable to distinguish between work that has been ignored and work that was attempted, but completed unsuccessfully. Moreover, this builds a skill too rarely discussed in the context of homework and academic achievement: the skill and habit of intellectual honesty. Leaders in professions, businesses, and academic institutions can all attest to the rare circumstances under which the words "I don't know" have been uttered. Nevertheless, the courageous people who say those words are often well regarded by their peers. When leaders express this trait, it becomes clear that honesty, rather than bluffs, is the acceptable code of conduct.

explore your options

What about Extracurricular Activities?

The research involving extracurricular activities is unambiguous. When students are participating in extracurricular activities such as sports, music, leadership, service, drama, debate, and a host of other wonderful activities, their academic achievement improves. Although these activities do take some time, and occasionally they even take time away from homework and academics, the overall research is not even a close call. Attendance and grades improve when students are busily involved in extracurricular activities, and the most effective schools seek to encourage every student, not just the most talented athletes and the most gifted musicians, to participate in activities beyond the classroom. Parents are well advised to encourage their children to participate in extracurricular activities. Moreover, schools must challenge themselves to give recognition to the most inclusive extracurricular activities in addition to the most exclusive extracurricular activities.

As valuable as extracurricular activities are, involvement can be carried to an unhealthy extreme. I know of children whose days begin with 7:30 chess club, followed by a full day of school, followed immediately by science club from 3:30 to 4:30. Religious school follows from 4:45 to 6:00. Eating a sandwich in the car, the child barely makes the 6:15 piano lesson. Basketball practice starts at 7:00 p.m. sharp and the child arrives home, exhausted, about 8:30 p.m. The cycle will repeat itself tomorrow, with soccer practice in place of basketball practice, a violin lesson replacing the piano lesson, and student council replacing science club. A reasonable rule might be, "one sport at a time" or "no more than one private lesson per week."

What If My Child Is Assigned to a Bad School?

The first question that must be considered is what makes a "bad" school. More often than not, parents evaluate schools the same way that real estate agents do, with a review of test scores. It is more than ironic that the same parents who seek out schools with high test scores express shock when those schools demonstrate that they take tests seriously. Moreover, it strikes administrators and teachers as deeply distressing when parents choose a school based on its academic excellence, and the same parents immediately try to change the policies of the school, expressing discontent that it is "too serious" and requires too much work for their children.

It is essential to identify what choice parents have in your school district. There is a national trend toward giving parents greater choice with respect to the assignment of students to different schools, but this is by no means a universal characteristic. Frequently, students are assigned to a school and parents have no choice within the public school system. Chapter 6 provides step-by-step procedures for exploring your school choice options.

Conclusion

When you are confronted with uncertainty, there is no substitute for information. While opinions and rumor abound, solid evidence and reliable information are frequently scarce. Because you want to have information that is directly relevant to *your* needs and the education of *your* children, there is no substitute for direct personal inquiry. You may be more comfortable with letters than with personal meetings or telephone conversations. However difficult the initiation of communication may be with the teachers and administrators at your children's schools, or the leaders at the district office, this challenge is worth the effort if you are able to begin the process of open dialogue, respectful communication, and accurate information.

seek reliable information

Chapter 5

What Your Child Is Expected to Know and Do in School

The academic standards at the back of this book can seem intimidating to parents, students, and teachers. You may experience many common apprehensions as you ask these questions: How can one child possibly do all that? How can a teacher possibly cover all of that material? What were these people thinking when they wrote all of these expectations for my children? This chapter puts the list of standards into focus by identifying some of the most important expectations for your children.

Before we begin, consider the most important question: What would parents be doing to help their children if we had no standards at all? We would probably do our best to build skills in reading, writing, and mathematics. We would help our children to understand that school is important, that diligence is a worthy character trait, and that perseverance in the face of difficulty is the way that one learns to master difficult tasks. In other words, if you simply followed your instincts as a good parent, you would impart to your child many of the most important elements of academic standards. With standards to augment common sense and good parenting, you need not guess at the details. You will understand what every student is expected to know and be able to do to become a successful student.

The inevitable question arises: Does my child have to master every standard in order to be successful? The straight answer is no. The details of academic standards—particularly with respect to social studies and science—represent more content than many teachers and parents understand. That even successful students have not mastered 100 percent of this material should be no surprise. In addition, each of you will find important information—perhaps things you learned in school—that appears to be missing from this chapter and from the state academic standards. This presents every teacher and school leader with a paradox: There are simultaneously too many and too few standards. The standards that exist require more time than is available in the school year; the standards that exist omit some subject matter that many parents and teachers find interesting or even vital. This paradox simply establishes what most parents are forced to admit rather early in the lives of their children: Perfection is not an option. The use of standards in school is no exception to this maxim. Therefore, use the standards as a guide, not a straitjacket. If you follow your instincts and help your child build academic skills in reading, writing, and mathematics, and if you consistently model and reinforce the development of sound character traits, your child will be successful in school.

Reading

Chances are that you began reading to your children while they were still babies By your early efforts, you were building a love of books, an understanding of the power of stories, and the belief that words on a page have meaning. In addition to reading, you probably provided plastic books on which your baby chewed, drooled, and even appeared to "read" as the vivid images captured the attention of the infant. As babies become toddlers and new words seemed to spring from their lips every day, reading together becomes a magical experience. Even before they know letters, very young children associate words with images and thus can fill in words in the picture books that parents are reading. When I ask parents about their favorite times of learning together with their children, these early days of eager discovery, quick mastery, joint experience, incredible wonder, and lots of laughter are the times recalled most fondly.

By the ages of four and five, the association between print and words is clear to most children, and they appear to "read" because they have memorized certain symbolic patterns. These so-called "sight words" help give children confidence, and therein lies one of the early misunderstandings about what it means to become a successful reader. While we naturally celebrate the ability of children to memorize symbols and their meaning, we also must understand that reading is more than the memorization of symbolic patterns. In order to become successful lifelong readers, we must build on the initial skill of memorization and add the following critical elements: decoding, comprehension, summarization, conclusions, and predictions.

As children enter adolescence, they naturally express a desire for more independence. Bedtime stories and long hugs give way to a peck on the cheek and a brief "good night!" Nevertheless, the fundamental need of middle school students is comparable to that of students in elementary school: Kids need to be competent, successful, and appreciated by the important adults in their lives. There is much in the lives of adolescents that seems out of control. Their bodies change, relationships are unstable, and emotions are out of control. One of the few things that offers stability to the adolescent is the mastery of academic skills, including reading. Parents who nurture and reinforce these skills provide reassurance, consistency, and stability to the teenager for whom these attributes are in very short supply.

successful reading

Literacy: Still the Most Essential Skill

Many parents and teachers of middle school students make the faulty assumption that reading proficiency is a certainty for fifth and sixth grade students. After all, they reason, children should have learned how to read and write in the first grade. Although it has been a few years since parents have heard their middle school children read a bedtime story, their ability to read directions, signs, and labels surely must indicate that literacy isn't a problem for these students. Such an assumption is fundamentally flawed for three reasons. First, many parents and teachers misunderstand what "good reading" really is. Many adults listen to a first grade child read aloud and exclaim, "My, what a good reader you are!" When the same child is identified a few years later as reading below grade level, the parents and teachers respond, "The test must be flawed. She is an excellent reader! In fact, she was able to read stories aloud without making a single mistake." Unfortunately, the oral pronunciation of words is not all of what "reading" really means. At the middle school level, students must be able to read long passages of 200 to 800 words silently; then they must be able to accurately recall and summarize the ideas, events, and people that were described in the passage. Good reading is much more than reading aloud.

The second reason that the presumption of "good reading" is potentially flawed is that students in elementary school tend to focus on fiction, while the reading requirements in middle school tend to be nonfiction. In one analysis of third grade reading I conducted last year, the ratio of fiction to nonfiction reading was 90 to 1. In middle school, however, students must be able to read nonfiction passages, including text on subjects such as social studies and science, in which students may not have a personal interest.

The third reason that parents must double-check their assumption that their child is a "good reader" is that the higher students progress in elementary school, the less detailed is the assessment of reading skill by teachers and school officials. Kindergarten and first grade teachers tend to keep detailed records of student progress in letter recognition and vocabulary development. These educators frequently maintain records that show which letters and words the child understands and where they will place particular emphasis in the weeks ahead. Teachers in the upper elementary grades discard such detailed record-keeping as their curriculum demands grow. Thus, a very bright and capable student can receive excellent grades, speak with confidence and assurance in class, impress most of the adults with whom he is in contact, and yet enter the sixth grade without the ability to read, comprehend, or write at a sixth grade level. In the upper elementary and early middle school grades, the discipline of reading gradually becomes a study of literature. Students and teachers discuss stories, characters, plots, and settings. Most of these discussions take place in groups, and there is little accountability for an individual student to read and understand the text. Indeed, the clever student can participate actively in a literature discussion, asking good questions and reflecting on the comments of classmates, without ever having read the text that is being discussed. Parents must therefore be willing to suspend their understandable confidence in their own children and ask the pointed question, "Can they really read and understand the pages of middle school textbooks?"

Whether or not reading is a problem for your child, there are two simple things that every family can do to improve the reading comprehension skills of every student. If your child is a superior reader, these ideas will elevate her skills to a higher level. If your child needs help in reading, you can quickly identify the areas where help is needed and build skills on a daily basis. Neither of these ideas will take more than 20 minutes of your time. First, have your child read aloud. The necessity to read aloud with clarity and confidence is important well beyond elementary school. Middle school students rarely get practice in the skill of oral reading, yet the development and maintenance of this skill is essential for their classroom success in middle school, high school, and beyond. Reading aloud can be a wonderful family activity and the selection of reading material can range from plays, in which each family member takes a part, to texts selected in turn by each member of the family In my family, we lingered around the dinner table for a few minutes every night and each person at the table, including children and adults, would read a paragraph. Sometimes it was an article about outer space, while other evenings it was a story. Often it was a brief article from an encyclopedia, usually hauled out to settle an argument. During certain seasons of the year, religious texts were read that were consistent with our family tradition. Whatever you select, these brief minutes will allow your children to develop confident reading skills in a safe and loving environment. If they make a mistake, the result will be your gentle encouragement rather than the snickering of classmates. If there is a serious problem in reading ability, you will learn about it firsthand and not be fooled by the awarding of a B in English class.

The second way families can improve the reading comprehension skills of middle school students is the "instant book report." Traditional book reports provide superficial summaries and evaluations of books and, at the middle school level, are written once every two or three months. The instant book report takes twenty minutes, with ten minutes of reading followed by ten minutes of writing. The child can select any text, although the parent may wish to alternate the genre between fiction and nonfiction. After ten minutes of silent reading, the child closes the book, takes out a piece of paper, and writes a brief summary of the text. If this is an activity that you do regularly, you also may wish to ask your child to compare the text of today's reading to the text that she read a few days ago. While the child is writing, the parent can read the text so that the actual reading passage can be compared to the child's summary.

These two reading strategies, reading aloud and reading silently before producing a written summary, are simple but powerful ways for parents of middle school students to get at the heart of what "good reading" really means. Because the number of students assigned to each teacher in middle school is significantly greater than was the case in elementary school, few middle school teachers have the time for this sort of individual attention to students and detailed analysis of reading ability. It is up to you, the parent, to provide this, and it only takes 20 minutes of your time.

Books: Just so Twentieth Century

This book, as with most of those published in the twenty-first century thus far, is written on a computer. Much of the research that I conduct comes from Internet searches and electronically published journals. If computers and electronic communication are to be the future of the written word, why should parents invest money and time in old-fashioned books? You might as easily ask why you should attend a live symphony orchestra concert when there are so many fine compact discs available. Why should you write a thank-you note with pen in hand rather than send an e-mail? The answer to these questions is that there are intangibles to the heft of a book and the resonance of the symphony hall, and to holding a letter that someone else took the time to write that are absent when technology, no matter how elegant or sophisticated, replaces physical contact.

There is, of course, an important role that technology will play in the future of our children. There are some wonderful computer programs that are successfully used to help children develop skills. As I write these words, my seven-year-old is explaining the nature of pulleys and levers to his five-year-old friend using illustrations from a clever science program. As with many education matters, this is not an "either/or" proposition. We can nurture a love and respect for books while encouraging an understanding of appropriate uses of technology. Our priorities, however, must be clear. My observation is that there are many more students who can troll the Internet than who can write a sentence with appropriate grammar, spelling, and punctuation.

the most effective strategy

Writing

Although most educators and parents properly place an exceptional emphasis on reading, we dare not neglect the importance of writing. It is also essential to recall that language development does not proceed in a neat linear fashion in which we first perfect speaking skills, then polish reading skills, and only then proceed to writing. In fact, as students improve their writing, they also improve their ability to read, particularly with regard to the advanced skills of comprehension, summarization, and prediction. Student proficiency in writing also is associated with improved student achievement in mathematics, social studies, and science. In fact, of all the strategies that teachers and parents can use to boost student achievement, improved formal writing is the single most effective strategy that provides benefits in every other area of the curriculum.

Some parents may question whether writing is really that important when state academic tests and college admissions tests are typically multiple-choice exams. The answer is not that there is some magic in a number two pencil, but rather that writing—particularly formal nonfiction writing—requires students to think, reason, analyze, and communicate. Those skills will help students deal with multiple-choice tests and every other challenge that they face in school. Indeed, the best teachers I have observed do not see writing as a trade-off with multiple-choice tests, but rather combine these two testing methods. They routinely require students not only to choose the correct response, but also require written explanations of why one response was chosen and another possible answer was rejected. Such an approach transforms multiple-choice tests from a guessing game into a challenging and engaging intellectual task.

Some parents and teachers regard writing with pen or pencil as an ancient craft, soon to be displaced by computers. I respectfully dissent. If we think of writing not merely as a means of communication, but also as a means to enhance thinking, reasoning, analysis, and communication, then writing will not "go out of style" until thinking goes out of style. Moreover, children and adults who are able to convey in handwritten form their deep emotions and sentiments such as sympathy, appreciation, and encouragement, will find that they have a far more profound impact on those with whom they communicate than if they are brought up to rely solely on a word processor. Technology will replace neither emotions nor the need to communicate them. Thus writing, including the ability to write legibly and without the aid of a computerized spell-checker, remains an essential characteristic of the educated child.

Rewriting: The Key to Improved Writing

Think of the things your child does well. Perhaps she plays soccer. Maybe he plays the violin or piano. She might be a great swimmer. Every child has something in which enjoyment and skill coincide. Now consider how that skill was developed. It never—not once—occurred with a single effort. Many soccer balls were kicked far from the net before that first glorious goal. A fair amount of screeching preceded the successful completion of "Minuet in G" on the violin. The first attempt at the G-major scale probably omitted the F-sharp. Skills are never developed in one-shot endeavors. Children know intuitively that practice makes perfect and that the remedy for failure is additional practice. Why then, is so much written schoolwork submitted on a one-shot basis? The habit of writing a rough draft, submission to a parent or teacher for correction, and rewriting, is not merely a habit for writing; it is a habit of mind that displays perseverance and character.

The Basics: Spelling, Grammar, Punctuation, and Legibility

Some of the best support for the proposition that the basics of English communication are important in every academic and vocational setting has come from several unexpected sources. The president of an urban electricians' union, for example, addressed an audience of technical school students and parents and provided a passionate defense for the literacy requirements. "Successful members of this union must be able to read and write instructions. Mistakes in writing can mean putting yourself and others at safety risk. We require people to be good writers." Many high schools have conducted focus groups of former students who were invited to share their responses to the question, "What do you wish you would have had in school?" With remarkable consistency, students in universities noted that they were required to write not only in English class, but in history, music, economics, and every other discipline. They needed more formal writing, they admitted. Individuals in technical schools and the world of work similarly expressed their concern that they were required to write on a regular basis and that they needed additional training to do so. Whether the former student was a dispatcher in a truck stop or an undergraduate in the Ivy League, the consistent theme was a request for more writing. Of course, none of these chastened high school graduates requested more writing during the course of elementary, middle, or high school classes. The role of teachers and parents in this and many other areas is not to give children what they want, but what they need. Writing is, in brief, a skill that they need, but rarely request.

It is important that parents and teachers are specific about what "writing" really means, for too often students have been left with the impression that aimless reflections in journals fulfill the requirement for written expression. Whatever merit journal writing may have, the self-absorbed and frequently scatological reflections of teenagers do not develop the formal writing skills that students need. They need to write paragraphs with topic sentences and essays with a clear beginning, middle, and end. They need models of good writing and clear criteria for what constitutes acceptable and exemplary composition. In any other area of skill development, specificity is essential. Children would laugh at the notion that they should be creative with regard to where the soccer ball should go. Thankfully, they do not find the need to be creative with regard to the tones to which the violin is tuned. Yet, there are remarkably creative and gifted soccer players and musicians. The strict application of structure, in other words, does not remove creativity, but rather creates a clear framework within which creative expression can occur.

The overwhelming majority of writing by students in elementary and middle schools is in the form of a creative narrative. While this genre of writing is important, it is not sufficient. Specifically, students must be able to write for several purposes. First, students must write to inform. That is, they must describe an object, sequence of events, person, or situation with clarity and accuracy. Second, students must write to analyze. Typically, analytical writing involves the comparison of two different events, people, or activities. When students write analytically, they carefully explain similarities and differences between the objects of their analysis. Third, students must write to persuade. Effective persuasive writing is not an expression of personal preference, but rather an argument supported by evidence, examples, and illustrations. Although the labels of these types of writing may vary from one class to another, students must understand differences between creative writing and description, analysis, and persuasion. Middle school students can be asked to compare different books and describe the characters, settings, and plots of novels. It is particularly important for students in middle school social studies and science classes to be able to express a conclusion and support it with evidence. My interviews with secondary school and college faculty members reveal that the single greatest deficiency among their students is writing, and in particular, nonfiction writing in the form of description, analysis, and persuasion. College students who persist in the illusion that a successful argument begins with the words "I feel" have, at some early point in their academic career, been denied the opportunity to learn the craft of writing.

Mathematics

The controversies involving mathematics education have mirrored the phonics vs. whole language debate. Typically, the terminology of the math wars includes "problem-solving" and "number operations," with advocates of the "new, new math" preferring the former over the latter and traditionalists taking the reverse point of view. While few thoughtful people doubt that problem-solving is a useful skill in mathematics, it is baffling to me that anyone would think that skill in solving mathematical problems can be developed without an understanding of calculation. Conversely, no mastery of the times tables replaces the necessity to read a story problem and write a clear explanation for a solution. The debate between these extremes implies a dichotomy that is illogical. Students must have both the ability to read and write about mathematics, as well as a sound grounding in the fundamentals of arithmetic.

One common source of friction is the use of calculators. Indeed, calculators are commonly used in math classes, based on the "obvious" proposition that students would be foolish not to make use of the best technology at hand. Evidence reported in the *Wall Street Journal* (December 15, 2000, p. A1) indicates that students who make frequent use of calculators in class perform at much lower levels on state tests than students who use calculators only two or three times a month. This is no surprise to the parent or math teacher who has witnessed a child instinctively reach for a calculator when asked to multiply three times three. Worse yet, if the student hits a wrong key and the screen says that the answer is 25, she may have been conditioned to place more confidence in the calculator than in her own understanding that three groups of three cannot conceivably yield a product of 25. This is not merely an issue of discipline and the "basics." Some of the most sophisticated mathematics at the secondary school and collegiate levels require students to be able to estimate. Their ability in "mental math," and their confidence in making a judgment about what a likely answer might be, is an important input into some statistical and financial equations. In sum, calculators do not replace the need for the disciplined thinking in mathematics any more than word processors replace the need for thoughtful analysis in an English class.

building sound skills

If You Are Intimidated by Math

It is possible, even likely, that your own experiences in mathematics were not favorable in school. Moreover, the format, content, and sheer size of mathematics textbooks can be intimidating. Nevertheless, there are many things you can do to help your children develop sound mathematical skills. In addition to the many activities suggested at the back of this book, there are four common household themes that will build the math skills of your children. These include games, money, time, and measurement. Children love games, and keeping score is normally part of this family activity Parents may be tempted to take on the scorekeeping duties in the name of accuracy or speed. This is a missed opportunity. My experience is that if one child is keeping score, every other child at the table will be doing the same thing, keeping an eagle eye out for errors. When the parent keeps score, children may passively accept the calculations. Money offers an exceptional opportunity to build mental math skills. If children are paid an allowance or compensated for chores, parents should make a point of providing money in different denominations and combinations. Middle school is a wonderful opportunity for budding entrepreneurs to mow lawns, baby-sit, sell popcorn and soft drinks, or engage in other creative ways to make money and, of course, keep careful track of the income and expenses of the enterprise. A regular review of the business records creates opportunities to practice the arithmetic involved in subtracting expenses from income to yield profit, and to introduce questions that involve common middle school challenges such as percents, decimals, fractions, and ratios. The power of these authentic situations is that they give genuine value and meaning to the field of mathematical problem-solving. These situations are no longer the academic questions of a textbook, but real-world situations that have relevance to your child's activities. How well does Pepsi sell compared to Dr. Pepper? How did sales change from week to week during the summer? If I charged a flat fee for the lawn job, how much did I make per hour?

Time is a theme that governs many households, yet the predominance of digital clocks prevents many children from learning to tell time or to solve problems regarding the intervals between different time periods. Daily reinforcement of these skills can occur with questions such as, "What time is it now, and how many minutes before school starts?" Finally, the theme of measurement offers abundant opportunities for the building of math skills in the kitchen, the yard, home construction jobs, or marking off athletic fields. Because measurement refers to space and volume, these lessons cannot be learned by reading a chapter in a math book about measurement. Students learn about measurement by measuring, by observing the impact of measurement mistakes, by making corrections, and by learning the carpenter's rule to "measure twice, cut once."

Science | a spirit of inquiry

As intimidating as mathematics may be, the science curriculum can be even more baffling to many parents. The traditional curriculum of weather, dinosaurs, and volcanoes has been replaced by an early emphasis on the physical, chemical, and biological sciences. Both state standards and school texts can present remarkably sophisticated challenges for students. Despite these challenges, there are several things that parents can do that will improve the scientific thinking of their children.

Parents can encourage a spirit of inquiry, helping children to understand that science is not just about providing answers, but also about asking questions. Real scientists are not just smart people who have all the answers. Even very famous scientists, such as Galileo, have been spectacularly wrong about many of their theories. Science advances through the process of generating a theory, developing alternative hypotheses, and then systematically testing those hypotheses. For science to advance, we must disprove hypotheses. This means that for every gain in scientific knowledge, some very smart scientist was proven wrong. This does not diminish the credibility or importance of scientific work. Indeed, the researcher's aphorism is, "We learn more from error than from uncertainty." This is a good rule in the lives of students as well. When they don't know the answer, testing an idea—even if such a test proves their previous conceptions to be untrue—is better than proceeding in ignorance.

Scientific observation can occur in the home every day when children pose the hypothetical question, "What will happen if I do this?" If we announce the answer, we deny our children the opportunity to generate a hypothesis and then test it through systematic observation. Children are full of "why" questions that are directly susceptible to the generation of hypotheses and systematic testing.

- **Why do some years have 365 days and other years have 366 days?**

- **Why is it colder in January and hotter in July in the Northern Hemisphere, but the other way around in the Southern Hemisphere?**

- **If I drop a penny and a baseball from the top of a ladder, which one will hit the ground first?**

The list is endless. The key is not for parents to attempt to become walking encyclopedias, but to build a spirit of inquiry and testing in which children are not afraid to generate thoughtful guesses and then test those guesses. Real scientists, and thoughtful students, are not afraid to routinely write the words, "My hypothesis was not supported by the evidence." This approach to learning values evidence over alchemy and thus is not only a sound intellectual trait, but an opportunity to build sound character as well.

Social Studies

The amount of content in social studies curricula can be overwhelming. Spanning the subjects of history, geography, civics, and economics, social studies texts can add many pounds to your child's backpack and nevertheless omit many important subjects. Despite the bewildering array of complex ideas in the subjects involved in social studies, parents can reinforce some fundamental understandings that every child should have.

The first and most important principle to understand is that advancement in social studies is directly related to student proficiency in reading and writing. Make no mistake: If your child needs help in reading and writing, then you and the teachers must devote time to these areas as a priority. Of course, it is possible to use reading texts that include history and government. There is, however, no substitute for absolute proficiency in literacy as an antecedent to the study of social studies. I have never heard a secondary school teacher say, "I wish that more students knew the capital of South Dakota," but I have heard hundreds of them say, "I wish that more students could read my textbook."

Government and Civics

At the end of the Cold War, President Gorbachev of the former Soviet Union famously said to General (now Secretary of State) Colin Powell, "General, you will have to find yourself another enemy." While Americans who grew up in the 1940s and 1950s rejoiced at the diminution of world tensions, and the reduction in the likelihood that our own children would face the prospect of nuclear war, the demise of the Soviet Union also changed conversations in schools and homes. For the last decade, we rarely talked about the difference between democracy and authoritarian forms of government with the same urgency that we did when our own form of government seemed to be threatened. These are distinctions that remain important and are among the fundamental concepts that students must know. If you can take your children to see any democratically elected body in action, it is worth the trip. If you live near the state capital, watch the legislature in session. Better yet, arrange to have your child serve as a page in one of the legislative chambers for a day. If distance from the capital prevents such an excursion, then take your children to a meeting of the school board, county commission, or city council. The concept of representative democracy is fundamental and every child should understand that one of the distinguishing parts of our heritage of freedom is the ability to vote, selecting men and women who do the public's bidding. Of course, parents who wish to encourage good civic behavior by their children must vote, and you may wish to consider taking your children with you to observe this most fundamental civic right and obligation. There can be little doubt in the aftermath of the presidential election of 2000 that every vote has an important influence on the future of the nation.

History

History has been the subject of the most hotly debated state standards. Part of this controversy stems from the idiosyncratic manner in which history has been taught in schools, with the principal source of differentiation being the personal preference of the teacher. Some teachers devote weeks to the building of scale models of the Coliseum as a substitute for the study of ancient Rome, while others devote the month of November to an historically inaccurate drama inevitably focusing on Pocahontas and John Smith. Other classrooms devote weeks to Custer's Last Battle, while others linger for months on the Civil War. Few, however, stop to ask what the study of history is all about and many leave students with the conviction that it is simply "a bunch of facts" that are regurgitated on demand. If the teacher deliberately avoided the fact-based approach to history, then students would have the impression that history is a series of disjointed dramas and personal stories. The presence of social studies standards offers the beginning of some coherence to the study of this discipline.

Let us first put to rest the "facts vs. themes" controversy. Students need to learn historical facts. It is preposterous to assume that students can apply higher order thinking skills to history, geography, and economics without understanding that the Civil War preceded Vietnam, that the Balkans are not the Baltics, and that there is rarely a singular cause for an historical or economic effect. While not every date is of equal importance, a sense of sequence in the broad sweep of history is essential if students are to have an appropriate context for their understanding of historical events, political decisions, and cultural artifacts of the time. The words of the song, "Battle Hymn of the Republic" have a profoundly different meaning for students who have studied the words as part of their understanding of 19th century history.

Parents can reinforce this understanding of historical context by talking about family history. Family trees and time lines can lend context that many children do not understand. If your children have parents, grandparents, or great-grandparents who fought in a war, then encourage serious family discussion about those events. For today's students, Vietnam is simply one more piece of history, as removed from their reality as the World Wars of the last century, or the many conflicts of centuries long past. If you can add profound family context to these events, the lessons learned by your children will have value far beyond a few paragraphs in a textbook. Every community has historical landmarks and most have museums. Although the events commemorated in those monuments may not be the focus of your school's textbooks, there is nothing to match the visual impression of personal observation. If your family has the resources to take a vacation, then plan to spend a week or more in the nation's capital. Let your children see the Constitution, the Declaration of Independence, and the words of Lincoln beneath his majestic statue.

adding context

Foreign Language, Music, and Art

Although this book focuses on the core academic areas of language arts, mathematics, social studies, and science, parents are wise to reinforce their children's pursuit of studies in foreign language, music, and art. At the very least, study of a foreign language will help to build English vocabulary, and at best will improve your child's understanding of other cultures. Much of the world's classic literature first appeared in languages other than English, and by opening the door to the study of other languages, you will provide a lifelong gift with which your children can explore other cultures and lands. Even a slight familiarity with another language allows your children to recognize the value of courtesy when they are guests in other nations.

The study of music is one of the most important disciplines for children. It is not necessary for your child to become a concert pianist or to play first chair in the saxophone section of the school band. The study of music, however, will improve your child's understanding of mathematics with the study of rhythm and notation. The study of songs will build your child's vocabulary and reading skills. The occasional performance will build confidence and presence.

The study of art allows your child a creative outlet that can be successfully combined with many other disciplines. Because vivid images are one of the best ways for children to acquire understanding and knowledge, the study of art should include not only the creation of original pieces of art, but trips to the museum and the observation of the art work of the world's great artists. The connection between art and written expression is particularly important. A wonderful way to build your child's skills in analytical writing is the comparison of two pieces of art. Moreover, students can illustrate their creative and nonfiction work with vivid illustrations that reflect their words.

respect, teamwork, and integrity

Behavior

No discussion of learning at home is complete without addressing the issue of behavior. Veteran teachers frequently complain of the extent to which behavioral education has been transferred from parents to schools, and teachers readily acknowledge that schools are ill-equipped to begin teaching respect, teamwork, and integrity in a classroom for six hours a day if those values were not taught before a child's schooling began and reinforced before and after the school day.

Although every family has its own code of behavior, these differences need not obscure some fundamental obligations that people, including school children, have in a civil society. Parents may differ about the need to call adults "sir" and "ma'am," but every parent has an obligation to instill in children a respect for the authority of teachers and school leaders. No amount of parental guilt due to absence and no amount of parental recollections of unsatisfactory relationships with their own parents justifies the wholesale abandonment of behavioral training. Even more shocking than the abandonment of parental attempts to instill codes of civil behavior in children is the frequent support of student behavior that is disruptive, rude, and dangerous, as if the school had an obligation to conform to the behavioral code of the children, rather than the reverse.

In addition to encouraging a fundamental respect for adult authority, parents can build sound behavior in their children by insisting upon good organization in everything from the toy box to the dresser, closet, and backpacks. The adage, "A place for everything and everything in its place" may not conform to the adults who routinely display messy desks and ridicule their more organized colleagues. Nevertheless, secondary school educators routinely speak of students who fail not because of poor intellectual skills, but due to lack of the most fundamental organizational skills. The teachers assumed that children would learn these skills at home, while parents assumed the children would pick up these traits at school. Meanwhile, school lockers resemble toxic waste dumps, completed homework assignments are lost in a backpack full of trash, and bright students flounder because they lack simple organizational skills and habits.

The most important consideration with regard to building strong organizational skills is to establish the fact that good student organization is a skill, not an inherited genetic trait. Writing assignments in a notebook, making daily lists of things that must be done, and putting away books and toys are not matters encoded in DNA; they are skills and habits that are taught, learned, practiced, and developed over time.

What to Do When You Can't Do it All: Power Standards

Having reached the end of this chapter and not yet confronted the list of standards at the end of this book, the skeptical reader might be tempted to exclaim, "Twenty minutes a day? He's got to be kidding! I could devote hours every day to the reading, writing, mathematics, science, music, and art, and never even get to the behavior and organizational stuff. Attempting to make a difference in 20 minutes is sheer fantasy."

Your skepticism is understandable. Moreover, this perception of standards and school curricula as overwhelming burdens is shared by many teachers and school leaders who know that even the most diligent teacher may not produce students who know and understand every single standard. Nevertheless, the plain fact remains that your time does matter and that 20 minutes a day makes a world of difference. Without question, the homes in which independent reading routinely takes place probably have other characteristics, including access to books, caring adults, quiet space, and time. Nevertheless, the evidence is clear. Student achievement can dramatically improve without transforming school and home into a joyless test prep center. Rather, the ideas in this book, implemented incrementally and balanced between academic and behavioral objectives, serve to have a clear and dramatic impact on student success.

Given the overwhelming number of standards and the many activities in this book, a fair question to ask is, "Where do we start?" The concept of "power standards" provides one mechanism for parents, teachers, and students to choose wisely among many available alternatives. The notion of power standards suggests that the choice is not necessarily based on popularity, but on impact. Power standards must pass three thresholds. First, they must have endurance. In other words, some information memorized for a particular test is liberated from our neurons within nanoseconds after the completion of a test. While the knowledge that Pb is the chemical symbol for lead may be of use when the *Jeopardy* category is Chemical Symbols, it is not a piece of knowledge that has endurance. While the scientific method endures, memorization of chemical symbols and, for that matter, the dimensions of the stegosaurus do not.

The second criterion for power standards is leverage. This chapter has already highlighted a skill that provides students with leverage, that is, it has impact on many different subjects. When students write more frequently, particularly when that writing includes formal submissions with rewriting based on teacher feedback, student achievement improves not only in writing, but in mathematics, social studies, and science.

Another example of leverage is the skill involved in creating tables, charts, and graphs, and the understanding necessary to draw inferences from the graphic representation of data. This requirement not only appears in the mathematics standards, but also in academic standards for science, social studies, and language arts. Time invested in the development of a skill with leverage will pay dividends in many different academic areas.

The third threshold that power standards must cross is that they be necessary for success at the next level of instruction. Whenever I have challenged teachers to narrow the focus of their curriculum and omit a chapter, activity, or unit, they frequently respond that "everything I do is important" and besides, "The children will need this information for the next grade." When I ask the same teachers to provide advice for a new teacher who has the responsibility for students in the next lower grade, the story changes. While the fifth grade teacher may insist that "everything I do is important," the sixth-grade teacher is quite willing to provide a very brief list of requirements for fifth grades. The fifth-grade teacher is similarly willing to provide clarity and focus for a suggested fourth-grade curriculum. In contrast to the lists of standards and test objectives that include scores of items and extend to several pages, the lists of requirements for the next lower grade that I routinely receive from teachers rarely exceeds a dozen items and seldom exceeds a single page. Part of this phenomenon may be the very human characteristic that it is easier to give advice than to take it. The inescapable conclusion, however, is that teachers and parents know that hasty and superficial coverage of massive amounts of curriculum is not as effective as thorough student knowledge of the most important elements of the curriculum.

While reasonable people may differ with regard to the ideal curriculum, no parent wishes students to be in a classroom where reading is not valued. Few parents would find competent the teacher who provides writing requirements only on rare occasions. In other words, while reasonable people may disagree about the universe of standards, most parents and teachers can apply the three criteria—endurance, leverage, and readiness for the next grade—and quickly arrive at a consensus on the most important pieces of information that are the non-negotiable. These are the areas of knowledge and skill that students must absolutely, positively have in order to be successful. This might mean that the scale model of the Coliseum gives way to improved reading instruction, that the eighteenth annual dramatization of Pocahontas yields to the need to master fractions, and the recollections of summer vacations are supplanted with a better understanding of the Constitution. In brief, power standards help teachers and parents make choices in the real world of limited time.

What's Worth Fighting For

Although it may appear that the burdens of standards are staggering, there are only a few areas on which parents must absolutely insist both with regard to student work at home and the curriculum in school. Those areas worth the assertion of parental authority include thinking, reasoning, and communication. If you find that students are only being asked to complete drill sheets rather than engage in deep and thoughtful analysis, it is essential that such practices are challenged with the evidence that the path toward greater student achievement lies not in mindless test preparation, but in extensive analysis, reasoning, and writing. If you find that students are taking exclusively multiple-choice tests and rarely if ever are required to write, then it is essential that such practices are challenged with the evidence that more frequent student writing not only builds thinking and reasoning skills, but also improves student performance on multiple-choice tests.

Although parents may not win every issue of contention over curriculum and testing, these discussions with teachers and school officials will make clear that the obligation of the parent is not merely to support homework and reinforce the skills required by the school. Sometimes the most important obligation of the parent is to provide complementary skills in those areas that the school is short-changing. If writing is underemphasized, then it is important that parents pay particular attention to writing requirements as part of your 20-Minute Learning Connection. If math calculation is underemphasized in the name of improved problem-solving techniques, then parents must make up the shortfall with an emphasis on the development of sound basic skills in addition, subtraction, multiplication, and division. If the discussion of literature takes precedence over the development of reading comprehension skills, then parents must give children the opportunity for independent reading—both aloud and silently—at home. Most importantly, parents must ensure that students can understand the text before them and write a brief summary that is accurate and complete.

When parents are proactive as advocates for their children, then they not only help future generations of children, but also immediately and decisively intervene in the educational lives of their own children.

be a proactive advocate

Chapter 6

Before School Begins: Planning for School Success

The 20-Minute Learning Connection begins long before children enter school. Part of the success of parent planning is a commitment to being proactive rather than reactive when dealing with school issues. This chapter addresses the strategies parents can use to maximize their influence on their children's educational opportunities.

Much of the recent discussion about parent choice in schools has been focused on the politically volatile issue of school vouchers. Although only a very few school systems in the nation offer publicly funded vouchers that parents may choose to use for a private school education for their children, there is frequently a great deal of choice that parents can and should exercise with regard to the educational opportunities for their children.

Choosing Schools

In some school districts, a parent's request for school "choice" is welcomed as an indication of positive involvement. Even some large urban school systems pride themselves on the claim that more than 90 percent of parents and children receive their first choice of school. In other school systems, however, choice of school is something exercised only by the administration, with boundary lines, program assignment, and bus schedules, all matters that are announced to parents, rather than decisions that invite participation and comparison among alternatives.

If you wish to get the straight story about parent rights and choice in your district, it is important that you ask the right questions. Figure 6.1 provides an easy guide to the specific questions you should ask school administrators in your district about your rights as a parent. Don't settle for a form letter or impromptu policy statement by a harried administrator. Ask the questions and write down the answers.

FIGURE 6.1
What Are My Choices?

School Administration Telephone Number:_____

Name of Administrator:_____

Introduction:

"Hello. My name is _____ and my child is a student in this district. I would like to ask some questions about the choices of schools available to my child. Are you the right person to talk with about this matter?"

If "no": "Thanks very much. Who should I speak with about this?"

 Name:_____

 Phone Number: _____

If "Yes": "That's great. Do you have a moment so that I can learn more about this?"

"Does the district have a voucher program that provides funding for private schools?"

❑ No

❑ Yes

❑ Details:_____

"Does the district have any charter schools?"

❑ No

❑ Yes

❑ Details:_____

"Is my child required to attend the school nearest to me, or may I select any of the public schools available?"

❑ Your child must attend local school. That is:_____

❑ Your child may choose any school.

❑ Your child may go to another school, but must deal with certain restrictions.

❑ Your child may go to another school, but families living close to each school have first priority, and people outside of the boundaries of that school are only permitted to enroll if there is space available.

❑ Additional details:_____

If no choice at all: "I understand that you are saying I have no choice of schools at all. Is that correct? So that I understand this clearly, are you saying that there are no situations in the school district at all in which students are attending a school other than their official assigned school? Could you please tell me about these exceptions to your normal policy?

If choice is available: "That's great. Is there a written policy that governs the choices that I have as a parent? Would you please send me a printed copy of that policy?"

"Just one more question. Where can I find information about the different schools? Is there an accountability report or other document that will provide detailed information about the enrollment, teaching staff, and academic programs of each school in the district?"

"Thank you very much."

Although most public school systems are far from a genuine market system in which consumers can make informed choices from among a variety of alternatives, there is frequently much more choice available than parents recognize. Although only a tiny minority of school systems offers publicly funded vouchers and only a few school systems offer charter schools that may appeal to some parents, virtually every school system with more than one school will provide some level of parent choice if the matter is pressed. The purpose for the inquiry is not necessarily to engage in political advocacy for vouchers, charters, or other forms of school choice. Rather, the purpose for your question is simply to ensure that you have the best possible information with which you can make a reasoned judgment.

choose wisely

Making the Best Choice

Once you have determined that you have some level of school choice, it is important that you choose wisely. The label of the school tells you very little about the quality of the curriculum and teachers. For example, some charter schools are among the very best in the nation; some charter schools have been abject failures. The label "charter" does little to assure a parent of educational quality. Rather, you must make specific inquiries about the curriculum, teaching, and leadership of the school. Sometimes these inquiries may be uncomfortable, as many schools have a history of operating free from parental scrutiny. Many other schools welcome parent questions and provide easy-to-understand accountability information for parents or any other member of the community. Regardless of the ease with which you acquire this data, the following questions will serve as a useful guide for your conversations about schools, curricula, teachers, and leadership.

Your inquiries must be specific. First, you'll want to know what the academic expectations of the school are. The assurance that "we are standards-based" or "we follow the state standards" is not sufficient. You deserve a direct answer to this question: "What is my child expected to know and be able to do at the beginning of the school year and at the end of the school year?" You should receive a specific list of the knowledge and skills with which your child should enter and leave each grade level. Anything less than a straightforward response to this inquiry is evidence that the school is "standards-based" in name only, and that curriculum anarchy prevails. The extent to which individual teachers can choose to make extraordinary departures from the curriculum is stunning to many parents. Some teachers offer little or no science, while others emphasize science to the exclusion of essential literacy programs. Some teachers invest extraordinary amounts of time in student performances, often with the enthusiastic encouragement and support of parents, omitting large amounts of academic requirements. A great number of teachers emphasize arts and crafts more than academic requirements. Kati Haycock, president of the Education Trust, recently observed that in classroom after classroom she witnessed more coloring assignments than reading, writing, and mathematics assignments. You must ask, "What is my child expected to know and be able to do?" The principal and individual teachers must be able to answer this question clearly and without hesitation. If the response is unclear to you, academic expectations will be the subject of mystery and ambiguity for your child.

Another important part of your consideration of curriculum is testing and assessment. Curriculum without testing is wishful thinking. All the elegant lesson plans, detailed curriculum documents, and heavy textbooks in the world have little impact if there is not a systematic method of determining the extent to which students are learning what is expected. Do not settle for unspecific assurances such as, "We do regular testing." Ask to see the results for the past two years of the state and district tests that are related to the academic standards and curriculum requirements of the school. Determine for yourself whether students in this school are learning what school leaders believe that students are learning.

Second, you want to know about the teaching qualifications of the staff. Teachers typically receive certifications for specific subjects, particular groups of grade levels, or both. While certification is no guarantee of quality, the evidence is overwhelming that students taught by noncertified teachers perform at significantly lower levels than students under the tutelage of certified teachers. Many school systems have emphasized reductions in class size. Unfortunately, they have filled some classrooms with well-intentioned, but untrained, people. You must insist that your child be taught by a certified teacher. In addition, the educational background and experience of the staff should be examined. Advanced degrees and extensive experience is no guarantee of quality, but you may wish to consider carefully whether your child should be in the classroom of a teacher with little or no experience.

Third, you want to learn about the leadership of the school. In some schools, the principal operates autonomously, with little or no oversight. In other schools, a collaborative decision-making body includes teachers, parents, and administrators. Sometimes these committees operate differently in practice than the theory with which they were originated. The best way for you to address this is to ask when the next meeting of the decision-making committee will be and plan to attend the meeting. Does the group make substantive contributions to the decision-making process? Do some groups dominate the discussion? Do parents have a real voice on matters such as curriculum, instruction, and policy? Finally, ask this specific question: "Can you give me an example of how parents have influenced the curriculum and instruction policies of the school?"

There is no doubt about this fact: You have a right to make these inquiries. Information about curriculum and teacher qualifications is not secret. If you receive anything less than completely forthcoming information, then you should make a written inquiry to your district superintendent. Figure 6.2 provides an example of how you can make these inquiries in a courteous and businesslike manner.

FIGURE 6.2
Inquiry Letter to School Superintendent

(name), Superintendent of Schools
(district name)
(address, city, state, zip)
Re: Information concerning _____ school
Dear (Dr./Ms./Mr.) _____:

On (date) I met with the principal of _____ school. The purpose of my meeting was to learn more about the curriculum, teaching, and leadership of the school my children may attend next year. I still have some questions about these matters and I would appreciate your assistance in responding to them.

With respect to the curriculum, I am particularly interested in the specific academic expectations of my children and how those expectations are assessed. If there are specific curriculum standards that every child is expected to meet, I would like to see them. In addition, I would like to know if there are district or state tests that address the extent to which the school has met those academic expectations in the past. I would also appreciate seeing the results from those assessments for the past two years. Please let me know if there are differences among the curriculum based on choices made by each teacher or if the curriculum is the same for each teacher. If there are differences, please elaborate on those differences.

With respect to the faculty, I would like to know about the subject matter and grade-level certification of the staff, their educational backgrounds, and teaching experience. If some faculty members have particular interests or areas of expertise, please share that information as well.

Finally, I am very interested to learn about the leadership of the school and particularly about the manner in which parents are able to participate in school decision-making. If there is a governing or advisory body in which parents participate, I would like to learn more about the operations of this group and when its next meeting will be held.

Thank you very much for your assistance.

Sincerely,

(your name)

be courteous but persistent

Choosing Teachers

Parent choice of teachers is a delicate subject. Reasonable people may disagree on the matter. Those advocating parent choice see it as a way of encouraging parent involvement and ensuring that parents have a vested interest in supporting the teacher and encouraging their child to succeed. Certainly most parents believe that they know their children better than anyone and are therefore best equipped to determine which teachers and educational programs are best suited for their children. Those opposing parent choice of teachers see this practice as an inequitable device in which activist parents get better teachers for their children than parents who do not have the time, ability, or interest to attempt to influence school administrators. Moreover, some administrators fear that parent choice is more of a popularity contest fueled by rumor than a choice based on professional abilities. In addition, some administrators worry that teachers might make unwise educational decisions in an attempt to be popular with parents. Finally, there is the concern that since teaching ability and popularity never will be equally distributed among various teachers in a grade level, some classes might be overburdened with too many students in a quest to meet the demands of parents.

Whatever the policy of your local school, it is important that parents take the time to understand the extent of their ability to influence the assignment of students to the classroom. Even if there is an official policy against parent choice, parents are entitled to ask questions about the differences among teachers with regard to certification, education, experience, and educational practices. While some of this information may be obtained through public documents, other matters, such as the educational practices of individual teachers, will only be revealed through interviews and observation.

When you make your initial inquiries about teachers, you will likely be told, "All of our teaching staff are excellent. Besides, we all have state standards, so you'll find that pretty much every class is the same. That's why we handle teacher assignment." You should be courteous but persistent in pursuing your inquiries. After you have learned the basics—certification, education, experience—you will need to dig deeper. Talk with your child's prospective teacher, preferably in the classroom. Plan to spend more time listening than talking. This is not the time for you to articulate your educational philosophy, but rather the time for you to determine what the philosophy and practices of the teacher will be. This is a difficult but important consideration: Your time is better spent finding a school and teacher that conform to your philosophy than attempting to convince a school and teacher that they should change their philosophies to agree with you.

Here are some things to notice as you enter the classroom:

❏ **Student work:** Is student work prominently posted around the room? If so, is there clear and specific feedback on what work is acceptable and what work needs improvement? Does every paper, including poor work, have a "smiley face," or does the teacher provide encouraging but clear guidance on how to improve? Are there samples of exemplary work that represent the educational target for students?

❏ **Class rules:** Are there high standards of behavior that are clear and unambiguous? Does the appearance of the classroom indicate that students take good care of their personal property and school property?

❏ **Teacher's desk:** Does the teacher set an example of organization and neatness?

❏ **Availability:** Were you welcomed into the classroom at any time or was your entry into the classroom restricted to specific pre-announced times? Were other parents actively volunteering, participating, and improving the learning environment?

Following is a list of things you should discuss with the teacher. It is absolutely important to take the time to listen to the responses without interruption. You want to solicit clear and unambiguous answers. You might need to draw the teacher out with some encouraging phrases such as, "Please tell me a little more about that."

❑ What should a child know and be able to do at the beginning of the school year? In other words, what preparation should a successful student have before coming to your class?

❑ What should a student know and be able to do at the end of this school year? Please be as specific as possible.

❑ How do you assess student progress? May I please see an example of one of the tests you routinely use to assess student progress? What is the consequence when a student does poorly on a test? Can you please provide an example of a time when you changed the curriculum based on your analysis of the assessment results of the class? If my child does badly on a test, how soon will I be informed? Are there reports of student progress other than the report card?

❑ Please tell me about your favorite things to teach. Are there certain areas for which you provide extra emphasis based on your personal interest and knowledge?

❑ Are there some areas that you are not as comfortable teaching? Are there certain areas that you tend to emphasize less as a result?

❑ As a parent, how can I be most supportive of my child's education? Are there particular things that the parents of students in your class should do?

❑ Please explain your homework policy. How much homework should students normally have? What is the consequence when a student fails to turn in homework?

❑ What is your policy with regard to parent volunteers in the classroom?

❏ **What is the practice of the school and your class with regard to extracurricular activities? If these activities occur during the regular school day, do students make up for lost instructional time? If so, please explain.**

❏ **May I please see a copy of the report card form? Please explain how grades or other marks on the report card are determined. Is there a written grading policy? May I please have a copy of it?**

❏ **What happens when students learn and complete their work at different levels of speed and proficiency? What assistance is provided to students who are slower or less proficient? What enrichment is provided to students who are quicker or more proficient? If enrichment work is provided, could you please show me an example of such a task?**

While these questions are certainly not exhaustive, they provide the basis for a continuing conversation and mutual understanding between parent and teacher. Even if there is absolutely no parent choice with regard to teacher and class assignment, this conversation will allow you and your child to begin the year with greater clarity and less ambiguity. Such a conversation also makes clear to the teacher that you are genuinely interested in the education of your children and that you are willing to be helpful and supportive of the teacher.

When You Need to Change Teachers

Many teachers are wonderful. They are dedicated professionals who work extra hours, take a personal interest in every child, and who are remembered by generations of students who were lucky enough to be in their classroom. Students in these classes may not come home every day having had fun, but they always come home having been challenged to do their best. Many teachers are solid practitioners, perhaps a little cynical because of their treatment at the hands of administrators and school boards. These teachers have had a few run-ins with parents, and those experiences left the teacher wondering whether the parents really wanted to support education or just wanted a babysitting service for their child. These teachers can provide a solid education for your children, but they are not the exceptional educators who will inspire a child to excellence. A few teachers are truly incompetent. Their classrooms are out of control, perhaps dangerous. Sometimes they scream; sometimes they are silent in the face of belligerent behavior that appears to be tacitly approved by their silence. They play favorites and the incomprehensibility of their evaluation system makes it impossible to tell how grades are awarded. Some of these terrible teachers embrace every new fad, sometimes to the exclusion of educational basics; others have learned nothing since they left college, perhaps decades ago. They rarely ask students to write, and the teacher's own writing is full of errors in grammar and spelling. Their personal understanding of the subjects that they teach rarely extends beyond the textbook, so that if there were errors in the science or social studies text, they would be unlikely to notice.

In the course of thirteen years of education, from kindergarten through the completion of high school, your children will probably have more than fifty different teachers, assuming one or more teacher for each elementary grade and six or seven teachers for each middle school and high school grade. Of these fifty teachers, some will be wonderful, some will be solid practitioners, and perhaps a very few will be incompetent. If that is the case, you have an obligation to intervene. In some cases, such as with an unclear grading policy, the situation may improve with a simple request. In most cases of a true incompetent, however, no amount of cajoling or complaining will change the fact that the person in the classroom is not equipped to do the job. Whatever the inconvenience, you will be less aggravated and your child will be better educated if you insist on a change. You may be able to change to a different teacher within your school or it may be necessary to change schools. In extreme cases, where the district and school administration are extremely uncooperative, it may be necessary to change to a different public school system or to find a charter or private school that will meet your child's needs. The impact of this disruption is negligible when compared to the impact of a lost year of learning.

If you request a change of teacher, you must have your facts straight. Present to the principal a written request, identifying the specific objections you have. If there were particular behaviors by the teacher to which you object, identify with as much specificity as possible the circumstances, the exact behavior (not the attitudes or motivation, just the behavior) that you observed, and precisely when it occurred. You should expect to have the principal listen to you politely, and then refuse your request for a change. In general, school administrators deplore change and are supportive of teachers in most instances of teacher-parent disagreement. Remain calm, make your case with clarity and specificity, and ask for a written notice of the principal's decision. If the decision is against your wishes, ask also for the written notice to include information on the next level of decision authority. There is no such thing as a decision that cannot be appealed, and you must pursue the matter with the district administration if necessary.

One final issue should be considered before you proceed to change teachers, schools, or systems. You must ensure that the alternative is genuinely better. That means that you have taken the time to have the same conversation with the prospective teachers in the other classrooms or alternative schools that you had with your child's current teacher. You cannot assume that simply because a school has a good reputation, is a charter school, is a private school, is exclusive, or is expensive that the individual classroom to which your child is assigned will be one of quality and challenge. There is no substitute for asking the questions listed above, starting with the simple, "What is my child expected to know and be able to do at the end of this year?"

get ready

Parents' Checklist for the Week Before School Begins

❑ Gradually begin to move your child's bedtime back (getting up at 6 a.m. can be quite a shock after "summer hours").

❑ Do any last minute shopping for school supplies. Try not to leave it all until the week before school starts, as the shelves may be stripped. Instead, try to start shopping for school supplies two or three weeks before school starts.

    ❑ Plan ahead. Know what you need to buy before you're in the store.

    ❑ Try office supply stores and warehouse stores. You'll find better prices.

    ❑ Try to involve your child in the shopping and decision-making. After all, these are the notebooks and pencils she'll be using.

❑ Let your child choose something special to wear or bring on the first day of school. A new backpack or his favorite shirt may help make things less overwhelming.

❑ If possible, visit school before it opens, and locate the places your child is likely to visit often. Once school begins, don't be surprised if your middle school student does not want you around to be helpful.

    ❑ Restrooms

    ❑ Counseling office

    ❑ Main office

    ❑ Nurse's office

    ❑ Gym

    ❑ Cafeteria

    ❑ Where to buy lunch tickets

    ❑ Locker

    ❑ Where to catch the bus

❑ Get a copy of the bell/class schedule and look it over along with a map of the school.

❑ If your child will be bringing a sack lunch to school, consult her on the menu.

❑ If your child will be walking to school or to the bus stop, make sure he is familiar with the route and with "safe places" along the way (friends' houses, stores you frequent, etc.).

❑ Be open, alert, and sympathetic to any and all questions about school, as well as to moods and behaviors that may indicate fear and anxiety on the child's part.

Parents' Checklist for the First Week of School

❑ Once again, be alert. Ask a lot of questions and make eye contact and affirming comments when your child answers. Make sure he knows you want to be involved and that you are listening to him.

❑ **Some direct questions to ask:**

  ❑ Where is your locker? Is it conveniently located? How often can you go to it? Do you have to carry all your books all day long?

  ❑ Where is lunch? Do you have someone to sit with? Do you know how to get through the lunch lines? Do you know where to buy lunch tickets?

  ❑ Are you having trouble with any kids?

  ❑ Are you thinking of trying out for any sports or plays, or joining any clubs? How can I help?

❑ **If you happen to have one of those kids who doesn't answer direct questions, here are some indirect ones to try:**

  ❑ What was your favorite part of the day?

  ❑ Was there a high part? What was it?

  ❑ Was there a low part? What was it?

❑ Pay close attention to any handouts your child brings home. The important guidelines and forms tend to be sent home in the first few weeks. If your child is not forthcoming with handouts, a "backpack search" may be in order.

❑ With your child, go over any homework, artwork, tests, or other papers she brings home. Talk openly about what was difficult and what was easy, her likes and dislikes about the assignment or project.

❑ Never be afraid to call the teacher! If something doesn't seem right or is simply unclear, a phone call at the beginning of the school year can often ward off bigger problems later.

❑ Realize that your child may be tired, overwhelmed, and even cranky the first week of school. Try to help him relax.

❑ Leaving notes of encouragement in a backpack or lunch box is a pleasant surprise that even older kids enjoy. Help them remember that you support them even if you can't be there.

The Emergency Supply Cabinet

We all remember running home from school one day saying, "Mom! I have a project due tomorrow! I have to make a replica of the Coliseum… do we have three pounds of clay and a yard of brown felt?" If it hasn't happened to you yet as a parent, it will. You can't get through even one child's school career without a school supply emergency of some sort. Here are a few things to keep on hand so that you'll be better prepared for such an occasion:

❑ **Glue and/or glue stick**

❑ **Construction paper**

❑ **Extra computer paper**

❑ **Extra toner or ink cartridge for the printer**

❑ **Blue and black ink pens**

❑ **Lined paper**

❑ **Poster board**

❑ **Colored pencils**

❑ **Markers**

❑ **Tape**

❑ **Scissors**

❑ **Ruler and/or yardstick**

❑ **Stapler and staples**

❑ **Paper clips**

❑ **Stickers**

❑ **Glitter**

- ☐ **Dictionary**
- ☐ **Thesaurus**
- ☐ **Atlas**
- ☐ **Globe**
- ☐ **Encyclopedia**

Chapter 7

But What Do I Do

Tomorrow?

The 20-Minute Learning Connection is not a quick fix. Rather, it is a commit-ment that will become a habit for you and for your child, leading to success in school as well as learning, discipline, intellectual development, discovery, and most importantly, the connections between parents and children that are far more important than any test or homework assignment. The path to this commitment, as with all great achievements, begins by recognizing what could go wrong and anticipating these devel-opments. One of the first things that might go wrong is that your child might not share your enthusiasm for spending these 20 minutes together every day. This chapter sug-gests some practical ways for dealing with the typical differences between what children want (freedom, television, and Nintendo) and what they need: guidance, discipline, and the development of skills and knowledge that will last them a lifetime. We will consider some typical responses of children who will resist your attempts to engage them in new and challenging enterprises.

"I Can't Do This!"

Perhaps the most frequent complaints of school children and, for that matter, adults, is the allegation that because they cannot do something, it must be impossible. I am reasonably certain that the young Michael Jordan did not sink his first basket, nor did Tiger Woods ace his first golf shot. Van Cliburn probably muffed a scale or two long before achieving stardom as a concert pianist. In the abstract, we know that hard work and many mistakes, along with an occasional dose of frustration, are part of learning. When the abstract becomes our reality, however, it is much easier to succumb to the logic that the past is prologue, and that what I was unable to do yesterday I cannot do today, nor will I ever be able to do it.

Children do not invent such a negative image of their ability to learn. They are taught this pernicious lesson through the example of many adults, including teachers and parents. Every parent knows that there is a wide gulf between pride in the accomplishment of a difficult task and the anxiety that preceded the first step toward such an achievement. Whether the challenge is the first step of the baby, the first word of the toddler, the first chapter of a book, the first soccer kick, or the first sonata, there is an inevitable sequence that includes challenge, doubt, failure, perseverance, and ultimate success. The chasm from challenge to success is a wide one, but it is not filled merely with obstacles and heartache. This path also includes encouragement, small victories, glimpses of future success, and growing confidence that the goal is worth the effort. When we hear the fear-filled complaint from children, "I can't do this!" our response must be more than superficial encouragement. Rather, we must provide an immediate shift in focus away from the insurmountable goal and toward an immediately achievable objective. In other words, our focus must continually be on what children can do now and our encouragement must be focused on the immediate next step. This establishes a clear incremental process: challenge, self-doubt, encouragement, small steps, and then, the next challenge.

"I Don't Have Any Homework! Why Should I Have to Do This?" learning

The 20-Minute Learning Connection offers parents an excellent opportunity to make learning part of life rather than mere drudgery confined to the school day. This habit can be developed as a routine, no more onerous than making one's bed or washing the dishes, and no less pleasurable than a short walk around the neighborhood or enjoying a hot cup of tea. Even though there are many other things to be done, parents and children still manage to engage in the ordinary duties and pleasures of everyday life. Learning ought to be one of those simultaneous duties and pleasures.

In order to develop the habit of learning, parents must counter the prevailing notion that the only context in which structured learning should take place is when homework is assigned by the teacher. Indeed, some parents may be skeptical about asking their children to engage in any additional activities because of what they have heard about excessive homework that today's children must endure. The myth of the sixth-grade student with five hours of homework every night should be challenged for what it is: either the result of the most grievous educational malpractice or, far more likely, the result of the fevered imagination of those who are persuaded by rumor rather than evidence. In fact, the far more common problem in many schools is the complete absence of homework, even at the secondary level. Teachers increasingly find that it takes too much time to grade, that students refuse to complete it, and that parents and even administrators fail to support the requirements that teachers place on students. When I hear complaints about excessive homework, including in my own home, I am generally inclined to examine the facts. The "five hours of homework" was, in fact, thirty minutes of homework, plus four and a half hours of phone calls, computer games, television, and other diversions. Even when there is an extensive homework assignment that might have required many hours of work, further investigation reveals that the teacher provided the requirement weeks in advance of the due date, and it was poor planning on the part of the student that caused all of the work to be required in a single sitting. The plain fact is that for the vast majority of middle school students and secondary students, the problem is not too much homework, but the habitual absence of homework that has convinced students that they ought to be liberated from anything resembling learning beyond the confines of the school day.

The skills and knowledge contained in this guide will, in fact, build confidence, speed, and efficiency in the completion of homework. Moreover, these activities offer the opportunity for parents and children to enjoy learning together, whereas the typical homework assignment is something that the teacher expects students to complete independently.

figure it out together

"It Doesn't Make Any Difference What I Do! I Just Don't Get It!"

I wish that I could offer a response to the frustration of a child that would mix the wisdom and certainty that Dr. Spock (the pediatrician and best-selling author, not the alien on *Star Trek*) offered to parents of the 1950s. Readers would recognize and challenge the superficiality of easy answers to challenging problems. In fact, children can become plagued by self-doubt, and their absolute knowledge that "I just don't get it" quickly becomes the ingrained belief that "I just *can't* get it." Here are some ideas to consider when dealing with a child who expresses feelings of inadequacy, self-doubt, and hopelessness.

First, recognize the value of these feelings. When children accurately say, "I don't get it," they are expressing the first step toward understanding. After all, it is far more difficult to convince someone to accept instruction when they think that they have the right answer and are unwilling to admit that they don't know everything. Thus, the parent's response to uncertainty and self-doubt should be clear and unequivocal affirmation. "You're right," the parent can acknowledge. "You don't know it. And you know what? You have to be *really* smart to know that you don't know something! Let's see if we can figure it out together..."

Second, determine what the child knows. For example, if the child is bewildered by the words of an authentic historical document, such as the Declaration of Independence, start with what your child knows. "So you're saying that the words of the Declaration of Independence are pretty strange, right? Well, let's start with what you already know. Why were the colonists angry at the British?" You might hear some answer about taxes or other colonial grievances that have been discussed in class. Then continue, "The Declaration of Independence includes a lot of reasons that the colonists were upset. Let's go through each one of them and put it into your own words."

Third, break the task into incremental steps. Too many textbooks, academic standards, and test requirements involve many different tasks masquerading as a single step. If the student does not recognize that there are many separate tasks, then frustration is inevitable.

For example, consider this typical item from an early middle school math test:

"Herb is a gardener who loves tomatoes. In fact, that is all he plants in his backyard garden. In his side yard he has a 12-square-foot garden with zucchinis and azaleas. In the front yard, he has a pond in the middle of his 32-square-foot flower garden. However, the backyard garden is all tomatoes. His backyard garden is 7 feet wide and 24 inches long. There are 4 tomato plants in each square foot. If each tomato plant has an average of 3 ripe tomatoes, how many tomatoes will Herb harvest?"

Some students might tackle this problem with gusto. In fact, they might do it so quickly that they will include information about the side yard and front yard gardens or forget to convert 24 inches into two feet. Other students will find the sheer quantity of information so overwhelming that they will become bogged down in some of the irrelevant details. An effective method of helping students tackle a multistep problem is the clear identification of each step. A good rule of thumb is this: If you are not sure whether you need to add an extra step, then add it. It is much less risky to have a step that you do not need than to skip a step that you did need.

Here is one approach to breaking this problem down into incremental steps.

First, circle the question—what am I supposed to know? In this case, the question is, "How many tomatoes will Herb harvest?" Whatever I do, I know that the final answer is not about feet or inches, it is about the number of tomatoes that Herb will harvest.

Second, make all the units the same. The garden is "7 feet wide and 24 inches long." To make these the same units, I need to know that there are 12 inches in one foot, and that 24 inches is the same as 2 feet. Third, draw a picture. Why? Because pictures are easier to understand than words. On some tests, students are required to draw a diagram for math problems. However, even when such a drawing is not required, it is a great idea to convert words into pictures because it makes the problem easier to understand. My picture might look like this:

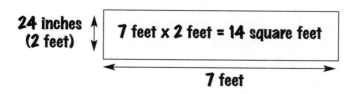

Fourth, write the problem in words. It might look something like this: "The number of tomatoes that Herb will harvest is equal to the number of tomatoes on one plant (3) times the number of tomato plants in one square foot of his garden (4) times the number of square feet in his garden (14)." Some tests require that students explain their answer in writing. However, even if it is a multiple-choice test and no one but the student will see the diagram and sentences, it is an excellent idea to write out the sentences that explain the answer. Fifth, put numbers with the words of the sentence. "The number of tomatoes that Herb will harvest is equal to 3 tomatoes per plant times 4 tomato plants per square foot times 14 square feet, or 168 tomatoes." Sixth, go back to the question in step one. Ask yourself, "Have I answered the question?"

This may seem to be a laborious process for a relatively simple math question. On the contrary, the easiest way to tackle this or any other math problem is to break it down into simple steps. Some of these steps will be the same on every single math problem, from fifth grade math through graduate school statistics. For example, the first step is always, "Circle the question—what am I supposed to know?" The last step is always, "Go back to the question in step one—have I answered the question?" This process is essential for a student to move beyond calculation into real mathematical problem solving. There are many students who know the times tables and math facts, but who cannot solve the problem of Herb's tomatoes. They do not read the problem carefully, they include irrelevant data, or they provide elaborate answers in square feet when the question is asking about the number of tomatoes that Herb will harvest.

This problem illustrates an important component of the 20-Minute Learning Connection. In this illustration, the parent was not imperiously demanding, "Don't you get it? It's 168 tomatoes!" Rather, the parent was breaking down a complex problem into steps and the child proceeded systematically through the problem.

"Everything Is Okay. Just Leave Me Alone!"

Self-reliance is a wonderful thing. A few school children still read Emerson's essay on the subject and are enjoined to revel in the independence of spirit enjoyed by that rare individual who is dependent on no other person. As a student and as a parent, I have experienced both sides of the tension that result when a parent wishes to be helpful and the child prefers to assert independence. It is at this point that the normal stress of homework can explode into a tearful confrontation. Thus, the parental response to "Just leave me alone" must be careful and measured.

Start with a positive statement. "You must be very confident to want to do thi yourself without any help. I am proud of you. Please show it to me when you are done. This is not a request; it is a requirement. If the Emersonian spirit is alive and well, your self-reliant student will submit flawless work that will elicit unrestrained praise. When that daydream is interrupted, however, it is far more likely that "Just leave me alone" was a way of saying, "I don't know how to do this, but I really don't want you to think that I'm stupid. If you would just stay away, then I won't know it, but at least you won't know that I don't know it."

This is a delicate point in a conversation with any child. Whether your child is in second grade (my youngest) or twelfth grade (my oldest), the need for independence is strong. There is a world of difference between the parent who in exasperation demands, "Let me show you how to do it right," and the parent who says gently but firmly, "I'm really proud of your independence. Please show it to me when you are done." Your time is limited. Invest it wisely. If the child's confidence is appropriate, then parental support for that confidence should follow. If the child needs help but will not admit it, then no humiliation is required. The certain knowledge that a loving and supportive parent will look at the final work product will lead to a request for help. For the strong-willed, independent child, the response to a request for help is far better than imposed assistance.

a positive beginning

Daily Checklist for School Success

Whether you have one child or six, checklists are helpful ways to transform the chaos of the morning into a positive beginning to the school day. While every family has its own rituals and requirements for the start of the day, here are some items you may want to include in a visible checklist for daily review by children and parents:

❑ **Assignment notebook complete.**

If not, call a friend, call the "homework hotline" if your school has one, or call the teacher at home. If it is not written down in the assignment notebook, it will not happen.

❑ **Backpack empty and repacked.**

Archaeologists of the future will find some student backpacks and be unable, in at least a few cases, to differentiate them from time capsules. The accumulation of literature, culture, and food represent the accumulation of epochs of civilization. Let your child find a better way to be famous than in the diorama of a natural history museum of future centuries. Empty the backpack completely every night and repack it, with a place for everything and everything in its place.

update the calendar

❑ **Projects, tests, and other important dates on the family calendar.**

There are few more discouraging moments than finding "important" notes squashed in the residue of the bottom of a backpack that involve dates that have already passed. There should be a single large family calendar that has everything from the volunteer activities and business trips of parents to the school activities, project due dates, and tests of children. Without such a combined calendar, conflicts are inevitable.

❑ **Homework checked.**

This does not mean homework done by the parent, nor does it imply homework completed at all. It means that the parent knows what has and has not been done. The child knows that accountability begins at home and that the requirements of the parents are at least as stringent as those imposed at school.

❑ **Long-term projects reviewed.**

The myth of "five hours of homework" is frequently revealed as the month-long project that has been concealed and postponed until the night before it is due. The requirement of fifteen minutes a night for twenty nights thus became five hours in a single night, with the teacher portrayed as the architect of student misery. While it is important that parents ask about projects due "tomorrow," it is equally important that future projects and tests become the subject of daily conversation.

The "Refrigerator Curriculum"

Ray Simon and Janine Riggs are leaders in one of the most remarkable stories of educational progress in the nation. Their "Smart Start" initiative in Arkansas focused on literacy and math and created nationally recognized progress among students of every economic and ethnic group in the state. Their methods were hardly revolutionary. They set high standards and clear expectations for every child. They also had the wisdom to know that parents were essential contributors to student success. One of their most successful innovations was the "Refrigerator Curriculum," so named because it was designed to be affixed next to student work proudly displayed on the refrigerator door. This document expressed on a single page the essential knowledge and skills that students needed for each grade level. Unless you have a large refrigerator, you will not have enough space to display every state standard. Nevertheless, you can identify the most important skills that your child must acquire, and reminders of those essentials should roughly correspond to the frequency with which you open the refrigerator door.

If your child's school does not offer a refrigerator curriculum, then consider creating one. The plain fact is that every standard and academic requirement is not of equal value. Determine those that are most important and reinforce them frequently. Ask your child's teachers and school administrators this simple question: "If I can't do everything that you'd like me to do at the end of the day, what are the most important things for my child to know and be able to do in order to be successful in the next grade?" When the question is phrased in this way, the response should be brief. It will not include a laundry list full of scores of standards. Rather, the list will include some academic requirements, a focus on literacy, and an emphasis on appropriate behavior, time management, and organizational skills. These are worthy of a place on your refrigerator door.

Conclusion

Advice about how to raise the perfectly behaved and flawlessly educated child can be overwhelming, unreasonable, and silly. There is simply too much to do and not enough time to do it all. One of the central themes of this book is that even on the typical day when perfection is elusive and you cannot "do it all," there are nevertheless important and constructive things you can do in order to make a positive difference for your child. As this chapter suggests, not every conversation is easy, nor is every offer of parental support welcomed by a child. Nevertheless, in 20 minutes you can update the calendar, check the backpack, help break a complicated problem down into small steps, provide some encouragement, and maybe even share a laugh. In other words, even on the busiest day, you can make a difference.

make a positive difference

Chapter 8

Standards and Tests in California

Putting It All Together: Standards, Tests, and Accountability

"Standards, Tests and Accountability"—the very words have the rhythm of "Lions, Tigers, and Bears" from Dorothy's scary walk along the Yellow Brick Road.

That which is unknown and mysterious is, to both students and adults, the source of fear and anxiety. This chapter will demystify middle school tests in California. While the tests are not easy, the more students know what to expect, the less fearful they will be. It is important to note that tests change from time to time and the California Department of Education regularly provides information for parents through their website at www.cde.ca.gov.

Is Test Preparation Unethical?

There is an important difference between mindless test drills and the teaching of a curriculum that is thoughtfully linked to the assessments that students must take. Although the phrase "teaching to the test" is often used critically by those who oppose any sort of testing, consider the alternative. If teachers did not link their curriculum to state assessments, then students would be set up for failure, with every test a mystery and every question a surprise. Inevitably, anger, frustration, fear, and anxiety would stem from the failure of schools to link their instruction to the requirements placed on students during tests.

Parents are rightfully concerned when they hear rumors that a thoughtful and rigorous academic environment has been transformed into a boot camp for test preparation. I personally have investigated many such claims, including the complaint that "all students do all day is prepare for the state tests." Each time I hear such a statement, I make a point of asking for more detail. "Tell me," I inquire, "about the schedule of the most test-obsessed teacher in the entire school. How much time every day is spent on test preparation? For how many weeks does such a regimen last?" The most recent inquiry resulted in the admission that the "test-obsessed" teacher devoted one hour a day for three weeks to test preparation. That is fifteen hours out of 1,080 instructional hours (180 school days x 6 hours a day), or about 1.4 percent of the time in school. That is not, by anyone's standards, an inappropriate obsession with test preparation. My typical recommendation to educators is that they devote about twenty minutes a week to the "life skill" of test taking. We teach students many life skills, including pedestrian and bicycle safety, avoidance of alcohol, tobacco, and drugs, and a variety of skills that extend beyond the academic curriculum of school. Test taking is also a skill that students use throughout their lives. Twenty minutes a week—about twelve hours a year—is hardly transforming American schools from an academic paradise into a test preparation boot camp.

Finally, let us consider the ethical issue itself. Even at twenty minutes a week, does test preparation cross an ethical boundary? Certainly, it would be unethical if a teacher were to procure questions from the state test, copy them, and encourage students to memorize the answers. Such behavior can result in felony convictions and jail time for teachers and administrators in some states. No thoughtful person recommends such behavior. It is, however, entirely fair and reasonable for teachers and school administrators to say, "This test will require reading and, more specifically, require students to write a summary of the stories and nonfiction passages that they read. This is not only a test requirement, but a requirement for any well-educated student. We would do this even if there were no state test. Therefore, every day when students read a passage in their textbook or read a story, we will require students to write a brief summary of what they have read."

This is good educational practice, not unethical "teaching to the test." The same is true of requirements for students to write, know their geography, or understand mathematics. It's just good education, not any sort of ethical breach. In fact, the real ethical challenge is presented by teachers who refuse to give students the information they need to be successful on tests and in the next grade. Some teachers refuse to acknowledge the value of aligning their curriculum with the skills and knowledge students need to succeed on tests. These teachers are committing an ethical violation as serious as the driver education teacher who sends students to take a driving test without an understanding of stop signs or the operation of the brake pedal.

reading, writing, and math

What Students Need to Know for the Tests

The most important clarification with regard to standards and testing is this: Students do not have to be proficient at every single standard to be successful on the California tests. In fact, the middle school tests in California cover only a small part of the school curriculum, with a particular emphasis on reading, writing, and mathematics. Although there has been discussion of additional history-social science and science tests, at this writing the tests in other subjects do not begin until secondary school. So if someone were to ask, "What does a student need to know and be able to do to be successful on the California tests?" the answer would be, "The student must read, write, and understand middle school-level mathematics."

The tests of most concern to middle school students in California include the Stanford Achievement Test, Ninth Edition (Stanford-9) and the California Standards Tests, both of which cover English language arts and mathematics, and both of which are administered to all middle school students in California—grades 6, 7, and 8. In addition, seventh-grade students are required to take a writing assessment. These tests are collectively known as the Standardized Testing and Reporting (STAR) program.

The Stanford-9 and California Standards Tests for English language arts include only multiple-choice questions. The seventh-grade writing assessment requires students to respond to a question or "prompt" and provide a well-organized essay or letter, using correct grammar, spelling, and punctuation.

The English language arts skills questions on the Stanford-9 and California Standards Tests require students to understand the meaning of common vocabulary words, spell correctly, identify misspellings, identify mistakes in sentences, and understand the meaning of reading passages that vary in length from a single sentence to several paragraphs. One of the best ways that parents can help students gain the essential knowledge, not only for the English language arts portions of the tests, but for success throughout the school years ahead of them, is to require students to read for at least 20 minutes, write a summary of what they have read, and then edit and correct their summary. While reading is important, the creation of a written summary, along with the editing and revision of that summary, provides one of the best ways to build the skills of thinking, comprehension, analysis, synthesis, understanding, and communication.

The math portions of the Stanford 9 and California Standards Tests also consist entirely of multiple-choice questions. In grade 8, the California Standards Test varies with the course in which the student is enrolled. Most students will take the grade 8 Algebra 1 course, while other students will take the Integrated Mathematics course. A few eighth-grade students who completed algebra in an earlier grade will take a geometry test in the eighth grade.

The mathematics skills questions on the Stanford-9 and California Standards Tests require students to read questions (this is very important: the "math" test is, in fact, very much a test of reading ability as well), understand what the question is asking, solve multi-step number operations (a mixture of addition, subtraction, multiplication, and division), and find the "next step" in solving mathematical problems. At the middle school level, students must master story problems involving decimals, percents, and fractions. Many of these problems involve money, such as discounts and taxes. This type of problem provides a perfect opportunity for parents to take advantage of the interest middle school children have in making more of their own financial deci-

important skills

sions and talking about financial matters in detailed terms that include real world calculations of percentages and fractions. Measurement is also an important skill for middle school mathematics, and everything from household projects to cooking a family meal offers opportunities for parents to reinforce their children's knowledge of linear, area, and volume measurements.

Make no mistake: math facts are important. Just as was the case when you were in school, students must know addition and subtraction facts from second grade on, and multiplication and division from third grade on. If your child is in a later grade and was told that, in the age of calculators and computers, math facts are not really important, then it is not too late to break out the flash cards and correct this omission in his or her education. If your child has a teacher who believes that learning the "times tables" and other drudgery is unimportant, then you need to seriously consider changing teachers. There are many areas in education about which reasonable people may differ, but this is not one of them. While the logical and analytical skills involved in mathematical problem-solving are important, they are not a replacement for understanding and knowing—and yes, that means memorizing—the facts of addition, subtraction, multiplication, and division. There is substantial evidence to indicate that students who are familiar with calculators, but who use them sparingly—only a few times a month—outperform students who are completely dependent upon calculators and must use them every day for simple mathematical operations.

Test Format and Test Preparation

For the most part, the tests are multiple-choice in format. This means that students can choose an answer from among the four or five possible responses provided on the test. The multiple-choice format has an important implication for students, teachers, and parents:

It is not only important to know the right answers to test questions, but also to find the wrong answers and eliminate them.

Although this may seem obvious to parents who have experience in taking multiple-choice tests, the implications for students are profound. This means that test taking need not be a game of mere memorization in which students conclude, "Either I know it or I don't, and if I don't, then I might as well give up." Rather, this focus on knowing both the right and the wrong answer gives students multiple opportunities to be successful on the test. It also gives students an incentive to persevere on a problem even if the right answer is not obvious to them. Most importantly, this insight gives teachers and parents the ability to move far beyond traditional practice tests and enhance the thinking and reasoning skills of students.

Consider this sample question:

Tamika and her family are making a round trip by car between New York and San Francisco. The distance between the cities is 2,921 miles. Her brother says that they should take the station wagon, but Tamika is concerned about the cost of gasoline and suggests the family take a smaller car instead. The station wagon consumes about one gallon of gas for each 18 miles traveled, while the smaller car consumes about one gallon of gas for each 25 miles traveled. If gas prices are $1.92 per gallon, how much money will the use of the smaller car save?

A) Cannot be determined from the information given

B) 7 miles per gallon

C) $174.48

D) $1,744.80

This could be a very time-consuming problem if each individual step is calculated. Let's use two different methods to solve this problem. First, let's solve the problem the slow way: Always start with the question: "How much money will the use of the smaller car save?" That tells us right away that the answer must be an amount of money—not miles, miles per gallon, or any of the other sorts of numbers provided in the problem. First, we need to know the total miles traveled. The total round trip distance is twice the one-way distance, or 2 x 2,921, or 5,842 miles. Next, we need to figure out the amount of gas each of the two cars would consume. With the station wagon traveling 18 miles on one gallon of gas, we can divide 5,842 total miles by 18 miles per gallon, with a result of 324.56 gallons consumed. With the smaller car traveling 25 miles on one gallon of gas, we can divide 5,842 total miles by 25 miles per gallon, with a result of 233.68 gallons of gas consumed. The difference in gasoline consumed is 233.68 subtracted from 324.56, or a difference of 90.88 gallons saved. With gasoline costing $1.92 per gallon, we then multiply $1.92 times 90.88, and determine that the smaller car would have saved a total of $174.48. That was a lot of work! There must be a faster and easier way to deal with this sort of multi-step problem.

Consider a different approach. Again, start with the question: "How much money do we save?" Let's estimate the round trip distance to be about 6,000 miles–3,000 miles each way. The smaller car gets 25 miles to the gallon, so for each 1,000 miles it travels, it uses 50 gallons of gas. Over a 6,000-mile trip, the smaller car will use about 300 gallons of gas. Gas costs about $2 per gallon, so the cost of gas for the smaller car is about $600. The larger car gets 18 miles to the gallon, or about a third less than the station wagon. Let's estimate that we'll save about $\frac{1}{3}$ of $600, or $200. Before spending any time on more calculations, let's see if the $200 estimate allows us to quickly answer this question and move on. In reviewing the choices, it's clear: the test writer is trying to catch students who read the question wrong with the choice of B: we're not looking for miles saved, but for money saved. Choice D will catch students who misplaced a decimal—something that is very easy to do when you are performing a lot of manual calculations. That leaves C as the clear choice—$200 is close enough to $174.48 so select that answer, save several minutes on the test, and move on to the next question.

The problem-solving section of math tests is challenging for many students, so it is a good idea to practice both ways—the slow way and the fast way—so that students build confidence both in calculation and in estimation. On the test, however, estimation can save a lot of time and avoid mistakes that frequently occur in a series of many different calculations. It is also important to know that, from an educational point of view, this sort of practice is not the "mindless test prep" that critics of standards and testing so frequently assail. In fact, this approach to the practice problem improves students' reasoning, reading, estimation, and problem solving—all skills that are essential even if state tests were eliminated tomorrow. Moreover, the habit of moving from the search for the right answer to the elimination of wrong answers builds a student's power of logic and reasoning, helping to improve success on tests for many years to come.

When parents and teachers analyze multiple-choice problems in this way, they are moving far beyond the low-level test preparation that critics of standards and testing have so frequently criticized toward the thinking skills that students need. It is fair to ask this question: If all tests were eliminated tomorrow, would my student still need to think, read, write, and compute? If you answered in the affirmative, then these exercises are not merely a matter of preparation for tests, but preparation for life.

Grade Seven Writing Assessment

The Grade 7 Writing Standards Test requires each student to produce one essay. Students typically have about an hour to create their essay. This is plenty of time for students to take their time, create an outline, write a rough draft, and then produce a final copy. Students who immediately start writing in response to the question frequently will submit an essay that is poorly organized. One of the most important skills that you can instill in your child is the habit of rewriting. Students should never presume that their first written product is their last. Most editors would argue that this is a good rule for authors of any age. By focusing on the habit of rewriting, parents provide both an intellectual and an emotional advantage for their children. The intellectual advantage is that one of the most important attributes of great writing is the result of editing, reflection, and rewriting. It is not, contrary to myth, the ability to express a completed thought on paper on the first draft. Successful writers must not only write, but rewrite and after thought, reflection, and feedback, rewrite yet again. This intellectual attribute is directly related to the emotional trait of persistence. Students will not have the ability to rewrite unless they have the emotional strength to persist in the face of difficulty and challenge. One of the most important gifts any parent can give to a child is the habit of persistence, resilience, and rising once again to a challenge. In simple terms, rewriting is an emotional and intellectual gift to students, and it is as important as the initial gifts of reading and writing that were bestowed by parents in the earliest days of literary exploration.

Does *Every* Student Have to Take the Test?

California laws and administrative regulations place a heavy emphasis on the inclusion of all students in testing. Virtually every student in grades 2 through 11 must take some form of assessment. The vast majority of students must take the tests that comprise the California STAR program. Spanish-speaking English learners who have been enrolled in California public schools less than twelve months at the time the tests are administered are required to take the Spanish Assessment of Basic Education (SABE). Students with special education needs, including students with learning disabilities and students with profound disabilities, must take the assessment with appropriate accommodations and adaptations unless their Individualized Education Plan (IEP) specifies in writing that the student must be excluded from testing. Even in those cases, the IEP must provide for other means of assessing student progress.

What If Parents Object to the Tests?

The California Department of Education provides the following guidance for parents who are opposed to the testing of their children:

Students for whom parents/guardians have submitted a written request that the students not be tested with all or any part of the test are to be exempted from testing in accordance with the parent/guardian's written requests. The parent/guardian must initiate the request, and the school district and its employees are prohibited from soliciting or encouraging the exemption of any student. Any information that is sent to parents/guardians notifying them of their right not to have their children tested must be sent to all parents/guardians in the same form. (California Department of Education website, www.cde.ca.gov, February 12, 2001)

What About the Other Tests in School?

Although the state-mandated standardized tests receive the lion's share of the publicity about testing in school, there are other tests that students routinely take that can have very significant consequences for future educational opportunities.

Some of these tests include so-called I.Q. (Intelligence Quotient) Tests and Aptitude Tests. These tests frequently are used to determine the eligibility of a student for "gifted and talented" programs or for participation in special education programs. Educational assessment experts have strong differences of opinion on what these tests mean. One leading national testing company explains "aptitude" as follows:

> A combination of characteristics, whether native or acquired, that are indicative of an individual's ability to learn or to develop proficiency in some particular area if appropriate education or training is provided. Aptitude tests include those of general academic (scholastic) ability; those of special abilities such as verbal, numerical, mechanical, or musical; tests assessing 'readiness' for learning; and tests that measure both ability and previous learning, and are used to predict future performance—usually in a specific field, such as foreign language, shorthand, or nursing. (Harcourt Educational Measurement website, www.hemweb.com/library/glossary)

Some scholars question the very existence of aptitude as a consistent quality in young students, arguing that interest, environment, and early education are all variables that change rapidly in the life of a young student. Moreover, the announcement of such a quality as aptitude can become a self-fulfilling prophecy. There are large numbers of students who have been told that they lack an aptitude in math and science based on a test at an early age. This test result discouraged these students and their parents from the pursuit of the more advanced—and potentially more interesting—science and math courses. Not surprisingly, the "predictions" appeared to be accurate, as these students did not perform well in high school and college on science and math tests. Consider the case of a student who is told, "You're going to be fat, so there is no reason for you to even consider diet, exercise, or a healthy lifestyle." When that student becomes an obese and unhealthy adolescent and adult, do we blame the student or would we question the wisdom of the prediction that, not surprisingly, came to fruition?

There is a cautionary tale from comic genius Matt Groening, the creator of the television series, *The Simpsons*. In one episode, Bart, the ne'er do well son of Homer and Marge, is accidentally identified as "gifted" when his test paper is switched with that of another student. As Bart exhibits the same behavior that had been routinely ridiculed and berated by teachers and school administrators, he is now applauded for his wise insights and extraordinary "gifts." The test had miraculous powers of prediction, though not in the way that its creators had intended. In this cartoon, as in real life, tests do a much better job of predicting the actions of the adults to read and believe the results than they do of predicting the success and failure of the students who take the tests.

Just as the term "aptitude" has been subject to debate among researchers, so also the term "intelligence" has been the subject of considerable controversy. Although the notion of measurable intelligence was regarded as a scientific fact in the early 20th century, researchers in the last two decades have cast considerable doubt on the notion of general intelligence. These complex controversies have filled volumes. For the purposes of this book, suffice it to say that a few things are fairly clear. First, the younger a student is, the more variable the scores on intelligence tests tend to be. Therefore, it is wise for parents to avoid reading too much into the results. Tuesday's gifted student may, with a little more fatigue and distractions, become Wednesday's student in need of special intervention. The same student, in turn, becomes Thursday's student who is destined for a career in music because of the chance playing of an engaging song on the radio and the ability of that student to replicate a music and rhythm pattern on the way to the office of the school psychologist.

These observations do not indict all tests administered to all students, but only indicate the obvious: the smaller the number of measurements, the greater the opportunity for error. No adult would submit to a life-changing decision based on a single test. If a physician prescribed surgery after a single blood pressure reading, we would demand more tests. We should be no less insistent on additional measurement when someone makes life-changing decisions that affect our children.

testing backlash

Questions for Teachers and School Leaders

The tests in California have consequences, both intended and otherwise, for students and parents. The most draconian consequence is the possibility of forcing a student to repeat a grade in school due to failure to pass a test. While there are many areas of educational research that yield ambiguous results, the issue of student retention is not one of them. In a tiny fraction of cases, such as those where a student started school at an inappropriately early age or where overly aggressive parents insisted on skipping the first or second grade, the requirement for a student to repeat a grade may be appropriate. In the vast majority of cases, however, the repetition of a grade is a classic example of the faulty logic demonstrated by repeating the same activity and expecting different results. It simply doesn't work. If the student has a reading deficiency, then the appropriate intervention is intensive and immediate reading instruction, not another year in which reading constitutes only 60 minutes a day of the curriculum. Because retention has such negative consequences for the students retained and, ultimately, for all students in the classroom, it is important that parents ensure that their students take the tests seriously, are well prepared, and perform well on them. Because the consequences of inadequate preparation are so serious, it is appropriate and fair for parents to ask these questions:

- **How is the curriculum in my child's class related to the California STAR program tests?**

- **What opportunities will my child have to become familiar with the requirements of the state tests?**

- **If my child is not making adequate progress toward preparation for the state tests, when and how will this be communicated to parents?**

- **What intervention plan does the school have for students who are having difficulty so that they receive this intervention long before the state tests are administered?**

- **Do the teachers and administrators in the school believe that these tests are important?**

While most parents have observed the obnoxious behavior of the Little League Dads, and their academic counterparts who are incessantly berating teachers and students about their performance, these questions are neither inappropriate nor intrusive. The unfortunate fact is that parents cannot assume that teachers know or care about tests. Despite substantial financial incentives that the state of California has created to encourage improved student performance, there is a backlash against testing, and many teachers and school administrators continue to regard the classroom curriculum to be the exclusive domain of the teacher. Thanksgiving plays, Halloween parties, and scores of hours devoted to dioramas, crafts, and coloring all have hallowed traditions and have been supported by generations of teachers, students and, indeed, parents. But none of these is more important than learning to read.

While the primacy of reading, writing, and mathematics may be obvious to some readers, a backlash to the standards movement has resulted in a growing number of places where an emphasis on academic excellence is regarded as politically incorrect. Even well-meaning parents have jumped on the bandwagon, opposing standards and testing, and decrying the increased emphasis on academics in the classroom. One wonders if the same parents would protest against the physicians who delivered the bad news that kids could benefit from cutting back on the corn chips, soda, and Twinkies. If those, too, were fixtures in classrooms for generations, a reduction in them might cause frowns and protests from students. Presumably, if the matter at hand were the health of our children, we would endure the whining about a reduction in junk food. There is no doubt about this point: Success in school, including proficiency in reading, writing, and mathematics, is a health issue. Students who are forced to repeat a grade are at substantially greater risk for dropping out of school later in life, and students who drop out of school exhibit a broad range of high-risk behaviors that threaten their very lives.

Test Preparation Without Test Anxiety: The Delicate Balance

The challenge for parents and teachers is the manner in which we convey this complex message to students. We want them to understand that the tests are important and we want them to be willing to work hard to learn in school. We also want them to have fun, enjoy school, love learning and most importantly, deal with the inevitable stress and anxiety that occur in school without becoming paralyzed by negative emotions. While the perfect balance may be elusive, we certainly know what does not work. Telling children that "It's no big deal" or "You're wonderful and you really don't need that stuff" may be comforting in the short term, but it lays a foundation of academic quicksand for students. False reassurances now lead to failure, stress, and anxiety later. By contrast, gentle but firm challenges now are necessary for the reduction of anxiety in the months to come. Many of these gentle but firm challenges occur in school under the guiding hand of a devoted, caring, and knowledgeable teacher. The vast majority of such challenges, however, must come from home where daily routines, including the 20-Minute Learning Connection, will give students confidence, skills, perseverance, and ultimately, success.

Chapter 9

Children with Special Needs

Your Rights As a Parent

I choose my words carefully here: The rights of people with disabilities are civil rights. The last century will be marked in history not only for technological advances, world wars, and economic booms and busts, but for the battle fought and won on behalf of the disadvantaged. If you are the parent of a child with special needs, whether the child is blind, hearing-impaired, cognitively disabled, or suffers from any other disability, then school officials are not doing you a favor when they provide accommodations for your child any more than your local officials do you a favor when they allow you to vote. Meeting the needs of persons with disabilities is a civic responsibility. Having those needs met is a right, not a privilege.

If you are already confident in the accuracy of the diagnosis of your child's needs, then you may wish to proceed directly to the end of this chapter and find more detailed information on organizations that are specifically oriented to the needs of your child. If, however, you do not know if your child has a learning disability or other special need, then this chapter may offer some ideas for you to consider as you enter this very complex and challenging area of education.

In the context of standards and testing, the discussions surrounding special needs students frequently have been polarized. At one extreme are those who stereotype every special needs student as cognitively unable to meet academic standards, and thus every effort is made to exclude these students from testing. At the other extreme are those who recognize no impairment that would interfere with testing and insist on including every child in testing. In reality, the essence of the legislation at all levels regarding children with special needs is designed to protect the *individual* needs of the child. This chapter, therefore, cannot provide guidance about all children except in the most general sense. Every sentence that follows must be interpreted through the parental lens that is best able to focus on the individual needs of your child. Whether your child is included or excluded from special education, whether your child meets academic standards with or without accommodations, and whether your child participates in regular state examinations or alternative examinations that are more appropriate, is not a matter of blind bureaucratic policy, but rather an individual decision made based on the individual needs of your child.

What Are Special Needs Anyway, and How Do I Know If My Child Has Them?

Some special needs are obvious. Children with profound physical, neurological, or developmental challenges clearly need additional assistance in order to deal with the challenges of daily life, including the challenges of a school environment. Other children may be unsuccessful in school, and yet there is no clear developmental or physical disability. How then can you tell if your child needs the additional assistance that is legally guaranteed? Parents must separate the normal challenges of daily life from the challenges faced by students with developmental impairments. As the complexity of pediatric neurology grows, the field is understandably intimidating for any parent. One thing is clear: Your child will never have any advocate that is more knowledgeable and caring about the individual needs of that child than a parent. Your lack of a professional credential must not limit you from playing an active role as the primary advocate for your child. In this respect, it is important for you to advocate accuracy. You are not an advocate either on behalf of participation in special education programs nor exclusion from them, but rather you are an advocate on behalf of accurate, complete, and meaningful diagnoses of your child's needs.

independent evaluation

The Limits of "Field Diagnosis"

The field of special education includes professionals who are gifted educators and diagnosticians. When your child is entrusted to this select group of educators, psychologists, and medical professionals, their wealth of experience and personal attention to each child, as well as their expert administration of a wide battery of tests and other diagnostic assessments, will provide a high probability that the diagnosis of your child's learning disability—or the absence of any disability at all—is accurate. Unfortunately, schools across the nation are governed by resource constraints, where one school psychologist may be assigned to serve the needs of more than a thousand students. Specialists in the diagnosis of learning disabilities are overwhelmed with the immediate needs of students whose needs are obvious and profound. In some cases, this leaves the diagnosis in the hands of amateurs who have neither the experience nor technical skills to make an accurate diagnosis. Here are the most important words in this chapter:

> *Before you allow your child to be categorized as "special education" or "learning disabled," it is imperative that you have an independent evaluation of your child done by an independent psychologist (doctor of psychology who specializes in learning disabilities and their diagnosis—not a practitioner, regardless of degree, who gives diagnostic tests on a part-time basis).*

Why is independent diagnosis so important? The literature is full of tests and questions that appear to create a link to potential learning disabilities. Among these "diagnostic questions" I have found, a parent might be alarmed to find the following:

- ❏ **Does the child have difficulty in understanding new concepts?**

- ❏ **Is the child restless in class?**

- ❏ **Does the child fidget in his seat?**

- ❏ **Does the child seem less mature than his classmates?**

By these standards, every one of my children would have sent alarm bells ringing on any given day, even though all of them have managed to perform at very high levels in school. Indeed, by these standards, I know of few children who would not send parents scurrying to a specialist in search of a diagnosis to these obvious "problems" which, in another age, we called normal childhood behavior. This does not diminish the very real presence of learning disabilities and the need for their diagnosis and treatment. Yet, when I hear of regular schools with no greater population of disabled children than the average, and more than thirty percent of the children have been labeled as "special education," then I must wonder if the problem is really with the children or in pervasive presumptions of disabilities and the need for accompanying accommodations when, in fact, the children are quite normal.

an important clue

Context: Where Does Your Child Excel?

One important clue to your child's needs is the context in which your child has difficulty and that in which your child excels. For example, a child who does not write well in class, but who at home is able to compose wonderful stories with exciting plots and characters does not have a writing disability, but rather has a disinterest in the type of writing that is presently being required in class. The child who refuses to read aloud in class may not have the suspected reading disability, particularly if the same child is able to read with enthusiasm when alone with Grandma. Some parents have been told that the requirement for multi-step mathematical problem-solving is developmentally inappropriate for their child, and yet the same child is able to engage successfully in playground games that require multi-step conditional problem-solving and to keep the score with meticulous accuracy.

Thus, the first step in your reflection on your child's learning needs is to ask the question, "Where does my child excel?" I have heard some parents and teachers insist that there is no response for such a question and that every activity involves failures. When I persist, I will sometimes get a shrug of the shoulders and the rueful observation that, "Well, at least he can excel at Nintendo!"

Curious, I persist. "Tell me more about this success in Nintendo."

"It's awful," the parent complains. "He'll sit there for two hours, hardly blinking an eye, and proudly announce that he has made the 'next level,' whatever that means. He even compares scores with seven other kids at school who seem to devote every recess period to talking about how to get better at the dumb game, and he rattles off their scores every night as if he were announcing the league standings for the NFL."

"Please let me make sure that I understand this," I respond. "This is a child who at school appears to have memory problems and a complete inability to focus and concentrate. Homework seems futile because the child cannot remember simple facts from the previous day. Just sitting and talking about schoolwork often provokes an angry and tearful confrontation and, eventually, you both give up and the child retreats to the Nintendo game, and that way at least you both get some peace and quiet. Is this a fair summary?"

"Every blessed night," the parent sighs.

"Okay, I want to make sure I understand this," I continue. "The child has memory problems, but gives a daily recitation of seven different changing Nintendo scores. The child has attention problems, yet remains engaged in a complex game with multiple levels for hours at a time. The child does not like to discuss even for a moment his areas of failure, but will revel at length in stories of his success. Let's think about where this child can excel. The child excels first when other students are similarly enthusiastic about the activity. The child also excels when there is immediate feedback—in fact, every few moments in a Nintendo game, the child knows if there is success or failure, and every session reveals whether a 'next level' has been achieved. And, it is fair to say that this child, like most humans, enjoys talking with those he loves and respects—his parents—about his successes much more than he enjoys dwelling on his failures. And when he talks with his friends, he talks about how to get better, not about how terrible his failures make him feel."

"So what?" the parents counter. "Playing Nintendo won't get him into college. In fact, it won't get him into the sixth grade, and that's what we're worried about right now."

"That's true, and as someone who (I trust my children will never make it to this chapter) has hidden the family Nintendo machine for several months now, I share your frustration with what seems like a mindless game that robs time from homework and other more appropriate pursuits. But let me share what I have learned from Nintendo and my good friend, Dr. Jeff Howard. Dr. Howard is the founder of the Efficacy Institute. He's a Harvard-trained psychologist who has devoted a good deal of his life to helping students on whom many other people have given up. Jeff doesn't like Nintendo games any more than I do, but he made me pay attention to what they offer that kids need. He asked me one day, 'How long would those kids be playing Nintendo if their scores were put in a package and given to them at the end of the week?' After I thought about it, I knew that the answer would be, 'Not very long.' Then Dr. Howard persisted, 'They stay focused on Nintendo because the feedback is immediate and relevant. They know when they succeed and, even if they fail, they have an immediate chance for redemption. When was the last time a homework assignment did that? In fact, it gets shoved into the parent packet and the child sees it at the end of the week, if ever, and the feedback inevitably focuses on their failure to do something that was required many days (an eternity for a fifth grader) earlier. Trust me—the kid can focus, memorize, and excel, but only if there is feedback that is timely and relevant, and only if the conversations about the activity focus on success rather than failure.'"

"So," the exasperated parent demands, "You and Dr. Howard want kids to play Nintendo?"

"Not at all," I offer reassuringly. "We just want students to apply the Nintendo Effect to the classroom and to family discussions of schoolwork. What would happen if we applied these rules to learning at school? First, feedback doesn't happen at the end of the week amidst a sea of red ink in the parent packet, but it happens right away. That means that you ask the teacher for immediate feedback, so that whenever there is an error, your child has the opportunity to correct it immediately. Teachers almost always have some free time built into the day, and this could be devoted to allowing your child to leave the school day with success rather than with ambiguity or failure. At the very least, your child could take the work home and deal with it Monday night rather than over the weekend—typically Sunday night after an exhausting weekend. Second, your child might be encouraged to talk with friends and parents about strategies to get better, and even an incremental gain—each time he reaches the 'next level'—is the cause of some celebratory phone calls. That might be a new chapter, a new reading level, or a new performance level in writing. Each gain may be, like Nintendo, only a few points, but it is at least as worthy of celebration as is game success."

The point of this extended dialogue is not to suggest that Nintendo will solve the development challenges of children. Rather, the central question must always be, "Where does my child excel?" Whether or not your child has a learning disability, the context, conversation, and process of those areas where your child excels will provide clues for application to other areas where your child needs help. This is one of many areas in which the lessons of special education can be broadly applied to every other area of education for learners of any age.

truth

Adaptations, Accommodations, and Truth

Children with special needs are entitled to the "least restrictive environment" for learning. They are also entitled to adaptations and accommodations that allow them to participate in regular classrooms to the maximum extent possible. The greatest entitlement, however, for students with special needs and their parents is the truth, including the truth about what the student has and has not yet accomplished. Too frequently, the discussions surrounding adaptations have as the underlying theme that an adaptation is equivalent to a loss of rigor. This is summed up in statements such as, "She was in special education, so I had to give her a B," or, "Sure, he passed the test, but only because he received special accommodations, so it really doesn't mean very much." There is a more appropriate way to discuss student achievement, and that is with an unwavering focus on truth.

If a child were blind, few people would presume that the Braille version of the test had less rigor than the printed version used by children with no visual impairments. In fact, some might argue that success on these tests by students who are blind requires more memory and better analytical skills than are required by other students. After all, the student reading Braille has to solve the Pythagorean theorem on a middle school math test, whether the problem about right triangles is posed in print or the problem is presented in the form of raised symbols. Now let's consider a child who has a different disability that is less obvious. The child has no guide dog, cane, or other external indicator of a disability, but nevertheless this student has an impairment that prevents the processing of printed text. The accommodation in such a case might include the presence of an adult to read the test. For another child with an attention deficit, the accommodation might include testing in a different room. For another child, there might be a scribe who writes the answers as dictated by the child. But all of these children must solve the problem with the Pythagorean theorem. In other words, the presence of an accommodation does not necessarily indicate a reduction of rigor. If these students can solve that equation, then it would be prejudicial in the extreme to conclude that they didn't "really" know that the square of the hypotenuse is equal to the sum of the square of the two sides.

Let's consider the case of a student who, perhaps due to a cognitive delay, does not correctly solve the problem. Rather than conclude that, "This child cannot do the Pythagorean theorem," or more broadly, that the child has a mathematics disability, we should focus our attention on truth and accuracy. We know what the child has not done yet, so what *can* this student do? Special educators are masterful at breaking standards and other academic requirements down into incremental tasks. In this example, the special educator might say that the real problem is text processing, not an inability to manipulate numbers. When the problem is presented as a story problem, the child "can't" do the Pythagorean theorem, but when the problem is presented with symbols and numbers, the child quickly calculates that $c^2 = a^2 + b^2$ or otherwise solves the problem without relying on text. Perhaps the student does not understand exponents, but does understand multiplication, or in this example, $c \times c = (a \times a) + (b \times b)$. Or perhaps the child does not yet grasp multiplication, but does understand the nature of addition as the total represented by groups of other numbers or objects. And so the task of incremental analysis continues. It is not done until we have more than the obvious information, such as the test item that the child missed. Our task as educators and parents remains incomplete until we have identified what the child can do, and the small incremental steps that are ahead of us, separating the present moment from the ultimate solution of the problem. A well-drafted Individualized Education Plan (IEP) will contain a series of such small increments, including a clear identification of what the student has already accomplished and the next steps to be accomplished.

The Individualized Education Plan (IEP)

The IEP is an important document that governs everything from classroom expectations to curriculum to assessment. This plan, as the name implies, must be focused on the individual needs of each student. While accommodations may be similar for several different students, the plan itself must be distinct, unique, and individual. The IEP is an evolving document, and the needs of your child may change. As a student gains skills, improves development, modifies behavior, or otherwise changes over the course of time, the IEP should also change.

The IEP is the result of the careful collaboration of a group of teachers, frequently labeled the IEP Team. This includes the classroom teacher, special education specialists, other specialists (such as speech pathologists), and school administrators. Parents should be personally involved in the IEP Team and should plan to attend meetings of the team. Your observations about the successes and challenges in the daily life of your child will provide valuable information that is more detailed and timely than may be obtained from classroom records.

Reporting Student Achievement of Standards— Beyond the Report Card

A frequent source of miscommunication between educators and parents has to do with the student report card. Many parents have contributed to this confusion by insisting that teachers must use a regular report card because parents perceive that this document is part of the "inclusion" to which their child is entitled. Although it is true that "regular" students routinely receive a traditional report card, this is among the many practices applied to regular education students that are of questionable value. For students who need very specific feedback on what they can do and have not yet done, the traditional report card provides inadequate information. Rather than focus on the report card, parents should focus on the imperatives of accuracy and fairness. What they really need to know is what standards their child has met and what specific incremental steps remain to be achieved in those areas where the student has not yet met a standard. When teachers and parents pretend that a standard has been met, or otherwise indicate achievement on a report card that is at variance with the facts, then the child does not benefit. In fact, when the adults in the system focus on factors other than objective indicators of real achievement, the child is left wondering what the meaning of success and failure really is. One of the best ways to resolve this dilemma is to make better use of the IEP and other documents that teachers and IEP members have collected. In fact, one of the best ways to individualize curriculum and instruction for a student with special needs is to start with an individualized report card that includes narrative descriptions, the IEP itself, evidence of student achievement in a portfolio, and narrative descriptions of what the child has achieved. This is far superior to the traditional set of letters and numbers that represent judgments which are typically inconsistent and poorly related to the individual needs of your child.

assistance and support

For Further Information

There are a number of national organizations devoted to helping parents of children with special needs advocate for their children. Because the needs of your child are likely to be complex and significantly different from the needs of other children, it might be helpful to find a group of parents across the nation who face similar challenges. You may feel that your circumstances are unique in your school, and thus you and your child can be made to feel very isolated. In fact, there are many parents who share the same challenges and successes, frustrations and triumphs. Here is a partial list of such organizations that you may wish to contact:

Children and Adults with Attention Deficit/Hyperactivity Disorder
(800) 233-4050
www.chadd.org

Council for Exceptional Children
(888) CEC-SPED
www.cec.sped.org

Learning Disabilities Association

(412) 341-1515

www.ldaamerica.org

National Center for Learning Disabilities

(888) 575-7373

www.ncld.org

National Information Center for Children and Youth with Disabilities

(800) 695-0285

www.nichcy.org

International Dyslexia Association (formerly, the Orton Dyslexia Society)

(800) 222-3123

www.interdys.org

Access America

www.disAbility.gov

Federation for Children with Special Needs

(617) 236-7210

www.fcsn.org

Alexander Graham Bell Association for the Deaf and Hard of Hearing

(202) 337-5220

www.agbell.org

American Foundation for the Blind

(800) 232-5463

www.afb.org

Autism Society of America

(800) 3AUTISM

www.autism-society.org

Brain Injury Association

(800) 444-6443

www.biausa.org

Tourette Syndrome Association, Inc.

(718) 224-2999

www.tsa-usa.org

20-Minute

Learning

Connection

Contact Numbers and Websites for the California Department of Education and National Resources

If you are interested in staying abreast of the latest educational policy as well as finding various ways to support and supplement your child's education, the numbers and sites below should prove helpful.

California Department of Education

http://www.cde.ca.gov/ci/

National Resources

U.S. Department of Education's Main Site
www.ed.gov
(800) USA-LEARN

Individuals with Disabilities Education Act (IDEA)
www.ed.gov/offices/OSERS/IDEA

National Assessment of Educational Progress (NAEP)
nces.ed.gov/nationsreportcard/site/home.asp
(202) 502-7458

National Center for Educational Statistics (NCES)
nces.ed.gov
(202) 502-7420

No Child Left Behind (President Bush's Statement on Education)
www.ed.gov/inits/nclb/index/html

Safe and Drug-free Schools
www.ed.gov/offices/OESE/SDFS
(800) 624-0100

PART II

CALIFORNIA

CONTENT

STANDARDS

with Home Learning Activities

California Content Standards* with Home Learning Activities

• English-Language Arts • Science • Math • History-Social Science

Annotated with Home Learning Activities by Abby Remer

The activities in this section are designed to help your child master the knowledge and skills required by the state of California for students in grades 6 through 8. Although there are many ways to approach the standards and activities, here are some suggestions:

• Read through the standards for all grades. This will help you understand how the "power standards" (see Chapter 5) apply to the California Content Standards. Although not every standard is of equal value, reading the complete set of standards will give you a general overview of the knowledge and skills the state expects your child's school to cover.

• Browse through the activities for your child's current grade, as well as previous grades. Many of the activities are appropriate for several grades, so it's best to choose those that will be most appealing to your child, rather than limiting your choice to those aligned to the standards for your child's grade. If your child especially enjoys writing, drawing, music, drama, or athletics, the icons will help you identify those types of activities.

• Look for activities that will build skills in an area where your child needs help in school. Ask your child's teacher to identify the standards your child needs to work on, and select corresponding activities for your 20-Minute Learning Connection.

• If you are concerned that the arts or physical education have been reduced at your child's school, this guide offers many opportunities to reinforce their importance at home. Icons for fine arts, performing arts, and physical education will help you identify activities in these categories.

Materials needed for each activity are identified by the following icons:

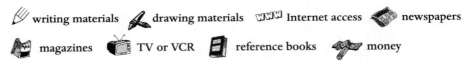

writing materials   drawing materials   Internet access   newspapers

magazines   TV or VCR   reference books   money

The following subject icons are used to indicate that more than one subject is covered by an activity:

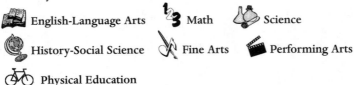

English-Language Arts   Math   Science

History-Social Science   Fine Arts   Performing Arts

Physical Education

CALIFORNIA

English-Language Arts Standards

Grades 6-8
(adopted December 1997, copyright 1998)

GRADE SIX

READING

1.0 Word Analysis, Fluency, and Systematic Vocabulary Development

Students use their knowledge of word origins and word relationships, as well as historical and literary context clues, to determine the meaning of specialized vocabulary and to understand the precise meaning of grade-level-appropriate words.

Word Recognition

1.1 Read aloud narrative and expository text fluently and accurately and with appropriate pacing, intonation, and expression.

Passionate words

 Have your child study, interpret, and present a moving speech, such as Martin Luther King Jr.'s 1963 "I Have a Dream" speech at http://web66.coled.umn.edu/new/MLK/MLK.html or at http://www.7cs.com/king.html, or perhaps President Lincoln's 1863 "Gettysburg Address" at http://lcweb.loc.gov/exhibits/gadd/. How will your child's understanding of the speech impact the way he presents it to others? Afterward, discuss how it felt to speak passionate words spoken by a real person in history.

Vocabulary and Concept Development

1.2 Identify and interpret figurative language and words with multiple meanings.

Words that sell

 If necessary, have your child use a dictionary to define the terms simile, metaphor, hyperbole, *and* personification. *Next, together explore advertisements in magazines and newspapers and identify examples of each term, seeing how they are used to sell a product. For example, what kind of hyperbole (exaggeration) is used in toy or food ads? Make sure to examine both words and images. Next, use examples from the Standard to create your own advertisements that will sell others on a personal idea, product, or activity. Make sure all of the words in your child's ad are spelled correctly and written legibly.*

1.3 Recognize the origins and meanings of frequently used foreign words in English and use these words accurately in speaking and writing.

Foreign language adventure

WWW *Have your child play an online game in which a foreign word (selected from among six languages) is spoken through your computer and your child clicks on the appropriate picture at http://www.magictheatre.com/laquiz.html. Then, help your child identify foreign words that have become part of the English language (such as taco, ciao, or cliché) and find their meanings and language of origin in the dictionary. Have your child be on "foreign word lookout" throughout the day, noting as many as possible while waiting on lines, in daily conversation, or on television.*

1.4   Monitor expository text for unknown words or words with novel meanings by using word, sentence, and paragraph clues to determine meaning.

Switch-aroo

Have your child read aloud from a favorite book or magazine. When he comes across an unfamiliar word, look together at the surrounding word clues. Repeat the sentence aloud, saying "blank" in place of the unknown word, and then continue on. Ask your child what other word(s) might be substituted for the unknown word in the sentence so that it still makes sense. For instance, "José's mother is proud of him because he is responsible. He always completes his chores on Saturday before he goes to the park." Ask your child to look for clues in the sentence that suggest a meaning for the unknown word. For example, José's mother is proud, so being responsible must be a good thing. Also, José does his work before he goes off to have fun. Then, ask your child to think of words that can be switched for the word responsible in the sentence; for instance, other words that might be used to describe José in this passage are dutiful, reliable, dependable, and trustworthy. Based on the surrounding word clues and the switched words, your child can conclude that a person who is described as responsible is "someone who does what he is supposed to do." Help your child understand whether the word(s) or definition he selected is close to the meaning of the original unknown word, asking him to use the dictionary as a resource. Ask your child to use the newly understood word in another sentence to enhance comprehension.

California Content Standards with Home Learning Activities

1.5 Understand and explain "shades of meaning" in related words (e.g., softly and quietly).

In other words

✍️ 📖 **CHILD'S FAVORITE BOOK** *Have your child select his favorite book, one that he believes is particularly well written. Go through the book and write down selected sentences, underlining the most evocative words or phrases. Then have your child read the sentences and write down suggestions for replacing the underlined word or phrase with related words. What slightly different tone, image, or connotation is conveyed by each choice? Have your child expand the list with a thesaurus, and consider some of these other possible choices. Ask him to write down and carefully consider many word choices before selecting the one that he feels is the best replacement for the original word or phrase. After your child writes his final selected words into the sentences you wrote, compare them to the author's original text. Discuss the differences and similarities in results and why the author might have made those particular word selections.*

2.0 Reading Comprehension (Focus on Informational Materials)

Students read and understand grade-level-appropriate material. They describe and connect the essential ideas, arguments, and perspectives of the text by using their knowledge of text structure, organization, and purpose. The selections in Recommended Readings in Literature, Kindergarten Through Grade Eight illustrate the quality and complexity of the materials to be read by students. In addition, by grade eight, students read one million words annually on their own, including a good representation of grade-level-appropriate narrative and expository text (e.g., classic and contemporary literature, magazines, newspapers, online information). In grade six, students continue to make progress toward this goal.

Structural Features of Informational Materials

2.1 Identify the structural features of popular media (e.g., newspapers, magazines, online information) and use the features to obtain information.

2.2 Analyze text that uses the compare-and-contrast organizational pattern.

Comprehension and Analysis of Grade-Level-Appropriate Text

2.3 Connect and clarify main ideas by identifying their relationships to other sources and related topics.

2.4 Clarify an understanding of texts by creating outlines, logical notes, summaries, or reports.

2.5 Follow multiple-step instructions for preparing applications (e.g., for a public library card, bank savings account, sports club, league membership).

Expository Critique

2.6   Determine the adequacy and appropriateness of the evidence for an author's conclusions.

2.7   Make reasonable assertions about a text through accurate, supporting citations.

2.8   Note instances of unsupported inferences, fallacious reasoning, persuasion, and propaganda in text.

3.0 Literary Response and Analysis

Students read and respond to historically or culturally significant works of literature that reflect and enhance their studies of history and social science. They clarify the ideas and connect them to other literary works. The selections in Recommended Readings in Literature, Kindergarten Through Grade Eight illustrate the quality and complexity of the materials to be read by students.

Structural Features of Literature

3.1   Identify the forms of fiction and describe the major characteristics of each form.

Narrative Analysis of Grade-Level-Appropriate Text

3.2   Analyze the effect of the qualities of the character (e.g., courage or cowardice, ambition or laziness) on the plot and the resolution of the conflict.

3.3   Analyze the influence of setting on the problem and its resolution.

3.4   Define how tone or meaning is conveyed in poetry through word choice, figurative language, sentence structure, line length, punctuation, rhythm, repetition, and rhyme.

Analyze this!

POEM Have your child select a favorite poem, or share one that you particularly like. Ask your child to imagine being an English professor teaching a class (household members) about the poem. Ask him to prepare the "lecture" by analyzing the poem as outlined in the Standard, paying particular attention to how tone or meaning is conveyed, and then taking "students" through the process of understanding the piece more deeply from his own findings. You, as one of the students, should pose questions or make observations about punctuation, rhythm, repetition, or rhyme to make the class more interesting and interactive.

3.5   Identify the speaker and recognize the difference between first- and third-person narration (e.g., autobiography compared with biography).

3.6   Identify and analyze features of themes conveyed through characters, actions, and images.

3.7   Explain the effects of common literary devices (e.g., symbolism, imagery, metaphor) in a variety of fictional and nonfictional texts.

Visual symbols

Both you and your child should each list something you really love (possibly chocolate chip cookies), some place you like being (a warm beach in wintertime), and an event that is exciting (a sports event or music concert). Then, on drawing paper, both of you should create evocative collages or drawn images, and write metaphors that describe these three things. (For example, you might write that chocolate chip cookies have "as many delicious chocolate chips as there are stars in the sky" to accompany pictures of gold speckled stars in the night sky.) You can mix your three selections together into one "poetic" composition, if you wish. Discuss how your words and images are both metaphors for the real things.

Literary Criticism

3.8   Critique the credibility of characterization and the degree to which a plot is contrived or realistic (e.g., compare use of fact and fantasy in historical fiction

WRITING

1.0 Writing Strategies

Students write clear, coherent, and focused essays. The writing exhibits students' awareness of the audience and purpose. Essays contain formal introductions, supporting evidence, and conclusions. Students progress through the stages of the writing process as needed.

Organization and Focus

1.1   Choose the form of writing (e.g., personal letter, letter to the editor, review, poem, report, narrative) that best suits the intended purpose.

1.2   Create multiple-paragraph expository compositions:

  a.   Engage the interest of the reader and state a clear purpose.

  b.   Develop the topic with supporting details and precise verbs, nouns, and adjectives to paint a visual image in the mind of the reader.

  c.   Conclude with a detailed summary linked to the purpose of the composition.

1.3   Use a variety of effective and coherent organizational patterns, including comparison and contrast; organization by categories; and arrangement by spatial order, order of importance, or climactic order.

Research and Technology

1.4   Use organizational features of electronic text (e.g., bulletin boards, databases, keyword searches, e-mail addresses) to locate information.

Zanzibar or Timbuktu I

✍ WWW Ask your child to pick a far away place she might like to visit, and then research the location with the tools mentioned in the Standard. Tell your child to take careful notes that will help in part II. 🌐

1.5 Compose documents with appropriate formatting by using word-processing skills and principles of design (e.g., margins, tabs, spacing, columns, page orientation).

Zanzibar or Timbuktu II

Ask your child to write song lyrics or a short narrative about a holiday in the locale she researched. Encourage her to incorporate as many details as possible from her research, so that her song or narrative is informative and descriptive as well as entertaining. After she creates a first draft of her work, have her edit for grammar, spelling, and punctuation. Have your child compose the document using word processing software and including all relevant aspects of the Standard.

EVALUATION AND REVISION

1.6 Revise writing to improve the organization and consistency of ideas within and between paragraphs

Sports editor

Attend a sports event together, or have your child read an article or watch a television show about a favorite sport, team, or player. Have your child write a brief summary about it and then pretend to be the sports editor of a newspaper, imagining this "first draft" just landed on his desk. What changes will your sports editor (child) make in terms of organization? Will he make the material chronological (say, if the article was an account of a game played), or narrative (if it was about the life of a sports hero)? What changes can he make for better consistency of ideas? Before going to "print," the sports editor (your child) should submit the final version to you, the "editor in chief" of the paper, supporting the reasons behind his changes.

2.0 Writing Applications (Genres and Their Characteristics)

Students write narrative, expository, persuasive, and descriptive texts of at least 500 to 700 words in each genre. Student writing demonstrates a command of standard American English and the research, organizational, and drafting strategies outlined in Writing Standard 1.0.

Using the writing strategies of grade six outlined in Writing Standard 1.0, students:

2.1 Write narratives:

Now what?

*✍ **MISCELLANEOUS HOUSEHOLD ITEMS** Explain to your child that you are going to give her a "set up" for a story, which she will then develop into a written narrative. For props, find two unrelated household objects, such as an eggbeater, toothbrush, or Halloween mask. For the "set up," hold the items in your hands and then walk into the room, stop short, and ask, "Now what?" It's up to your child to take it from there, using the elements in the Standard to write a gripping tale, edited for correct spelling, grammar, punctuation, and tone.* 🎬

  a. Establish and develop a plot and setting and present a point of view that is appropriate to the stories.
  b. Include sensory details and concrete language to develop plot and character.
  c. Use a range of narrative devices (e.g., dialogue, suspense).

2.2 Write expository compositions (e.g., description, explanation, comparison and contrast, problem and solution):

  a. State the thesis or purpose.
  b. Explain the situation.
  c. Follow an organizational pattern appropriate to the type of composition.
  d. Offer persuasive evidence to validate arguments and conclusions as needed.

2.3 Write research reports:

a. Pose relevant questions with a scope narrow enough to be thoroughly covered.

b. Support the main idea or ideas with facts, details, examples, and explanations from multiple authoritative sources (e.g., speakers, periodicals, online information searches).

c. Include a bibliography.

2.4 Write responses to literature:

Dear author

✍ Have your child write a letter to the author of one of his favorite books sharing his interpretation of it. Your child should include the items listed in the Standard (2.4 a–c) in his correspondence, editing the letter for correct spelling, punctuation, grammar, and tone. Submit the letter to the book's publisher, or write back to your child in the author's voice.

a. Develop an interpretation exhibiting careful reading, understanding, and insight.

b. Organize the interpretation around several clear ideas, premises, or images.

c. Develop and justify the interpretation through sustained use of examples evidence.

2.5 Write persuasive compositions:

Put it in writing

✍ The next time your child asks for something—a later bedtime, a larger allowance, permission to stay outside longer—ask her to put it in writing, using all of her literary powers of persuasion, as listed in Standard 2.5 a–c.

a. State a clear position on a proposition or proposal.

b. Support the position with organized and relevant evidence.

c. Anticipate and address reader concerns and counterarguments

WRITTEN AND ORAL ENGLISH LANGUAGE CONVENTIONS

The standards for written and oral English language conventions have been placed between those for writing and for listening and speaking because these conventions are essential to both sets of skills.

1.0 Written and Oral English Language Conventions

Students write and speak with a command of standard English conventions appropriate to this grade level.

Sentence Structure

1.1 Use simple, compound, and compound-complex sentences; use effective coordination and subordination of ideas to express complete thoughts.

Grammar

1.2 Identify and properly use indefinite pronouns and present perfect, past perfect, and future perfect verb tenses; ensure that verbs agree with compound subjects.

Punctuation

1.3 Use colons after the salutation in business letters, semicolons to connect independent clauses, and commas when linking two clauses with a conjunction in compound sentences.

Capitalization

1.4 Use correct capitalization.

Cap it off

Look through the arts & entertainment section of the newspaper with your child and circle the instances where capitalization is used. Note all the different cases, including titles of books and musical compo-

sitions, names of individuals and organizations, and so forth. Also find the use of capitalization in quotations.

Spelling

1.5 Spell frequently misspelled words correctly (e.g., their, they're, there).

  NOTE CARDS *Together, write commonly misspelled words on individual note cards: too, two, to; their, there, they're; affect, effect, and so forth. You can add others to the file over time. Have your child write a definition (using a dictionary if necessary) for each variation of the word on its own note card. Then shuffle the deck and have your child randomly select a card. For this word, your child should give its definition, use the word correctly in a sentence, and then spell and define any of the same sounding words related to it. Use the cards in the deck to check your child's answers.*

LISTENING AND SPEAKING

1.0 Listening and Speaking Strategies

Students deliver focused, coherent presentations that convey ideas clearly and relate to the background and interests of the audience. They evaluate the content of oral communication.

Comprehension

1.1 Relate the speaker's verbal communication (e.g., word choice, pitch, feeling, tone) to the nonverbal message (e.g., posture, gesture).

Turn on a television drama without the sound and briefly watch the action, having your child keenly observe how the actors convey ideas through body language. Discuss what you can infer from certain movements, facial gestures, or lack of them in the segment. Next, try to mime out a short conversation between the two of you, using only body language but no speech.

1.2   Identify the tone, mood, and emotion conveyed in the oral communication.

1.3   Restate and execute multiple-step oral instructions and directions.

Cooking 101

 RECIPE, INGREDIENTS Help your child learn to cook something that has a fairly simple recipe. Take your child through the steps, either reading aloud from a recipe book or reciting the steps from memory. Your child should restate each step in his own words and then execute the steps in order. The final step is sharing the delicious result!

Organization and Delivery of Oral Communication

1.4   Select a focus, an organizational structure, and a point of view, matching the purpose, message, occasion, and vocal modulation to the audience.

1.5   Emphasize salient points to assist the listener in following the main ideas and concepts.

Appetizer news

 RADIO Listen to a radio news report together as you prepare a meal. Have your child take notes on the report, knowing that he will be a newscaster at the dinner table. As an "appetizer" at the beginning of the meal, have your child "broadcast" the story, briefly summarizing the major points with supporting evidence from the newscast.

1.6   Support opinions with detailed evidence and with visual or media displays that use appropriate technology.

1.7 Use effective rate, volume, pitch, and tone and align nonverbal elements to sustain audience interest and attention.

Make em' laugh

WWW 📖 *Have a joke-telling festival in your household, where each teller tries to increase the humor through facial expressions and gestures. Funny hats and costumes are encouraged! Can't think of a good joke? Most libraries have joke books, and there are joke collections on websites as well.* 🎬

Analysis and Evaluation of Oral and Media Communications

1.8 Analyze the use of rhetorical devices (e.g., cadence, repetitive patterns, use of onomatopoeia) for intent and effect.

Snap, crackle, pop

✍️ *Describe <u>onomatopoeia</u>—the use of words whose sounds suggest their meaning. Think of some examples together (sizzle, snap, pop, crackle, and the like), having your child create movements that enhance the sound as he says it aloud.* 🎬 🚲

1.9 Identify persuasive and propaganda techniques used in television and identify false and misleading information.

2.0 Speaking Applications (Genres and Their Characteristics)

Students deliver well-organized formal presentations employing traditional rhetorical strategies (e.g., narration, exposition, persuasion, description). Student speaking demonstrates a command of standard American English and the organizational and delivery strategies outlined in Listening and Speaking Standard 1.0.

Using the speaking strategies of grade six outlined in Listening and Speaking Standard 1.0, students:

2.1   Deliver narrative presentations:

You are there

Ask your child to close her eyes for a moment and think of a favorite place. Then without saying the name of the location, have your child describe as much as possible about it and her experience there. Can you guess the location from the description? Reverse roles and then discuss which aspects of the descriptions were most helpful in imagining the place. Afterward, both of you should draw your location and discuss how visual representations capture things that words might not, and vice versa. (For example, art might convey the exact color of the ocean or lake at a location, but not the sounds of the waves.)

a.   Establish a context, plot, and point of view.

b.   Include sensory details and concrete language to develop the plot and character.

c.   Use a range of narrative devices (e.g., dialogue, tension, or suspense).

2.2   Deliver informative presentations:

a.   Pose relevant questions sufficiently limited in scope to be completely and thoroughly answered.

b.   Develop the topic with facts, details, examples, and explanations from multiple authoritative sources (e.g., speakers, periodicals, online information).

2.3   Deliver oral responses to literature:

a.   Develop an interpretation exhibiting careful reading, understanding, and insight.

b.   Organize the selected interpretation around several clear ideas, premises, or images.

c.   Develop and justify the selected interpretation through sustained use of examples and textual evidence.

2.4   Deliver persuasive presentations:

a.   Provide a clear statement of the position.

b.   Include relevant evidence.

c.   Offer a logical sequence of information.

d.   Engage the listener and foster acceptance of the proposition or proposal.

2.5   Deliver presentations on problems and solutions:

a.   Theorize on the causes and effects of each problem and establish connections between the defined problem and at least one solution.

Cause and effect I

Upon returning from an event to which you and your child arrived late, sit down together and sketch out a diagram that charts the circumstances that led to being late. For instance, did someone not get up on time or not prepare to leave in advance or forget something at home and have to return? On the left side of a piece of paper, have your child write down the factor(s) in a box labeled "cause(s) that contributed to being late." In a box in the middle, have your child write the effect, "arrived late." What steps can you take to prevent lateness again? Have your child list all of them in a final box labeled "solutions" on the right side of the paper. Ask your child to brainstorm solutions to the problem. Move to the second part of the activity.

b.   Offer persuasive evidence to validate the definition of the problem
and the proposed solutions.

Cause and effect II

DIAGRAM FROM PART I Have your child examine the solutions and prepare evidence to validate which one of the solutions he thinks will be most effective. Ask your child to prepare a brief oral presentation outlining the problem and providing persuasive evidence for his recommended solution. Review the sheet before your next outing!

California Content Standards with Home Learning Activities

READING

1.0 Word Analysis, Fluency, and Systematic Vocabulary Development

Students use their knowledge of word origins and word relationships, as well as historical and literary context clues, to determine the meaning of specialized vocabulary and to understand the precise meaning of grade-level-appropriate words.

Vocabulary and Concept Development

Identify idioms, analogies, metaphors, and similes in prose and poetry.

1.2 Use knowledge of Greek, Latin, and Anglo-Saxon roots and affixes to understand content-area vocabulary.

> **It's Latin to me**
>
> **WWW** *Together, click on the "Latin Word List" and "Grammar Aid" at the bottom of the page at http://www.nd.edu/~archives/latgramm.htm. Each letter of the alphabet has a separate page with Latin words. Together, try to locate as many familiar words or stems (roots) as possible. For stems, have your child come up with words in which the root is used, such as "nauta," which means* sailor *in Latin, and is used in the word* <u>nautical</u> *(relating to the sea, navigation, or ships).*

1.3 Clarify word meanings through the use of definition, example, restatement, or contrast.

2.0 Reading Comprehension (Focus on Informational Materials)

Students read and understand grade-level-appropriate material. They describe and connect the essential ideas, arguments, and perspectives of the text by using their knowledge of text structure, organization, and purpose. The selections in *Recommended Readings in Literature, Kindergarten Through Grade Eight* illustrate the quality and complexity of the materials to be read by students. In addition, by grade eight, students read one million words annually on their own, including a good representation of grade-level-appropriate narrative and expository text (e.g., classic and contemporary literature, magazines, newspapers, online information). In grade seven, students make substantial progress toward this goal.

Structural Features of Informational Materials

2.1 Understand and analyze the differences in structure and purpose between various categories of informational materials (e.g., textbooks, newspapers, instructional manuals, signs).

2.2 Locate information by using a variety of consumer, workplace, and public documents.

2.3 Analyze text that uses the cause-and-effect organizational pattern.

Comprehension and Analysis of Grade-Level-Appropriate Text

2.4 Identify and trace the development of an author's argument, point of view, or perspective in text.

2.5 Understand and explain the use of a simple mechanical device by following technical directions.

Expository Critique

2.6 Assess the adequacy, accuracy, and appropriateness of the author's evidence to support claims and assertions, noting instances of bias and stereotyping.

Critique the critic

WWW *Have your child read a critic's review of a movie, television show, or album in which she is interested. Ask your child to "grade" the critic in terms of how well he or she supported any claims (e.g., "It was the best show ever..." "The singer's first album was far superior...") and where the critic might have been biased—perhaps toward or against the show, movie, or particular performer—and any evidence of stereotyping. Have your child write her own "A+" review on the same topic, correcting the inadequacies or inaccuracies she noted in the critic's original piece.*

3.0 Literary Response and Analysis

Students read and respond to historically or culturally significant works of literature that reflect and enhance their studies of history and social science. They clarify the ideas and connect them to other literary works. The selections in *Recommended Readings in Literature, Kindergarten Through Grade Eight* illustrate the quality and complexity of the materials to be read by students.

Structural Features of Literature

3.1 Articulate the expressed purposes and characteristics of different forms of prose (e.g., short story, novel, novella, essay).

Narrative Analysis of Grade-Level-Appropriate Text

3.2 Identify events that advance the plot and determine how each event explains past or present action(s) or foreshadows future action(s).

What's next?

***CHILDREN'S BOOKS** Help your child enhance her ability to predict and extend ideas by using existing information. While reading aloud from a book, newspaper, or magazine article, stop occasionally and ask your child to predict what happens next. Ask which events or clues in the story led to her predictions. You also can sharpen predicting abilities by repeating the activity with television shows (asking at commercial breaks what your child thinks will happen next), or by pausing movies on the VCR. When you complete the book, television show, or movie, ask your child to restate what happened in the story in order to clarify ideas, and then extend these concepts by explaining why she thinks the story unfolded as it did.*

3.3 Analyze characterization as delineated through a character's thoughts, words, speech patterns, and actions; the narrator's description; and the thoughts, words, and actions of other characters.

3.4 Identify and analyze recurring themes across works (e.g., the value of bravery, loyalty, and friendship; the effects of loneliness).

3.5 Contrast points of view (e.g., first and third person, limited and omniscient, subjective and objective) in narrative text and explain how they affect the overall theme of the work.

Literary Criticism

3.6 Analyze a range of responses to a literary work and determine the extent to which the literary elements in the work shaped those responses.

WRITING

1.0. Writing Strategies

Students write clear, coherent, and focused essays. The writing exhibits students' awareness of the audience and purpose. Essays contain formal introductions, supporting evidence, and conclusions. Students progress through the stages of the writing process as needed.

Organization and Focus

Random funny story.

✍ TWO PAPER BAGS On individual pieces of paper, write down 10 miscellaneous nouns (e.g., robot, avocado, penguin, ignition, spotlight) and place them in a bag; do the same for 10 miscellaneous verbs (e.g., hiccup, snooze, scramble, correct, twist, corrupt). Then have your child randomly select five words from each of the two bags. Using the words he selected, ask him to make notes or outline his ideas, and then write a story paying particular attention to Standards 1.1–1.3. Afterward, review your child's writing together, making sure that the organization is logical and that all claims are supported, as well as correcting any mistakes in capitalization, punctuation, or spelling.

1.1 Create an organizational structure that balances all aspects of the composition and uses effective transitions between sentences to unify important ideas.

1.2 Support all statements and claims with anecdotes, descriptions, facts and statistics, and specific examples.

1.3 Use strategies of notetaking, outlining, and summarizing to impose structure on composition drafts.

Research and Technology

1.4 Identify topics; ask and evaluate questions; and develop ideas leading to inquiry, investigation, and research.

1.5 Give credit for both quoted and paraphrased information in a bibliography by using a consistent and sanctioned format and methodology for citations.

1.6 Create documents by using word-processing skills and publishing programs; develop simple databases and spreadsheets to manage information and prepare reports.

Evaluation and Revision

1.7 Revise writing to improve organization and word choice after checking the logic of the ideas and the precision of the vocabulary.

2.0 Writing Applications (Genres and Their Characteristics)

Students write narrative, expository, persuasive, and descriptive texts of at least 500 to 700 words in each genre. The writing demonstrates a command of standard American English and the research, organizational, and drafting strategies outlined in Writing Standard 1.0.

Using the writing strategies of grade seven outlined in Writing Standard 1.0, students:

2.1 Write fictional or autobiographical narratives:

> **Ho-hum life**
>
> *Ask your child to write a fictional narrative of a day in the life of an ant (or your household pet). Have your child address all the elements listed in Standard 2.1 a–c to create an engaging narrative about an ordinary day from an extraordinary point of view. Have your child illustrate the tale after editing the text for correct spelling, punctuation, and grammar.*

a. Develop a standard plot line (having a beginning, conflict, rising action, climax, and denouement) and point of view.

b. Develop complex major and minor characters and a definite setting.

c. Use a range of appropriate strategies (e.g., dialogue; suspense; naming of specific narrative action, including movement, gestures, and expressions).

2.2 Write responses to literature:

Kid's view

WWW *Tell your child that she can see her own opinions online. Have your child visit www.Amazon.com, www.bn.com, or another book-selling site that encourages visitors to post reviews. Search for a book that she has read. On the page displaying the book, select the option of writing your own review. Have your child compose her own review, as described in the Standard, and then post it on the website.*

a. Develop interpretations exhibiting careful reading, understanding, and insight.

b. Organize interpretations around several clear ideas, premises, or images from the literary work.

c. Justify interpretations through sustained use of examples and textual evidence.

2.3 Write research reports:

Consumer report

WWW *RESEARCH MATERIALS AS LISTED IN SECTION C OF THE STANDARD Have your child research the very best sneakers (or backpack or sports equipment) on the market and write a "consumer report" supporting her findings, conveying them as described in the Standard.*

a. Pose relevant and tightly drawn questions about the topic.

b. Convey clear and accurate perspectives on the subject.

c. Include evidence compiled through the formal research process (e.g., use of a card catalog, *Reader's Guide to Periodical Literature*, a computer catalog, magazines, newspapers, dictionaries).

d. Document reference sources by means of footnotes and a bibliography.

2.4 Write persuasive compositions:

a. State a clear position or perspective in support of a proposition or proposal.

b. Describe the points in support of the proposition, employing well-articulated evidence.

c. Anticipate and address reader concerns and counterarguments.

2.5 Write summaries of reading materials:

Dining out

 Ask your child to imagine that she runs a restaurant selection business. In her imaginary business, clients telephone and ask for opinions about the best places to eat. It's up to your child to read restaurant reviews and summarize the reviewer opinions for the clients so they can make informed decisions about where to eat. Have your child use reviews in magazines, books, or newspapers, or those online at the Zagats website at http://www.wplj.com:5146/get/zagats/. After reading each review, your child should summarize the author's message to you (the client). You can refine the activity by having clients request specific locales, types of cuisine, price ranges, and so forth.

---

a. Include the main ideas and most significant details.

b. Use the student's own words, except for quotations.

c. Reflect underlying meaning, not just the superficial details.

WRITTEN AND ORAL ENGLISH LANGUAGE CONVENTIONS

The standards for written and oral English language conventions have been placed between those for writing and for listening and speaking because these conventions are essential to both sets of skills.

1.0 Written and Oral English Language Conventions

Students write and speak with a command of standard English conventions appropriate to the grade level.

Sentence Structure

1.1   Place modifiers properly and use the active voice.

> **Modify what?**
>
> *Together, learn about misplaced and dangling modifiers and also the active voice at http://www.gabiscott.com/bigdog/ or research these topics at the library. After you've researched modifiers and the active voice, write 10 to 15 sentences on a piece of paper; some of the sentences should have misplaced or dangling modifiers, some should be written in the passive voice, and others should be completely correct. Have your child read through the sentences and identify and correct the mistakes. When he is finished, read through the sentences with your child and discuss his answers. For more practice, have your child play with existing sentences selected from the daily newspaper by changing the placement of the modifiers to alter the meaning of the sentences. Your child also should determine if the sentence is in the passive voice and if so, rewrite it in the active voice.*

Grammar

1.2   Identify and use infinitives and participles and make clear references between pronouns and antecedents.

1.3   Identify all parts of speech and types and structure of sentences.

1.4   Demonstrate the mechanics of writing (e.g., quotation marks, commas at end of dependent clauses) and appropriate English usage (e.g., pronoun reference).

> **He said, she said**
>
> *Show your child that adults sometimes use "air quotes" (two curled fingers from each hand held up like quotation marks) to indicate that they are repeating someone else's words verbatim. Ask your child to describe*

her day at school, recalling conversations with friends and teachers in as much detail as possible. Ask your child to use "air quotes" when she is repeating the exact words of her teachers and friends, or when quoting her own exact words. Play along with your response, using "air quotes" as you continue the discussion—"What did you say when the teacher said (air quotes), 'Rehearsals for the school play begin this afternoon'?"

Punctuation

1.5 Identify hyphens, dashes, brackets, and semicolons and use them correctly.

Right mark

 Read all about punctuation marks by clicking on each term at http://grammargirl.9ug.com/toc.html or by researching the topic at the library. Then have your child circle an example of each type of punctuation in the daily newspaper, explaining why the particular punctuation mark is used in each situation. Refer back to the website or reference books if necessary.

Capitalization

1.6 Use correct capitalization.

Spelling

1.7 Spell derivatives correctly by applying the spellings of bases and affixes.

LISTENING AND SPEAKING

1.0. Listening and Speaking Strategies

Deliver focused, coherent presentations that convey ideas clearly and relate to the background and interests of the audience. Students evaluate the content of oral communication.

Comprehension

1.1   Ask probing questions to elicit information, including evidence to support the speaker's claims and conclusions.

Hiring help

Tell your child to imagine that she runs a zoo, and you are coming to interview for a job. Have your child interview you as the prospective employee, asking about your talents, interests, and experience as it relates to working in the zoo. Before the interview, discuss with your child some of the different types of jobs available at zoos, including the individuals who feed and care for the animals, the ticket takers at the gates, the veterinarians who care for the animals' health, the architects who design the habitats for the animals, and so on. Then discuss some of the characteristics of good zoo employees: individuals who love animals, individuals who are knowledgeable about each of the animals' preferred diets and habitats, individuals who are observant (to notice when animals are sick or need things), individuals who are strong (for moving feed bags and equipment), and so forth. Explain to your child that, during the interview, she should paraphrase your answers to each question to make sure she understands your response. At the end of the interview, ask your child which job she might place you in and why. Ask your child to cite the specific interview responses that led to her decision.

1.2   Determine the speaker's attitude toward the subject.

1.3   Respond to persuasive messages with questions, challenges, or affirmations.

Organization and Delivery of Oral Communication

1.4   Organize information to achieve particular purposes and to appeal to the background and interests of the audience.

Tips for talking

Have your child read through the tips on effective talks at http://www.si.umich.edu/~pne/acadtalk.htm#Heading3. Then, ask your child to prepare a weather (or sports) report to present at dinner tonight, using the checklists to help during the planning and rehearsal process.

1.5 Arrange supporting details, reasons, descriptions, and examples effectively and persuasively in relation to the audience.

1.6 Use speaking techniques, including voice modulation, inflection, tempo, enunciation, and eye contact, for effective presentations.

Analysis and Evaluation of Oral and Media Communications

1.7 Provide constructive feedback to speakers concerning the coherence and logic of a speech's content and delivery and its overall impact upon the listener.

1.8 Analyze the effect on the viewer of images, text, and sound in electronic journalism; identify the techniques used to achieve the effects in each instance studied.

2.0 Speaking Applications (Genres and Their Characteristics)

Students deliver well-organized formal presentations employing traditional rhetorical strategies (e.g., narration, exposition, persuasion, description). Student speaking demonstrates a command of standard American English and the organizational and delivery strategies outlined in Listening and Speaking Standard 1.0.

Using the speaking strategies of grade seven outlined in Listening and Speaking Standard 1.0, students:

2.1 Deliver narrative presentations:

a. Establish a context, standard plot line (having a beginning, conflict, rising action, climax, and denouement), and point of view.

b. Describe complex major and minor characters and a definite setting.

c. Use a range of appropriate strategies, including dialogue, suspense, and naming of specific narrative action (e.g., movement, gestures, expressions).

2.2 Deliver oral summaries of articles and books:

a. Include the main ideas of the event or article and the most significant details.

b. Use the student's own words, except for material quoted from sources.

c. Convey a comprehensive understanding of sources, not just superficial details.

2.3 Deliver research presentations:

Top tunes I

 Ask your child to research an up-and-coming singer or band and decide whether the singer/band will succeed. Have her use entertainment industry data as well as research collected from the Internet, newspapers, magazines, and other sources. (Your child might want to consider using a similar singer/band as a comparison for the purposes of gathering sales information and other data.) Help your child plan her research first, looking at all the sections of the Standard as outlined in 2.3 a–d. After your child collects, tabulates, and organizes all the data from published and personal sources, move on to "Top tunes II."

a. Pose relevant and concise questions about the topic.

b. Convey clear and accurate perspectives on the subject.

c. Include evidence generated through the formal research process (e.g., use of a card catalog, Reader's Guide to Periodical Literature, computer databases, magazines, newspapers, dictionaries).

d. Cite reference sources appropriately.

2.4 Deliver persuasive presentations:

Top tunes II

 Have your child use the information from the first part of this activity to present information at an imaginary entertainment conference at which top record company executives (household members and friends) will listen to your child's report on whether this singer/band will be the next big thing.

a. State a clear position or perspective in support of an argument or proposal.

b. Describe the points in support of the argument and employ well-articulated evidence.

READING

1.0 Word Analysis, Fluency, and Systematic Vocabulary Development

Students use their knowledge of wordorigins and word relationships, as well as historical and literary context clues, to determine themeaning of specialized vocabulary and to understand the precise meaning of grade-level-appropriate words.

Vocabulary and Concept Development

1.1 Analyze idioms, analogies, metaphors, and similes to infer the literal and figurative meanings of phrases.

1.2 Understand the most important points in the history of English language and use common word origins to determine the historical influences on English word meanings.

1.3 Use word meanings within the appropriate context and show ability to verify those meanings by definition, restatement, example, comparison, or contrast.

Defeat the book

 Explain to your child that he is going to play a game against the thesaurus. First, have your child select a word that is new to him in a glossary. (Try looking in textbooks, cookbooks, and how-to books for a glossary.) Have your child read the definition of the new word in the dictionary and then write the definition in his own words on a piece of paper.

Now, have your child list as many synonyms for the word as possible. Feel free to help your child by giving him hints when he runs out of ideas. When your child's list is complete, have him compare the synonyms he came up with to those listed in the thesaurus, to see which list had more synonyms—and to discover ones he might have missed or that were surprising. Finally, your child should be able to use the new word in a sentence that clearly demonstrates an understanding of its definition.

2.0 Reading Comprehension (Focus on Informational Materials)

Students read and understand grade-level-appropriate material. They describe and connect the essential ideas, arguments, and perspectives of the text by using their knowledge of text structure, organization, and purpose. The selections in *Recommended Readings in Literature, Kindergarten Through Grade Eight* illustrate the quality and com-plexity of the materials to be read by students. In addition, students read one million words annually on their own, including a good representation of narrative and expository text (e.g., classic and contemporary literature, magazines, newspapers, online information).

Structural Features of Informational Materials

2.1   Compare and contrast the features and elements of consumer materials to gain meaning from documents (e.g., warranties, contracts, product information, instruction manuals).

New product papers

 NEW PRODUCT Ask your child to imagine that he just has been hired to develop the appropriate consumer materials for a product. But first your child will have to research each type of document. Have him study the packaging of a new product that comes with a warranty, product information (perhaps on the package), and instruction manual. Ask your child to underline or highlight the key information in each document and then summarize what each document is meant to accomplish. (Warranties guarantee a product for a period of time. Product information explains what the product does. Instruction manuals spell out how to set up and

use the item.) Now, have your child select a gadget in the house and write the warranty, product information, and instruction manual for it. Once complete, and edited for correct spelling, punctuation, and grammar, have him present the entire package (product and accompanying papers) to someone in the household. Have the person read each document to see if it clearly accomplishes what your child intended. If there are ambiguities, have your child "go back to the drawing board," and make changes to the document(s) accordingly.

2.2   Analyze text that uses proposition and support patterns.

Comprehension and Analysis of Grade-Level-Appropriate Text

2.3   Find similarities and differences between texts in the treatment, scope, or organization of ideas.

2.4   Compare the original text to a summary to determine whether the summary accurately captures the main ideas, includes critical details, and conveys the underlying meaning.

Short vs. long

 Have your child read a summary (either online or in a newspaper or magazine) of a book she has read. Ask your child to grade the summary, from A+ to F according to how accurately it captured the main idea, critical details, and primary underlying meaning of the book. Then, have your child write an A+ summary, editing the work for organization, meaning, and correct spelling, grammar, and punctuation.

2.5   Understand and explain the use of a complex mechanical device by following technical directions.

2.6   Use information from a variety of consumer, workplace, and public documents to explain a situation or decision and to solve a problem.

Expository Critique

2.7   Evaluate the unity, coherence, logic, internal consistency, and structural patterns of text.

3.0 Literary Response and Analysis

Students read and respond to historically or culturally significant works of literature that reflect and enhance their studies of history and social science. They clarify the ideas and connect them to other literary works. The selections in *Recommended Readings in Literature, Kindergarten Through Grade Eight* illustrate the quality and complexity of the materials to be read by students.

Structural Features of Literature

3.1 Determine and articulate the relationship between the purposes and characteristics of different forms of poetry (e.g., ballad, lyric, couplet, epic, elegy, ode, sonnet).

A rose by any other name

Together, explore the online glossary of poetic terms available at http://cluster.wwa.com/~rgs/glossary.html, which includes helpful examples from well-known poets. For each form of poetry listed in the standard, have your child write a definition in his own words to demonstrate understanding. Then ask your child to write a poem that fits the definition of one of these types of poetry. Before he begins composing his poem, help him select a theme for his work, such as love, friendship, or the passage of time. Then, hold a poetry reading night in your household. Have different members read their own poetry or favorite poems by other poets to one another, and then ask your child to identify the form (listed in the Standard) of each example.

Narrative Analysis of Grade-Level-Appropriate Text

3.2 Evaluate the structural elements of the plot (e.g., subplots, parallel episodes, climax), the plot's development, and the way in which conflicts are (or are not) addressed and resolved.

3.3 Compare and contrast motivations and reactions of literary characters from different historical eras confronting similar situations or conflicts.

Different strokes for different folks

TWO BOOKS ABOUT HISTORICAL FIGURES Have your child select two biographies about historical figures from different time periods who encountered similar circumstances (such as obstacles to civil rights, political conflict, or personal hardship). Have your child read both books and take notes about the differences and similarities between the two people and their experiences and reactions, as outlined in the Standard. From the notes, ask your child to draw a "portrait" of each person, with supporting visual images that convey the differences and similarities discovered (such as similar backgrounds, different methods to achieve the same goal, etc.).

3.4 Analyze the relevance of the setting (e.g., place, time, customs) to the mood, tone, and meaning of the text.

3.5 Identify and analyze recurring themes (e.g., good versus evil) across traditional and contemporary works.

3.6 Identify significant literary devices (e.g., metaphor, symbolism, dialect, irony) that define a writer's style and use those elements to interpret the work.

Literary Criticism

3.7 Analyze a work of literature, showing how it reflects the heritage, traditions, attitudes, and beliefs of its author. (Biographical approach).

WRITING

1.0 Writing Strategies

Students write clear, coherent, and focused essays. The writing exhibits students' awareness of audience and purpose. Essays contain formal introductions, supporting evidence, and conclusions. Students progress through the stages of the writing process as needed.

Organization and Focus

1.1 Create compositions that establish a controlling impression, have a coherent thesis, and end with a clear and well-supported conclusion.

1.2 Establish coherence within and among paragraphs through effective transitions, parallel structures, and similar writing techniques.

1.3 Support theses or conclusions with analogies, paraphrases, quotations, opinions from authorities, comparisons, and similar devices.

Research and Technology

1.4 Plan and conduct multiple-step information searches by using computer networks and modems.

Blood cell tale I

 WWW Assign your child the task of telling the story of blood traveling around the human body from the point of view of a single cell. Help your child plan and conduct research online, typing in different key words (like blood, cell, humans) and using major Internet search engines, as well as checking online science journals and reference sites. Have your child take notes either by hand or on the computer and then continue with part II.

1.5 Achieve an effective balance between researched information and original ideas.

Blood cell tale II

 WORD PROCESSING PROGRAM Ask your child to review the information from part I and use it as the basis for a creative story, building a "persona" or character for the blood cell as it travels through a human body. Explain that your child should strike a balance between the imaginary aspects of the cell "speaking" and that of the science behind the activity.

Evaluation and Revision

1.6 Revise writing for word choice; appropriate organization; consistent point of view; and transitions between paragraphs, passages, and ideas.

2.0 Writing Applications (Genres and Their Characteristics)

Students write narrative, expository, persuasive, and descriptive essays of at least 500 to 700 words in each genre. Student writing demonstrates a command of standard American English and the research, organizational, and drafting strategies outlined in Writing Standard 1.0.

Using the writing strategies of grade eight outlined in Writing Standard 1.0, students:

2.1 Write biographies, autobiographies, short stories, or narratives:

a. Relate a clear, coherent incident, event, or situation by using well-chosen details.

b. Reveal the significance of, or the writer's attitude about, the subject.

c. Employ narrative and descriptive strategies (e.g., relevant dialogue, specific action, physical description, background description, comparison or contrast of characters).

2.2 Write responses to literature:

a. Exhibit careful reading and insight in their interpretations.

b. Connect the student's own responses to the writer's techniques and to specific textual references.

c. Draw supported inferences about the effects of a literary work on its audience.

d. Support judgments through references to the text, other works, other authors, or to personal knowledge.

2.3 Write research reports:

First-hand history

PRIMARY SOURCE MATERIALS SUCH AS FAMILY MEMORABILIA, LETTERS, GOVERNMENT RECORDS, PHOTOGRAPHS, NEWSPAPER CLIPPINGS, CERTIFICATES, AND SO FORTH Have your child study the history of a relative (perhaps yourself, a grandparent, aunt, or uncle) up close by examining <u>primary sources</u> (those created during the time period being studied, including photographs, letters, and personal memorabilia). Help *your child assemble a variety of primary sources and piece together a "history" of the person's life, creating a mini exhibition on a table, counter, shelf, or other open flat space. Have your child create labels that explain each item and what it reveals about the person's history. Afterward, discuss the difference between studying history with these primary sources, and <u>secondary sources</u>, which are materials prepared later by people who studied the primary sources, such as textbooks, biographies, or documentaries. Have your child create her own secondary source by writing an introductory essay to the exhibition. Make sure your child's essay is legibly written and correctly spelled and punctuated.*

a.   Define a thesis.

b.   Record important ideas, concepts, and direct quotations from significant information sources and paraphrase and summarize all perspectives on the topic, as appropriate.

c.   Use a variety of primary and secondary sources and distinguish the nature and value of each.

d.   Organize and display information on charts, maps, and graphs.

2.4   Write persuasive compositions:

a.   Include a well-defined thesis (i.e., one that makes a clear and knowledgeable judgment).

b.   Present detailed evidence, examples, and reasoning to support arguments, differentiating between facts and opinion.

c.   Provide details, reasons, and examples, arranging them effectively by anticipating and answering reader concerns and counterarguments.

2.5   Write documents related to career development, including simple business letters and job applications:

a.   Present information purposefully and succinctly and meet the needs of the intended audience.

b.   Follow the conventional format for the type of document (e.g., letter of inquiry, memorandum).

2.6   Write technical documents:

a. Identify the sequence of activities needed to design a system, operate a tool, or explain the bylaws of an organization.

b. Include all the factors and variables that need to be considered.

c. Use formatting techniques (e.g., headings, differing fonts) to aid comprehension.

WRITTEN AND ORAL ENGLISH LANGUAGE CONVENTIONS

The standards for written and oral English language conventions have been placed between those for writing and for listening and speaking because these conventions are essential to both sets of skills.

Written and Oral English Language Conventions

Students write and speak with a command of standard English conventions appropriate to this grade level.

Sentence Structure

1.1 Use correct and varied sentence types and sentence openings to present a lively and effective personal style.

1.2 Identify and use parallelism, including similar grammatical forms, in all written discourse to present items in a series and items juxtaposed for emphasis.

1.3 Use subordination, coordination, apposition, and other devices to indicate clearly the relationship between ideas.

Grammar

1.4 Edit written manuscripts to ensure that correct grammar is used.

Fine tuning

 Have both you and your child create separate campaign leaflets, imagining you are running for president of your neighborhood association. What will you write to convince others that you should be elected? What

personal characteristics, experiences, and ideas will you try to get across? Swap leaflets and critique one another's writing. What is clear, unclear, strong, weak, confusing, and so forth? Then each edit your own work as indicated in the Standard, and rewrite the final leaflet on plain paper, adding illustrations that will attract voters to your words.

Punctuation and Capitalization

1.5 Use correct punctuation and capitalization.

Spelling

1.6 Use correct spelling conventions.

Spell-check and hunt

WWW *Have your child play the fun online game to see how she does with spelling at http://www.funbrain.com/spell/index.html. Have your child move from "easy" to "hard." Next, customize your own hidden-word hunt game, which you can print out, using vocabulary from popular books at http://www.funbrain.com/detect/.*

LISTENING AND SPEAKING

1.0 Listening and Speaking Strategies

Students deliver focused, coherent presentations that convey ideas clearly and relate to the background and interests of the audience. They evaluate the content of oral communication.

Comprehension

1.1 Analyze oral interpretations of literature, including language choice and delivery, and the effect of the interpretations on the listener.

1.2 Paraphrase a speaker's purpose and point of view and ask relevant questions concerning the speaker's content, delivery, and purpose.

Organization and Delivery of Oral Communication

1.3 Organize information to achieve particular purposes by matching the message, vocabulary, voice modulation, expression, and tone to the audience and purpose.

1.4 Prepare a speech outline based upon a chosen pattern of organization, which generally includes an introduction; transitions, previews, and summaries; a logically developed body; and an effective conclusion.

1.5 Use precise language, action verbs, sensory details, appropriate and colorful modifiers, and the active rather than the passive voice in ways that enliven oral presentations.

1.6 Use appropriate grammar, word choice, enunciation, and pace during formal presentations.

1.7 Use audience feedback (e.g., verbal and nonverbal cues):

a. Reconsider and modify the organizational structure or plan.
b. Rearrange words and sentences to clarify the meaning.

Analysis and Evaluation of Oral and Media Communications

Fad diets

 With your child, examine newspaper, magazine and TV advertisements for diets and weight-loss foods. Decipher which claims seem likely and which do not (such as losing 10 pounds in 2 days). How does the fact that the advertiser's claims are printed in a newspaper or magazine affect what you might believe about them? Would you be more or less likely to believe the claims if they were printed in a scientific or medical journal? How about if they were confirmed by a "real person" (as opposed to a paid actor) on TV? What if you heard the claims from a friend? Based on your conclusions, discuss the methods advertisers use to persuade customers to buy other categories of products (toys, clothes, sneakers, etc.).

1.8 Evaluate the credibility of a speaker (e.g., hidden agendas, slanted or biased material).

1.9　Interpret and evaluate the various ways in which visual image makers (e.g., graphic artists, illustrators, news photographers) communicate information and affect impressions and opinions.

2.0 Speaking Applications (Genres and Their Characteristics)

Students deliver well-organized formal presentations employing traditional rhetorical strategies (e.g., narration, exposition, persuasion, description). Student speaking demonstrates a command of standard American English and the organizational and delivery strategies outlined in Listening and Speaking Standard 1.0.

Using the speaking strategies of grade eight outlined in Listening and Speaking Standard 1.0, students:

2.1 Deliver narrative presentations (e.g., biographical, autobiographical):

Who's coming to dinner?

 Have your child imagine inviting any guest in the world—a known person from the past or present—to dinner. In order for your child to make the guest feel welcome, he must do some research, finding out as much information as possible about the person (online, in the library, or in person). Have your child use this information to tell you (and other household members) all about the person without ever saying the fictional dinner guest's name. Your child should address as many aspects of the Standard a–c as possible. You must try to guess who the person is from your child's presentation to find out who you'll be dining with tonight!

a.　Relate a clear, coherent incident, event, or situation by using well-chosen details.

b.　Reveal the significance of, and the subject's attitude about, the incident, event, or situation.

c.   Employ narrative and descriptive strategies (e.g., relevant dialogue, specific action, physical description, background description, comparison or contrast of characters).

2.2   Deliver oral responses to literature:

Dinner review

At dinner ask your child, and then everyone else at the table, to give a short description of a book (or magazine article) they are reading or have read recently, addressing sections a–c in the Standard. You might hold a "dinner review" once a week so that everyone can share their responses to what they are reading on a regular basis.

a.   Interpret a reading and provide insight.

b.   Connect the students' own responses to the writer's techniques and to specific textual references.

c.   Draw supported inferences about the effects of a literary work on its audience.

d.   Support judgments through references to the text, other works, other authors, or personal knowledge.

2.3   Deliver research presentations:

a.   Define a thesis.

b.   Record important ideas, concepts, and direct quotations from significant information sources and paraphrase and summarize all relevant perspectives on the topic, as appropriate.

c.   Use a variety of primary and secondary sources and distinguish the nature and value of each.

d.   Organize and record information on charts, maps, and graphs.

2.4   Deliver persuasive presentations:

a.   Include a well-defined thesis (i.e., one that makes a clear and knowledgeable judgment).

b.   Differentiate fact from opinion and support arguments with detailed evidence, examples, and reasoning.

c.   Anticipate and answer listener concerns and counterarguments effectively through the inclusion and arrangement of details, reasons, examples, and other elements.

d.   Maintain a reasonable tone.

2.5   Recite poems (of four to six stanzas), sections of speeches, or dramatic soliloquies, using voice modulation, tone, and gestures expressively to enhance the meaning.

Director's call

Ask your child to imagine that you are a film director, and that you would like to "audition" her for a part in your upcoming movie. For the tryout, you would like your child to recite a single poem, excerpt from a speech, or dramatic soliloquy. Help direct your child to make the proper volume and gesture adjustments as she tries out for the newest blockbuster.

CALIFORNIA

Science

Grades 6-8

(adopted October 1998, copyright 2000)

Focus on Earth Science

Plate Tectonics and Earth's Structure

1. Plate tectonics accounts for important features of Earth's surface and major geologic events. As a basis for understanding this concept:

Colliding, sliding plate

 For an overview of plate tectonics, together visit http://www.pbs.org/wgbh/aso/tryit/tectonics/intro.html. Then explore the "Plate Tectonics and People" section at http://pubs.usgs.gov/ publications/text/dynamic.html to see how the earth's constant movement underfoot affects humankind. (If you prefer, research plate tecton-

ics using library resources.) Have your child use the research to write and illustrate a dramatic story, with correct grammar, spelling, and punctuation that conveys an imaginary person's exciting experience resulting from shifting and colliding plates.

a. Students know evidence of plate tectonics is derived from the fit of the continents; the location of earthquakes, volcanoes, and midocean ridges; and the distribution of fossils, rock types, and ancient climatic zones.

b. Students know Earth is composed of several layers: a cold, brittle lithosphere; a hot, convecting mantle; and a dense, metallic core.

Baked Earth

COOKING INGREDIENTS AS MENTIONED IN THE ACTIVITY Together, create a yummy cross-section of the Earth, with a different tasty treat for each layer. Begin by having your child toss together 1 ½ cups crushed graham crackers, one well-beaten egg, ¼ stick butter, and ¼ cup brown sugar. Blend well and spread the mixture, which will be the earth's "core," in a 9-inch pie pan. Bake in a 350 degree oven until the sugar and butter melt. Remove to let the "core" harden. On top, pour 16 ounces semisweet chocolate, softened and melted in a microwave, or carefully and slowly on the top of the stove. (Help your child with this step as the chocolate is hot.) This is the Earth's movable "mantle." Let cool and then, finally, sprinkle completely with lightly toasted nuts of your choice, making the brittle lithosphere or Earth's outer shell. Before chowing down, have your child explain each of the Earth's layers to anyone sharing the dessert. Keep leftovers covered in the refrigerator.

c. Students know lithospheric plates the size of continents and oceans move at rates of centimeters per year in response to movements in the mantle.

d. Students know that earthquakes are sudden motions along breaks in the crust called faults and that volcanoes and fissures are locations where magma reaches the surface.

Shake, rattle, and explode

WWW *INGREDIENTS FOR EXPLODING VOLCANO, MUSIC Using reference books or the Internet, together explore earthquakes and plate tectonics (online at http://wwwneic.cr.usgs.gov/neis/plate_tectonics/rift_man.html). Then read about volcanoes at http://library.thinkquest.org/17457/english.html. Ask your child to define the difference between volcanoes and earthquakes (as described in the Standard) in his own words. Then build your own exploding volcano with simple kitchen ingredients as described at http://www.spartechsoftware.com/reeko/Experiments/volcano.htm. While working on the experiment, listen to music that parallels the energy of the earth's transformation, such as Russian composer Modest Moussorgsky's "A Night on Bald Mountain" (best known from the Disney movie* Fantasia).

e. Students know major geologic events, such as earthquakes, volcanic eruptions, and mountain building, result from plate motions.

f. Students know how to explain major features of California geology (including mountains, faults, volcanoes) in terms of plate tectonics.

g. Students know how to determine the epicenter of an earthquake and know that the effects of an earthquake on any region vary, depending on the size of the earthquake, the distance of the region from the epicenter, the local geology, and the type of construction in the region.

Shaping Earth's Surface

2. Topography is reshaped by the weathering of rock and soil and by the transportation and deposition of sediment. As a basis for understanding this concept:

Weathering change hunt

WWW *Together, examine the pictures of the many different forms of weathering at http://www.geo.duke.edu/geo41/wea.htm and http://www.geo.duke.edu/geo41/wea2.htm. Have your child take extensive notes and make small sketches and then go out into the "field" (any natural area). Your child earns one point for every different type of real-life weathering she can find, using her notes as a reference.*

a. Students know water running downhill is the dominant process in shaping the landscape, including California's landscape.

b. Students know rivers and streams are dynamic systems that erode, transport sediment, change course, and flood their banks in natural and recurring patterns.

River travel

Together, enjoy the animated explanations of saltation, traction, solution, suspension—the four processes by which rivers transport their natural loads—at http://library.thinkquest.org/28022/transport/index.html. Research the terms in the above Standard using reference books or an Internet search engine. Have your child draft and revise lyrics for a song (with correct spelling, punctuation, and grammar) about the different processes that occur in rivers and streams. Your child can set her lyrics to a favorite tune or create her own music.

c. Students know beaches are dynamic systems in which the sand is supplied by rivers and moved along the coast by the action of waves.

d. Students know earthquakes, volcanic eruptions, landslides, and floods change human and wildlife habitats.

Heat (Thermal Energy) (Physical Science)

3. Heat moves in a predictable flow from warmer objects to cooler objects until all the objects are at the same temperature. As a basis for understanding this concept:

a. Students know energy can be carried from one place to another by heat flow or by waves, including water, light and sound waves, or by moving objects.

b. Students know that when fuel is consumed, most of the energy released becomes heat energy.

c. Students know heat flows in solids by conduction (which involves no flow of matter) and in fluids by conduction and by convection (which involves flow of matter).

SILVER SPOON, CUP OF HOT CHOCOLATE Make a cup of hot chocolate that's too steamy to drink right away. Show your child that one way to cool it down more quickly is to put in a metal (preferably silver) spoon. Have your child place the spoon in the mug and very carefully put his fingers on the part of the stem nearest the hot liquid. Ask your child to note as the heat transfers into the cool metal spoon, rising upward. Then, have your child describe what this experiment illustrates. (Heat always moves from hotter to cooler objects.) But there's more to it. This is an example of <u>conduction</u>—the movement of heat through a material without the flow of matter. What is it that moves to create the heat? Ask your child to rub his hands together very fast for 30 seconds. What happens to his palms? They heat up! The rubbing hands create warmth. When heat travels by conduction, the atoms likewise vibrate quickly, producing heat. As they jostle ever faster, they strike cold, slow-moving atoms next to them, thereby making these neighboring atoms vibrate and thus heat up as well. The vibrating atoms transfer—ping-pong style—the heat/vibrations up through the cooler material. Now your child should be able to explain to a friend or household member not only how to cool off a hot drink more quickly, but why it works! To learn about convection, the second part of this Standard, see the activity for Standard 4.c.

    d.   Students know heat energy is also transferred between objects by radiation (radiation can travel through space).

Energy in the Earth System

    4.   Many phenomena on Earth's surface are affected by the transfer of energy through radiation and convection currents. As a basis for understanding this concept:

    a.   Students know the sun is the major source of energy for phenomena on Earth's surface; it powers winds, ocean currents, and the water cycle.

    b.   Students know solar energy reaches Earth through radiation, mostly in the form of visible light.

    c.   Students know heat from Earth's interior reaches the surface primarily through convection.

Warm air rising

SPACE HEATER OR RADIATOR Have your child stand in a small, cool room, such as a bathroom. Turn on the radiator or a space heater and ask your child to stand nearby with hands raised about shoulder height. Have your child note when the heat reaches her hands. Ask your child to explain what this reveals about the direction in which hot air moves. (Hot air is lighter than cold, so it rises, while cool air sinks.) Eventually the whole room will become warm because as the hot air rises, the cold air sinks toward the heater, becomes warm, and rises, pushing down cold air, and so forth. This up and down movement of air is called <u>convection currents</u>. *Have your child create a mime or short dance piece titled "Convection Currents" that physically and visually embodies this type of movement. Learn about convection currents in liquid in "Cold toes, warm torso" in Standard 4d.*

d. Students know convection currents distribute heat in the atmosphere and oceans.

Cold toes, warm torso

WWW *BODY OF WATER Stand in a pool, lake, or ocean (or you can even have your child sit in a bathtub) in which the water on top is warmer than at the bottom. Ask your child to deduce what this indicates about the weight of warm water versus cold water. (Warm water weighs less and tends to rise, whereas cooler water, weighing more, tends to sink.) To extend this activity, together learn more about convection and try your hand at the "Thought Experiment" at http://ethel.as.arizona.edu/~collins/astro/subjects/convection2.html.*

e. Students know differences in pressure, heat, air movement, and humidity result in changes of weather.

Ecology (Life Science)

5. Organisms in ecosystems exchange energy and nutrients among themselves and with the environment. As a basis for understanding this concept:

a. Students know energy entering ecosystems as sunlight is transferred by producers into chemical energy through photosynthesis and then from organism to organism through food webs.

Eating green I

Can humans make their own food? What organism on earth can? Green plants can turn sunlight into a meal! Learn all about photosynthesis, its role in food/energy production, and the food chain either online using an Internet search engine, or from reference books. From the research, have your child draw images to illustrate each step along the way in the photosynthesis process. Afterward, move to part II.

b. Students know matter is transferred over time from one organism to others in the food web and between organisms and the physical environment.

Eating green II

Now that you have seen how plants make food from the sun's radiant energy, have your child complete a simple <u>food web</u>, which involves the flow of energy from the sun to green plants to animal consumers. Have your child divide a large piece of drawing paper into three horizontal bands. Ask your child to sketch the sun and its radiant energy in the top band, and then have your child sketch plants that grow from the sun's energy in the second band, and finally, animal consumers (including humans) in the bottom band. Ask your child to expand and refine his diagram by referring back to his reference books or with information from http://edu.leeds.ac.uk/~edu/technology/epb97/forestfdchn.htm.

c. Students know populations of organisms can be categorized by the functions they serve in an ecosystem.

d. Students know different kinds of organisms may play similar ecological roles in similar biomes.

What's a biome?

Together, research biomes, either using reference books or by taking a virtual tour with pictures and information of various biomes located on the world map at http://www.cotf.edu/ete/modules/msese/earthsysflr/biomes.html. <u>Biomes</u> are distinct ecological communities of plants and animals living together in a particular climate. Next, have your child select two biome examples (such as a desert and a tropical savannah) and conduct further research in order to draw at least

two parallels between the similar role different plants or animals play in each environment. (For instance, your child could investigate which animals are the hunters and scavengers in the two types of locales.) Afterward, have your child use her research as the basis for a labeled drawing that reflects an understanding of the environmental and ecological differences and similarities in each biome.

e. Students know the number and types of organisms an ecosystem can support depends on the resources available and on abiotic factors, such as quantities of light and water, a range of temperatures, and soil composition.

It's a small world

LARGE, CLEAR PLASTIC SODA BOTTLE WITH TOP CUT OFF, GRAVEL, SMALL PLANTS, ROCKS, BRANCHES, MOSS, PLASTIC WRAP Explain to your child that he is going to create a small ecosystem at home. If possible, first visit a local plant store and examine various terrariums. Then, help your child create an example at home using either the simple online instructions at http://www.nsc.org/ehc/kids/terrariu.htm or a reference book on how to build terrariums (such as a children's book of science experiments). Have your child create an illustrated "viewer's information poster" to display by the container, adding information and observations about the ecosystem of the terrarium over time. The poster should address the living organisms as well as abiotic factors (those without life, such as water, temperature, soil, and so forth). Afterward, discuss what limitations the terrarium has in fully representing the natural environment. (Do animals, insects, and changes in weather interact in the terrarium as they do in a real environment?)

Resources

6. Sources of energy and materials differ in amounts, distribution, usefulness, and the time required for their formation. As a basis for understanding this concept:

a. Students know the utility of energy sources is determined by factors that are involved in converting these sources to useful forms and the consequences of the conversion process.

b. Students know different natural energy and material resources, including air, soil, rocks, minerals, petroleum, fresh water, wildlife, and forests, and know how to classify them as renewable or nonrenewable.

Old energy, new ideas

WWW 📖 *Together, learn why the nonrenewable energy sources of coal, oil, and natural gas are called fossil fuels using library references or online at http://www.energy.ca.gov/education/story/story-html/chaptero5.html. (The term "fossil" comes from the fact that they were formed during the time of the dinosaurs.) Next, have your child try to name as many renewable energy sources as possible. To augment the list, try the "Renewable Energy Crossword Puzzle" at http://www.energy.ca.gov/education/puzzles/puzzles-html/crossword1.html.*

c. Students know the natural origin of the materials used to make common objects.

Natural materials race

🖐 *Give your child and other players five minutes to find examples of household objects that have natural materials as part of their construction. (Leather bags or gloves, wool sweaters or scarves, wood furniture, houseplants, natural sponges, and food in the refrigerator are examples.) After you call "time" at five minutes, have contestants come back and share their findings, checking one another to make sure the materials are natural. Whoever has the largest variety wins!*

Investigation and Experimentation

7. Scientific progress is made by asking meaningful questions and conducting careful investigations. As a basis for understanding this concept and addressing the content in the other three strands, students should develop their own questions and perform investigations. Students will:

a. Develop a hypothesis.

b. Select and use appropriate tools and technology (including calculators, computers, balances, spring scales, microscopes, and binoculars) to perform tests, collect data, and display data.

c. Construct appropriate graphs from data and develop qualitative statements about the relationships between variables.

d. Communicate the steps and results from an investigation in written reports and oral presentations.

e. Recognize whether evidence is consistent with a proposed explanation.

f. Read a topographic map and a geologic map for evidence provided on the maps and construct and interpret a simple scale map.

g. Interpret events by sequence and time from natural phenomena (e.g., the relative ages of rocks and intrusions).

h. Identify changes in natural phenomena over time without manipulating the phenomena (e.g., a tree limb, a grove of trees, a stream, a hillslope).

GRADE SEVEN

Focus on Life Science

Cell Biology

1. All living organisms are composed of cells, from just one to many trillions, whose details usually are visible only through a microscope. As a basis for understanding this concept:

Cell basics

WWW *Explain to your child that* <u>cells</u> *are the basic units of life. Simple organisms are made of one; humans are made of 10 trillion (10,000,000,000,000) cells! Together, bring a cell visually to life, learning about basic cell components as your child follows instructions for making a squeezable model at http://gslc.genetics.utah.edu/basic/cell/index.html.*

a. Students know cells function similarly in all living organisms.

b. Students know the characteristics that distinguish plant cells from animal cells, including chloroplasts and cell walls.

The sun's taste

OPTIONAL: SAMPLE OF CHLOROPHYLL FROM HEALTH FOOD STORE Using life science or biology reference books (or an encyclopedia), or searching online, explore the similarities and differences between plant and animal cells. Have your child create a chart, with "plant cells" and "animal cells" in columns across the top, and listing the characteristics that they have in common, and the ones that are particular to a certain kind of cell. For instance, in plant cells, <u>chloroplasts</u>, resembling incredibly tiny footballs, contain chlorophyll, which helps make food for the plant. To taste the dark green building block of life, buy an organic bottle of chlorophyll at your local health food store. Enhance half a glass of juice (or water) with a tablespoon a day. Besides its nutrients, chlorophyll helps freshen breath.

c. Students know the nucleus is the repository for genetic information in plant and animal cells.

Cellular commander

Why do nose cells look different from toenail cells, eye cells, and so forth? Together, discover how the nucleus serves as the "control center" of the cell using reference books or by typing "nucleus" into an Internet search engine. Afterward, have your child create a persuasive argument (in a clear and articulate manner) for why the nucleus should be referred to as the "brain" of the cell. Your child should cite her research as support for the argument.

d. Students know that mitochondria liberate energy for the work that cells do and that chloroplasts capture sunlight energy for photosynthesis.

A cell's choppers

<u>Mitochondria</u> convert the chemical energy contained in food into energy the cell uses to grow, divide, and function. Have your child investigate this cellular "digestion" using reference books

or by typing mitochondria into an Internet search engine. Ask your child to give a "cell digestion" talk during dinner to household members, explaining the way this process occurs in cells. Your child's discussion should be clear and articulate and presented in a logical, easily understandable manner. Afterward, have your child solicit nicknames from diners for mitochondria, such as "tiny powerhouses" or "mini power plants," to make sure everyone understands the importance of mitochondria and their function.

e. Students know cells divide to increase their numbers through a process of mitosis, which results in two daughter cells with identical sets of chromosomes.

Whose tosis?

LONG YELLOW STRING BEANS, LONG GREEN STRING BEANS, LARGE DINNER PLATE, TWO SMALL DESSERT PLATES First learn about mitosis, the process of cell division at http://esg-www.mit.edu:8001 /esgbio/cb/mitosis.html. To reinforce the concept visually, use string beans (representing chromosomes) and plates to recreate the diagram on the website. First, have your child place four green string beans and four yellow string beans on a large plate (representing the cell, as seen in the website diagram). Continue the mitosis process as illustrated. Pair up the string beans with similar colors (two yellow sets and two green sets), then align them vertically down the center of the plate, and finally divide them up onto two smaller plates—with one set of green and one set of yellow on each. Each "daughter" cell should now look like the original.

f. Students know that as multicellular organisms develop, their cells differentiate.

Genetics

2. A typical cell of any organism contains genetic instructions that specify its traits. Those traits may be modified by environmental influences. As a basis for understanding this concept:

California Content Standards with Home Learning Activities

Cellular story

WWW 📖 *Together, begin with the basics about cells and genetics. Information can be found in reference books about life science, or click on the right-hand arrow on the "Cells Are Us" website at http://www.icnet.uk/kids/cellsrus/cellsrus.html to follow an illustrated story of how we all began from two cells, and the role of DNA and chromosomes. Have your child retell the story of his coming into being in his own words, from the cellular point of view! The narration should be logical, chronological, and engaging, demonstrating a clear understanding of the material studied.* 📖

b. Students know sexual reproduction produces offspring that inherit half their genes from each parent.

c. Students know an inherited trait can be determined by one or more genes.

d. Students know plant and animal cells contain many thousands of different genes and typically have two copies of every gene. The two copies (or alleles) of the gene may or may not be identical, and one may be dominant in determining the phenotype while the other is recessive.

e. Students know DNA (deoxyribonucleic acid) is the genetic material of living organisms and is located in the chromosomes of each cell.

Kitchen lab!

✍ 🔬 **WWW** *MATERIALS LISTED ON THE WEBSITE Why don't people look like dogs, or kittens like tangerines? It's all a matter of a chemical substance called <u>DNA (deoxyribonucleic acid)</u> carried inside chromosomes. DNA carries the information that makes every living thing different from all others. Together, conduct your own DNA experiment in the kitchen using instructions at http://gslc.genetics.utah.edu/basic/howto/index.html. As an extension, have your child investigate the growing use of DNA profiling (or fingerprinting), and its use in criminal cases. Ask your child to write and illustrate a nerve-tingling crime story with a clearly articulated plot and characters (using correct spelling, punctuation, and grammar) about a crime solved with DNA evidence.* 📖 ✍

Evolution

3. Biological evolution accounts for the diversity of species developed through gradual processes over many generations. As a basis for understanding this concept:

   a. Students know both genetic variation and environmental factors are causes of evolution and diversity of organisms.

   b. Students know the reasoning used by Charles Darwin in reaching his conclusion that natural selection is the mechanism of evolution.

Interviewing Charles D.

WWW 📄 *Have your child study the life and work of Charles Darwin, using library resources (such as an encyclopedia or short biography), or by typing "Charles Darwin" into an Internet search engine. Afterward, you should play the role of a graduate student gathering first-hand history for your thesis, interviewing Mr. Darwin (your child) about his life and scientific work. (Have your child help you come up with a list of relevant and probing interview questions before taking on your roles.) As you conduct the interview, have someone knowledgeable about Darwin "coach" the two of you during the scene. Your child's answers during the interview in the role of Charles Darwin should demonstrate an understanding of his work and life, as well as an ability to speak clearly and articulately.* 📖 🎬

---

   c. Students know how independent lines of evidence from geology, fossils, and comparative anatomy provide the bases for the theory of evolution.

   d. Students know how to construct a simple branching diagram to classify living groups of organisms by shared derived characteristics and how to expand the diagram to include fossil organisms.

   e. Students know that extinction of a species occurs when the environment changes and that the adaptive characteristics of a species are insufficient for its survival.

Here today, gone tomorrow

WWW 📖 *Together, investigate the causes of extinction and endangered species using reference books, or online at http://library. thinkquest.org/25014/english.index.shtml. Have your child select one of the endangered species and cover it from a television reporter's point of view. Your child should research, assemble, and present the information as a "news flash" on a nightly newscast (right before or after dinner to assembled family members), using correct diction and clearly articulated ideas.* 📖 🎬

Earth and Life History (Earth Science)

4.   Evidence from rocks allows us to understand the evolution of life on Earth. As a basis for understanding this concept:

a.   Students know Earth processes today are similar to those that occurred in the past and slow geologic processes have large cumulative effects over long periods of time.

b.   Students know the history of life on Earth has been disrupted by major catastrophic events, such as major volcanic eruptions or the impacts of asteroids.

c.   Students know that the rock cycle includes the formation of new sediment and rocks and that rocks are often found in layers, with the oldest generally on the bottom.

d.   Students know that evidence from geologic layers and radioactive dating indicates Earth is approximately 4.6 billion years old and that life on this planet has existed for more than 3 billion years.

e.   Students know fossils provide evidence of how life and environmental conditions have changed.

Fossil hunt

✏️ **WWW** 📖 *Together, learn about fossils using reference books, such as an earth science book, or online by typing "fossil" into an Internet search engine. Then go on a fossil hunt at http://www.dmns.org/denverbasin2/ fossil/. If you don't have Internet access, you can bring your child to a natural* *history or field museum to look at fossils and how they are excavated. Have your child take "field notes" during your fossil investigation, analyzing the information to summarize in a clear, articulate manner, everything people can learn about the past from studying fossils.*

f.   Students know how movements of Earth's continental and oceanic plates through time, with associated changes in climate and geographic connections, have affected the past and present distribution of organisms.

g.   Students know how to explain significant developments and extinctions of plant and animal life on the geologic time scale.

Structure and Function in Living Systems

5.   The anatomy and physiology of plants and animals illustrate the complementary nature of structure and function. As a basis for understanding this concept:

a.   Students know plants and animals have levels of organization for structure and function, including cells, tissues, organs, organ systems, and the whole organism.

b.   Students know organ systems function because of the contributions of individual organs, tissues, and cells. The failure of any part can affect the entire system.

c.   Students know how bones and muscles work together to provide a structural framework for movement.

d.   Students know how the reproductive organs of the human female and male generate eggs and sperm and how sexual activity may lead to fertilization and pregnancy.

e.   Students know the function of the umbilicus and placenta during pregnancy.

f.   Students know the structures and processes by which flowering plants generate pollen, ovules, seeds, and fruit.

g. Students know how to relate the structures of the eye and ear to their functions.

Physical Principles in Living Systems (Physical Science)

6. Physical principles underlie biological structures and functions. As a basis for understanding this concept:

a. Students know visible light is a small band within a very broad electromagnetic spectrum.

b. Students know that for an object to be seen, light emitted by or scattered from it must be detected by the eye.

c. Students know light travels in straight lines if the medium it travels through does not change.

d. Students know how simple lenses are used in a magnifying glass, the eye, a camera, a telescope, and a microscope.

Little watery lens

WWW 📖 *KEY WITH HOLE AT TOP, GLASS OF WATER, BOOK WITH FINE PRINT Together, read about lenses at http://www.opticalres.com/kidoptx. html, or use library materials. Then, have your child create a mini microscope lens. Dip a key with a hole at the end into a glass of water. Make sure the drop of water stays in the hole. Look through the water drop, reading fine print from a book. Have your child slowly move the key/lens around to read the text. Ask your child to describe in his own words the function of a lens. (Lenses make things seen through them look larger.)*

e. Students know that white light is a mixture of many wavelengths (colors) and that retinal cells react differently to different wavelengths.

The color of light

WWW 📖 *Together, explore what colors are absorbed and reflected when you see a red apple, green tree, or brown desk by researching white light and wavelengths online at http://www.colormatters.com/see color.html, or by using a reference book that contains information about physical science. Continue this activity while walking or driving through the neighborhood, having your child identify the absorbed and reflected colors of objects that you see along the way.*

f. Students know light can be reflected, refracted, transmitted, and absorbed by matter.

g. Students know the angle of reflection of a light beam is equal to the angle of incidence.

h. Students know how to compare joints in the body (wrist, shoulder, thigh) with structures used in machines and simple devices (hinge, ball-and-socket, and sliding joints).

i. Students know how levers confer mechanical advantage and how the application of this principle applies to the musculoskeletal system.

j. Students know that contractions of the heart generate blood pressure and that heart valves prevent backflow of blood in the circulatory system.

Interior roller coaster ride

Together, view a diagram of the circulatory system (using reference materials or online at http://library.thinkquest.org/10348 /find/content/graphics/bloodcir.html). Then, have your child research and take notes about its major components. Ask your child to use the information to invent song lyrics about the journey of a blood cell starting at the heart, traveling through the body as though it were on an invigorating amusement park roller coaster ride. Your child's lyrics should demonstrate an understanding of the circulatory system and contain correct spelling, grammar, and punctuation, and also an imaginative and evocative use of words.

Investigation and Experimentation

7.   Scientific progress is made by asking meaningful questions and conducting careful investigations. As a basis for understanding this concept and addressing the content in the other three strands, students should develop their own questions and perform investigations.

Ripening methods

NOT QUITE RIPE BANANAS, BROWN PAPER AND PLASTIC BAGS Ask your child to conduct an experiment to help you determine the best method for ripening bananas. Have your child take three similarly unripe bananas and place them in the sun on a windowsill to ripen. For this experiment, place one banana in a brown paper bag, place another in a plastic bag, and leave the third banana uncovered. Have your child note their rate of ripening twice a day, recording the information on a piece of paper. Encourage your child to include touch, taste, and smell in her observation methods. Finally, ask your child to draw a chart or diagram mapping the experiment and then evaluate the information. What is her "expert" opinion on the best method for ripening bananas?

Students will:

a. Select and use appropriate tools and technology (including calculators, computers, balances, spring scales, microscopes, and binoculars) to perform tests, collect data, and display data.

b. Use a variety of print and electronic resources (including the World Wide Web) to collect information and evidence as part of a research project.

c. Communicate the logical connection among hypotheses, science concepts, tests conducted, data collected, and conclusions drawn from the scientific evidence.

d. Construct scale models, maps, and appropriately labeled diagrams to communicate scientific knowledge (e.g., motion of Earth's plates and cell structure).

e. Communicate the steps and results from an investigation in written reports and oral presentations.

GRADE EIGHT

Focus on Physical Science

Motion

1. The velocity of an object is the rate of change of its position. As a basis for understanding this concept:

Velocity races I

Before heading to the velocity races activity, discuss this major concept of motion with your child. <u>Velocity</u> is the rate at which a body moves in space in a given direction. Velocity is expressed in distance and time, such as miles per hour or meters per second. Why aren't speed and velocity the same thing? Speed indicates the rate of motion, but not the direction. Look at the formula for computing uniform velocity (where the distance and direction traveled in each unit remains the same): velocity = distance ÷ by time. Now, continue to part II.

a. Students know position is defined in relation to some choice of a standard reference point and a set of reference directions.

b. Students know that average speed is the total distance traveled divided by the total time elapsed and that the speed of an object along the path traveled can vary.

c. Students know how to solve problems involving distance, time, and average speed.

Velocity races II

STOP WATCH, MEASURING TAPE, PING PONG BALL First, have your child prepare a score chart with a column for each contestant's name, distance traveled, time elapsed, and velocity. Then measure the "race course," say, the length of a room at home. (Make the distance an even number so it's easily divisible by each person's time.) Next, hold a timed competition in which every player (household members and friends) pushes a ping-pong ball the length of the "course" with his or her nose (or crawls backwards across the room). Have your child fill in the chart after each person's turn, and then use the formula d/t = v to find out the velocity for each player.

d. Students know the velocity of an object must be described by specifying both the direction and the speed of the object.

e. Students know changes in velocity may be due to changes in speed, direction, or both.

f. Students know how to interpret graphs of position versus time and graphs of speed versus time for motion in a single direction.

Forces

2. Unbalanced forces cause changes in velocity. As a basis for understanding this concept:

a. Students know a force has both direction and magnitude.

b. Students know when an object is subject to two or more forces at once, the result is the cumulative effect of all the forces.

c. Students know when the forces on an object are balanced, the motion of the object does not change.

Arm wrestle

Explain that you will arm wrestle with your child to explore a scientific idea about force. Both take a neutral arm wrestling position. Then, have your child exert a moderate force, which she should keep constant throughout the experiment. Explain that you will change the amount of your own force, from very little to a lot. First, exert just a tiny bit so that your child's hand tips yours over. Then slowly add more force so your hands come into balance, and then, finally, exert more force so your child's hand goes down. Repeat the experience switching roles and having your child speed up the process just a little, noting how much more quickly your clasped hands change location.

d. Students know how to identify separately the two or more forces that are acting on a single static object, including gravity, elastic forces due to tension or compression in matter, and friction.

Staying in place

Together, explore aspects of <u>gravity</u>, a natural force that makes or tends to make objects move toward the center of earth, using a reference book (such as an encyclopedia or physical science book), or online at http://library.thinkquest.org/27585/frameset_intro.html. Afterward, have your child look at a photograph of a scene with a lot of people involved in various activities. (You can find one in a newspaper or magazine.) Ask your child to redraw the scene, imagining that gravity does not exist. How will this affect the elements in the scene? Where will all the elements in your child's anti-gravity drawing end up?

e. Students know that when the forces on an object are unbalanced, the object will change its velocity (that is, it will speed up, slow down, or change direction).

f. Students know the greater the mass of an object, the more force is needed to achieve the same rate of change in motion.

Rock pitch

Go outdoors and tell your child you are going to test his baseball pitching arm by enhancing sensitivity to the mass of the ball. For this exercise though, your child won't be using balls. Have your child find three rocks of different masses—light, medium, and heavy. Next, mark the "pitcher's mound" where your child should stand. Then mark "home plate," drawing in the dirt or placing something on the ground that's easy to see (a bright sweater or jacket). Stand out of the way as your child tosses each rock toward the plate, repeating the activity until each rock makes it over home plate. After your child perfects his "pitching arm," ask what he learned about the amount of force needed to make each rock hit the same place. Your child should be able to articulate that the heavier the mass, the stronger the force needed in his pitching arm.

g. Students know the role of gravity in forming and maintaining the shapes of planets, stars, and the solar system.

Structure of Matter

3. Each of the more than 100 elements of matter has distinct properties and a distinct atomic structure. All forms of matter are composed of one or more of the elements. As a basis for understanding this concept:

a. Students know the structure of the atom and know it is composed of protons, neutrons, and electrons.

Edible atom

GUMDROPS, TOOTHPICKS, MINIATURE MARSHMALLOWS Together, learn about protons, neutrons, and electrons in science reference books, or by taking a virtual tour of atoms at http: //education. jlab.org/atomtour/. Then, help your child create an edible atomic model. Have your child select gumdrops to represent protons and neutrons (using a different color to represent each), connecting them with toothpicks into circular forms. Then add small, lightweight electrons, using miniature marshmallows.

b. Students know that compounds are formed by combining two or more different elements and that compounds have properties that are different from their constituent elements.

A substance by any other name

Learn the chemical names of substances you and your child encounter on a regular basis (salt, sugar, water, etc.) and substitute these names in your regular conversation for a day. So, you would say, "Please pass the NaCl (sodium chloride) at dinner, instead of asking for the salt, or you might say, "Be sure to turn off the H_2O when you're done with your shower."

c. Students know atoms and molecules form solids by building up repeating patterns, such as the crystal structure of NaCl or long-chain polymers.

d. Students know the states of matter (solid, liquid, gas) depend on molecular motion.

e. Students know that in solids the atoms are closely locked in position and can only vibrate; in liquids the atoms and molecules are more loosely connected and can collide with and move past one another; and in gases the atoms and molecules are free to move independently, colliding frequently.

f. Students know how to use the periodic table to identify elements in simple compounds.

Earth in the Solar System (Earth Science)

4. The structure and composition of the universe can be learned from studying stars and galaxies and their evolution. As a basis for understanding this concept:

a. Students know galaxies are clusters of billions of stars and may have different shapes.

b. Students know that the Sun is one of many stars in the Milky Way galaxy and that stars may differ in size, temperature, and color.

c. Students know how to use astronomical units and light years as measures of distances between the Sun, stars, and Earth.

d. Students know that stars are the source of light for all bright objects in outer space and that the Moon and planets shine by reflected sunlight, not by their own light.

e. Students know the appearance, general composition, relative position and size, and motion of objects in the solar system, including planets, planetary satellites, comets, and asteroids.

Reactions

5. Chemical reactions are processes in which atoms are rearranged into different combinations of molecules. As a basis for understanding this concept:

The tiniest substance

WWW 📱 *SUGAR, OPTIONAL MAGNIFYING GLASS, PERIODIC TABLE Have your child look at a single grain of sugar (with a magnifying glass, if possible). Ask if this is as small as the substance gets. One tiny sugar crystal is made up of millions of sugar molecules! A <u>molecule</u> is the smallest particle of a substance that retains all the properties of the substance. Molecules themselves are made of atoms. Learn more about molecules and atoms, elements and compounds at http://www.nyu.edu/pages/mathmol/text book/compounds.html, or by researching the topic in a physical science book or encyclopedia. Then, have your child use a periodic table (online at http://pearl1.lanl.gov/periodic/) to identify the type of atoms and their number in a molecule of sugar when written as $C_{12}H_{22}O_{11}$. (12 carbon atoms, 22 hydrogen atoms, 11 oxygen atoms). Also, ask your child how many atoms are in a single molecule of sugar (45).* 1,2,3

a. Students know reactant atoms and molecules interact to form products with different chemical properties.

b. Students know the idea of atoms explains the conservation of matter: In chemical reactions the number of atoms stays the same no matter how they are arranged, so their total mass stays the same.

c. Students know chemical reactions usually liberate heat or absorb heat.

d. Students know physical processes include freezing and boiling, in which a material changes form with no chemical reaction.

Forever changing

PLASTIC BAG, FOOD COLORING OR INK Have your child fill a plastic bag about a third of the way full with water tinted with food coloring or ink for easy observation. Blow some air into the bag and then tie it tightly closed. Have your child describe the water's state within the bag as it sits on the counter (liquid). Next, place the bag in direct sunlight. Have your child periodically check the bag until he can see the vapor that rises from the water when heated. Have your child describe this state too (gas). Finally, place the bag into the freezer and have your child describe the water in this final state (frozen). Afterward, note how all these physical changes occurred without any chemical reaction!

e. Students know how to determine whether a solution is acidic, basic, or neutral.

Chemistry of Living Systems (Life Science)

6. Principles of chemistry underlie the functioning of biological systems. As a basis for understanding this concept:

a. Students know that carbon, because of its ability to combine in many ways with itself and other elements, has a central role in the chemistry of living organisms.

Long live carbon!

Together, learn about the importance of carbon in the online, interactive detective game "Carbon is 4 Ever" at http://www.spinaweb.ie /showcase/1124/content/intro.htm. Afterward, have your child phrase, clearly and succinctly, in her own words, the importance of carbon in living organisms.

b. Students know that living organisms are made of molecules consisting largely of carbon, hydrogen, nitrogen, oxygen, phosphorus, and sulfur.

c. Students know that living organisms have many different kinds of molecules, including small ones, such as water and salt, and very large ones, such as carbohydrates, fats, proteins, and DNA.

Periodic Table

7. The organization of the periodic table is based on the properties of the elements and reflects the structure of atoms. As a basis for understanding this concept:

a. Students know how to identify regions corresponding to metals, nonmetals, and inert gases.

Periodic super heroes

Have your child identify which elements in the periodic table are in solid, liquid, and gas form at their normal temperature and pressure. (Examples of periodic tables can be found on the Internet, including http://EnvironmentalChemistry.com/yogi/periodic/.) **Ask your child to create a "super hero" with characteristics of two elements, such as the Amazing He-Fe Man (helium-iron), or Au-O Wonder Woman (gold-oxygen). What special abilities will the hero have because of his or her chemical makeup?**

b. Students know each element has a specific number of protons in the nucleus (the atomic number) and each isotope of the element has a different but specific number of neutrons in the nucleus.

c. Students know substances can be classified by their properties, including their melting temperature, density, hardness, and thermal and electrical conductivity.

Density and Buoyancy

8. All objects experience a buoyant force when immersed in a fluid. As a basis for understanding this concept:

a. Students know density is mass per unit volume.

Bulk up

WWW *INGREDIENTS LISTED AT WEBSITE Explain that* <u>density</u> *is the amount of mass an object has compared to its volume, or size. To gain a better understanding, together try the cool egg, salt, and water experiment to see how density changes using the instructions at http://library.think quest.org/11771/english/hi/chemistry/dense.shtml.*

b. Students know how to calculate the density of substances (regular and irregular solids and liquids) from measurements of mass and volume.

c. Students know the buoyant force on an object in a fluid is an upward force equal to the weight of the fluid the object has displaced.

d. Students know how to predict whether an object will float or sink.

Investigation and Experimentation

9. Scientific progress is made by asking meaningful questions and conducting careful investigations. As a basis for understanding this concept and addressing the content in the other three strands, students should develop their own questions and perform investigations. Students will:

Curatorial care

MEASURING TAPE, INDOOR/OUTDOOR THERMOMETER, COMPASS
Ask your child to imagine that she is a museum curator and she is going to install a huge, bizarre sculpture made out of cotton candy that stands four feet wide and five feet high. Before the wacky artist will ship the work, he has sent the curator (your child) special installation instructions: "My fabulous new work of a pink plant created from cotton candy, which is as light as air, needs special attention in your exhibition. Because it is made out of spun sugar, the room cannot be warmer than 68 degrees Fahrenheit or it will begin to melt. Also, you will need to face it toward the east as the plant believes it needs to see the sun rise in the morning. (It told me so itself.) Please let me know when you have secured a proper space." Have your child use a tape measure, thermometer, and compass to decide which room in your gallery (your home) can accommodate this chic work of art. Your child will need to find a space that is big, tall, and cool enough; she must also determine which way is east, to orient the artwork in the right position once it arrives from the artist's studio.

a. Plan and conduct a scientific investigation to test a hypothesis.

b. Evaluate the accuracy and reproducibility of data.

c. Distinguish between variable and controlled parameters in a test.

d. Recognize the slope of the linear graph as the constant in the relationship $y = kx$ and apply this principle in interpreting graphs constructed from data.

e. Construct appropriate graphs from data and develop quantitative statements about the relationships between variables.

f. Apply simple mathematic relationships to determine a missing quantity in a mathematic expression, given the two remaining terms (including speed = distance/time, density = mass/volume, force = pressure × area, volume = area × height).

g. Distinguish between linear and nonlinear relationships on a graph of data.

CALIFORNIA

Math

Grades 6-8
(adopted December 1997, copyright 1999)

GRADE SIX

By the end of grade six, students have mastered the four arithmetic operations with whole numbers, positive fractions, positive decimals, and positive and negative integers; they accurately compute and solve problems. They apply their knowledge to statistics and probability. Students understand the concepts of mean, median, and mode of data sets and how to calculate the range. They analyze data and sampling processes for possible bias and misleading conclusions; they use addition and multiplication of fractions routinely to calculate the probabilities for compound events. Students conceptually understand and work with ratios and proportions; they compute percentages (e.g., tax, tips, interest). Students know about π and the formulas for the circumference and area of a circle. They use letters for numbers in formulas involving geometric shapes and in ratios to represent an unknown part of an expression. They solve one-step linear equations.

Number Sense

1.0 Students compare and order positive and negative fractions, decimals, and mixed numbers. Students solve problems involving fractions, ratios, proportions, and percentages:

Nutty mixed fractions

✐ (OPTIONAL) NUTS, PENCIL Use visual aids to help your child understand how to write <u>mixed numbers</u> (consisting of whole numbers and fractions). First write the improper fraction $^9/_5$ on a piece of paper. In <u>improper fractions</u> the numerator (top number) is equal to or greater than the denominator (bottom number). Have your child lay a pencil horizontally on the table and then place 9 nuts on top of this "fraction line" and five nuts underneath it. Explain that this fraction equals more than a whole and there is another way to write it: as a mixed number. Have your child "divide" the number five, (the amount of the denominator of the 5 nuts below) into the numerator of 9 nuts on top. Your child should remove 5 of the top nuts (leaving 4 on top). Have your child move these 5 just to the left of the pencil fraction line, assembling them to create the number 1. Now, looking at the nuts, ask your child to articulate the entire equation, which is a mixed fraction = $1\,^4/_5$. Give your child more written improper fractions to translate, seeing how quickly she can transform them into nutty mixed fractions. Finally, if possible, explore fractions further at the All About Fractions web site http://www.aaamath. com/fra.html.

1.1   Compare and order positive and negative fractions, decimals, and mixed numbers and place them on a number line.

1.2   Interpret and use ratios in different contexts (e.g., batting averages, miles per hour) to show the relative sizes of two quantities, using appropriate notations (a/b, a to b, a:b).

Batter up I

Ratio means relationship. It is a comparison between two numbers. (For instance, if there are 2 adults and 3 children watching television, this would be written as $^2/_3$, 2:3, or 2 to 3.) Explain that when written as 2:3, the colon is an abbreviation for the division sign. Batting averages can also be expressed as ratios. Together, watch a little league or professional baseball game and have your child keep score for each player, writing down the number of base hits and times at bat. At the end of the game, have your child express each player's batting average as a ratio. Batting averages are calculated by taking the number of hits out of 100 times at bat, and multiplying the result by 10. A batting average of .300, means that the batter gets 30 hits out of every 100 times at bat; this can be expressed in a ratio form as 30:100. Learn more about ratios at http://www.mathleague.com/help/ratio/ratio.htm. Now move on to the "Batter up II" activity (Standard 3.3 in Statistics, Data Analysis and Probability).

1.3   Use proportions to solve problems (e.g., determine the value of N if $^4/_7 = {}^N/_{21}$, find the length of a side of a polygon similar to a known polygon). Use cross-multiplication as a method for solving such problems, understanding it as the multiplication of both sides of an equation by a multiplicative inverse.

"Please sir, may I have some more?"

Explain to your child that she has just been hired by the city's best restaurant to cook a dream meal for the sports team or musical group of her choice. The meal should be sumptuous and plentiful, enough for 60 people, because everyone will be bringing friends and family. First, have your young chef select the recipes she will make for an appetizer, main course, and dessert. Then have her write each selected recipe on a separate sheet of paper, including the number of servings it provides. Now your chef has to convert the recipes to feed 60 guests. Together, review the helpful information about proportion and ratios at http://www.learner.org/exhibits/dailymath/cooking.html or research these terms in reference books. Have your chef write out the newly converted recipe on the original papers. Help check that the math is correct and then, for more math practice, have her make a shopping list with the quantity of all the items you would need to buy. Using approximate costs, have your child figure out how much the grocery bill will run, and then divide the sum by 60 people to determine the cost per person.

1.4 Calculate given percentages of quantities and solve problems involving discounts at sales, interest earned, and tips.

Catalog delight

 GIFT CATALOG, CALCULATOR Have your child imagine that she has just received a $1,000 check from a mysterious benefactor. The note with the check said your child could buy whatever she wanted with the money, as long as she also bought gifts for others in the household as well. Also, she is required to make all of her purchases from one catalog. Have your child select her purchases (keeping a running estimate of her total) and then fill out the catalog order form. In order to complete the form, she should total the order and calculate the sales tax and shipping costs as indicated in the instructions. If her total after sales tax and shipping exceeds her $1,000 budget, ask her to revise her order. Ask her to make all of her calculations first, and to use the calculator to check her work. For additional fun, together play the Estimated Total Price with Sales Tax and Tip game at http://www.aaamath.com/rat68-tip-estimate.html, which requires similar calculations.

2.0 Students calculate and solve problems involving addition, subtraction, multiplication, and division:

3 for $1.00

 Visit the supermarket together and find sales where an item costs less if you buy it in bulk (e.g., 3 peaches for $1.00 or one peach for $.39). Have your child create a two-column chart listing "sale price per unit/item" and "regular price per unit/item." For each example you discover in the store, have your child use division to discover the unit price for the items if bought in bulk, and then compare this to how much each unit would cost if bought at the regular price. While on line or at home, have your child do the math for all the items you bought on sale to tell you exactly how much money you saved today!

2.1 Solve problems involving addition, subtraction, multiplication, and division of positive fractions and explain why a particular operation was used for a given situation.

2.2 Explain the meaning of multiplication and division of positive fractions and perform the calculations (e.g., $5/8 \div 15/16 = 5/8 \times 16/15 = 2/3$).

2.3 Solve addition, subtraction, multiplication, and division problems, including those arising in concrete situations, that use positive and negative integers and combinations of these operations.

Home banking

 SPARE BANK BOOK FOR RECORDING BANK ACCOUNT TRANS-ACTIONS OR NOTEBOOK, CALCULATOR Obtain a spare bank account transaction book for your child (or have her recreate the format on a page of notebook paper, using an empty page from your own bank book as a model). Have your child begin by listing the amount of money she has in savings. Each day for a week your child should add in any deposits, such as earnings from chores, gifts, or allowance, and subtract any money used for expenses, including gifts, food, entertainment, and hobbies. (For this activity you can also have your child select an amount to have in her pretend savings, and then make imaginary transactions each day.) Every night have your child calculate how much additional money she will earn through interest, using the rate of 4% per day (multiplying the evening's savings total by .04). Have your child check her answers for the entire day's transactions, including the interest earned, with a calculator. You can "donate" the money to your child's bank each night that all the calculations are made correctly.

2.4 Determine the least common multiple and the greatest common divisor of whole numbers; use them to solve problems with fractions (e.g., to find a common denominator to add two fractions or to find the reduced form for a fraction).

Algebra and Functions

1.0 Students write verbal expressions and sentences as algebraic expressions and equations; they evaluate algebraic expressions, solve simple linear equations, and graph and interpret their results:

Rainy day predictions

BOWL, RULER On a rainy day have your child place a bowl outside and measure the depth of the water after 20 minutes. Have your child use the equation: 20 minutes = x amount of water to create algebraic equations to predict how much water will accumulate in the next 5 minutes, 15 minutes, and 30 minutes. (To extend the activity just add more time units.) Have your child chart the difference between her predictions and the actual measurements using a bar graph. (If necessary, see an online version at http://www.mathleague.com/help/data /data.htm or find examples in library resources.) While your child is waiting for the time to pass between measurements, have her write, edit, and revise a poem (using correct spelling and punctuation) that captures the mood, tempo, and atmosphere of the rainy day and uses the imagery of the accumulating rain in the bowl.

1.1   Write and solve one-step linear equations in one variable.

1.2   Write and evaluate an algebraic expression for a given situation, using up to three variables.

Juicy expressions

WASHED GRAPES, LARGE SERVING PLATE, CUTTING BOARD, OR CLEAN COUNTER TOP, INDIVIDUAL NOTE CARDS MARKED WITH PLUS, MINUS, AND MULTIPLICATION SIGNS AND PARENTHESES Explain to your child that you are going to compute edible algebraic expressions. First on plain paper, write the example: $3a^2 - b$. Then write: a = 3 and b = 7. Now ask your child to translate the written expression, using grapes and the note cards on a large serving plate, cutting board, or clean countertop. (3 grapes [3 grapes x 3 grapes] – 7 grapes) Now have your child *solve the expression, if necessary reviewing the "order of operations" with library materials, schoolmath textbooks, or online at http:// www.harcourt school.com/glossary/math/glossary8.html. ([3 x 9] − 7 = 27 − 7 = 20 grapes) Repeat the activity, substituting other equations and have your child solve with grapes, eating the final answers after each round! For more information and reinforcement on algebraic equations, click on each "equations" section at http://pittsford. monroe.edu/jeffer son/calfieri/algebra/AlgebraMain.html or type the word* algebra *into any major Internet search engine.*

1.3   Apply algebraic order of operations and the commutative, associative, and distributive properties to evaluate expressions; and justify each step in the process.

1.4   Solve problems manually by using the correct order of operations or by using a scientific calculator.

Operating order

COTTON BALLS, BAND AIDS, Q-TIPS, SMALL BOX Create a visual demonstration to clarify for your child the concept of <u>order of operations</u> in an algebraic expression. Explain that you are going to write an algebraic expression that will represent the first aid items your child will then assemble into a first aid kit. Write the following equation with plenty of space between each symbol on a large piece of paper: x + 3y + z + 2x + x(2 + 6) = First Aid Kit. Now write out a key: x = cotton balls, y = Band Aids, z = Q-tips. Have your child place the corresponding number of first aid items on the paper under their respective symbols (e.g., 3 Band Aids under 3y). Your child should notice that cotton balls (x) appear in the equation three times. First, perform any operations with parentheses (i.e., 2 + 6 = 8). The equation now looks like this: 1 cotton ball + 3 Band Aids + 1 Q-tip + 2 cotton balls + 1 cotton ball x 8. Next multiply and divide, whichever comes first, from the left to the right of the equation (1 cotton ball x 8 = 8 cotton balls.) Have your child group the 2 and the 6 cotton balls together in the equation. The equation is now: 1 cotton ball + 3 Band Aids + 1 Q-tip + 2 cotton balls + 8 cotton balls. Finally, add or subtract, whichever comes first, from left to right. Have your child rearrange the cotton balls to represent this last function (11 cotton balls

+ 3 Band Aids + 1 Q-tip) and then place them in their individual groups into a first aid box. To further reinforce the concept, together review information about order of operations at http://www.math.com/school/sub ject2/lessons/S2U1L2GL.html or research the term using library resources.

2.0 Students analyze and use tables, graphs, and rules to solve problems involving rates and proportions:

2.1 Convert one unit of measurement to another (e.g., from feet to miles, from centimeters to inches).

Recipe switch-a-roo

RECIPE AND INGREDIENTS, MEASURING TOOLS, U.S. VOLUME UNIT CHART Together review the breakdown of U.S. volume units for teaspoons, tablespoons, ounces, pints, quarts, etc. using a chart from a basic recipe book or online at http://www.aaamath.com/mea69-us-vol ume.html. (If you use the website, scroll down to the "Play" section for fun interactive games that test your volume memory.) Next, find a recipe to cook together. When measuring the ingredients, have your child put his knowledge of units of measure to work. Tell him that he needs to measure the ingredients accurately, but he cannot use the unit of measure called for in the recipe. So, for example, if the recipe calls for a tablespoon of an ingredient, he must use an equivalent measure (three teaspoons) instead. Tell your child that this is an "open book test," so he can consult the measurement chart as often as necessary. Enjoy the completed recipe together!

2.2 Demonstrate an understanding that rate is a measure of one quantity per unit value of another quantity.

2.3 Solve problems involving rates, average speed, distance, and time.

3.0 Students investigate geometric patterns and describe them algebraically:

3.1 Use variables in expressions describing geometric quantities (e.g., $P = 2w + 2l$, $A = {}^{1}\!/_{2}\, bh$, $C = \pi\, d$—the formulas for the perimeter of a rectangle, the area of a triangle, and the circumference of a circle, respectively).

Quick perimeter

RULER Draw several different sized rectangles or parallelograms on a piece of paper. Have your child add up the sides for each figure to determine the perimeter (the distance around the edge of a multisided figure). Help your child write out the mathematical equation needed to calculate the perimeter of the first figure: l (length) + w (width) + l (length) + w (width) = perimeter. Look at the formula together (l + w + l + w), and ask your child if he can suggest a way to shorten it. Which numbers repeat? Both the length and width repeat twice, so you use multiplication to shorten the process: 2 x (l + w) = perimeter. Have your child plug in the numbers for length and width to see how quick this method is. For the remaining rectangles and parallelograms, time your child using the addition only method and then the method that uses multiplication to see which method is most efficient.

3.2 Express in symbolic form simple relationships arising from geometry.

Ancient geometry

No one knows how old geometry is, but the ancient Egyptians and Babylonians used it some 5,000 years ago. The Egyptians, for instance, applied geometry when re-marking land boundaries after the Nile River flooded every year (and, of course, when creating their pyramids). Have your child research ancient Egyptian agriculture using library resources or online at http://www.sd83.bc.ca/schools/hpes/highland/agriculture.html. Have your child take detailed notes while conducting this research and use this information as the basis for a large drawing depicting fertile ancient Egyptian crops growing near the Nile River. Have your child sketch land plots (drawn to scale, using inches for yards) that are regular and irregular polygons, and ask your child to

label the perimeter of each plot (the sum of a polygon's sides) and identify the types of crops grown. Ask your child to present his drawing to you and other household members, and have him explain the research upon which his drawing is based.

Measurement and Geometry

1.0 Students deepen their understanding of the measurement of plane and solid shapes and use this understanding to solve problems:

1.1   Understand the concept of a constant such as π; know the formulas for the circumference and area of a circle.

Constant π

4 DIFFERENT SIZE LIDS, STRING, MEASURING TAPE Share that the circumference of any circle is slightly more than 3 times that of its diameter. π, which is the relationship between the circumference and the diameter, remains constant (approximately 3.14) no matter how large or small the circle! Help your child prove that this is true. Ask him to create a chart with three vertical columns labeled "Circumference," "Diameter," and "Circumference Divided by Diameter." Have your child use string and a measuring tape to measure the circumference and diameter of four different-sized lids. (To find the circumference, wrap a piece of string around the outside of the lid, lay the string down in a straight line, and then use the measuring tape to see how long the string is.) Ask your child to divide the diameter into the circumference for each example and place the number, written as a decimal, in the column labeled "Circumference Divided by Diameter." What whole number appears in each answer? (3). All the answers will be close to 3.14, either slightly more or less. Have your child continue the experiment by measuring a very large circle, such as the bottom of a trash pail, and a tiny one, such as a dime, to see that π still remains constant. Your child has just proved that circumference = π × diameter.

1.2 Know common estimates of π (3.14; 22/7) and use these values to estimate and calculate the circumference and the area of circles; compare with actual measurements.

1.3 Know and use the formulas for the volume of triangular prisms and cylinders (area of base × height); compare these formulas and explain the similarity between them and the formula for the volume of a rectangular solid.

2.0 Students identify and describe the properties of two-dimensional figures:

Pie puzzle

COMPASS, PROTRACTOR, CLOCK Have your child draw two large circles of different sizes using a protractor; then cut out the circles. Next, ask your child to draw five diameter lines within both circles. Each diameter should be a different distance from any of the others so that the "slices" aren't uniform in size. Now, have your child use the protractor to find the degree of the angle for each pie segment, writing down the corresponding number on its "slice." Have your child total the measurements to make sure the sum equals 360 degrees. Cut up the two pies into segments and mix them in a pile. Using the marked degree calculations on each slice, have your child reconfigure the two circles as quickly as possible, trying to beat his time in each successive round.

2.1 Identify angles as vertical, adjacent, complementary, or supplementary and provide descriptions of these terms.

Missing-angle stomach strength

RULER, PROTRACTOR Together, review the definition of complementary angles (two angles whose sum is 90°) and supplementary angles (two angles whose sum is 180°). Definitions and visual representations also appear at http://www.mathleague.com/help/geometry/angles.htm. Then, have your child practice mental addition and subtraction. Draw an acute angle within a right angle, writing the angle's measurement (say 52°). How

fast can your child find the complementary angle? (38°) Conduct the same activity for supplementary angles, and then continue to help your child increase his speed and recognition of the two types of angles. Now, turn the game into a physical exercise. Say the degree measurement of an angle aloud. Your child will look at the protractor and then, sitting on the floor with legs stretched out ahead, use his legs to imitate the base of the protractor. Your child will now lean backward or forward to create a correct visual representation of the angle you stated. If you say 40°, your child will lean back just a bit more than halfway between upright (90°) and flat on the floor (0°). You then will call out either supplementary or complementary and your child will calculate the degree measurement of the new angle necessary to make the equation complete. (If you call out "complementary at 40°," your child will say "50°." If his calculation is correct, he gets to sit to the complementary (upright) or supplementary (prone) position to rest his abdominal muscles.

2.2   Use the properties of complementary and supplementary angles and the sum of the angles of a triangle to solve problems involving an unknown angle.

2.3   Draw quadrilaterals and triangles from given information about them (e.g., a quadrilateral having equal sides but no right angles, a right isosceles triangle).

Statistics, Data Analysis, and Probability

1.0 Students compute and analyze statistical measurements for data sets:

1.1   Compute the range, mean, median, and mode of data sets.

> ### Average m & ms
>
> *SCHOOL MATH TEXTBOOKS, m & ms (OPTIONAL HANDFUL OF MIXED NUTS), GRAPH PAPER Have your child review the terms mode, mean, and median, online at http://www.mathleague.com/help/data/ data.htm or use library materials or school math textbooks. Repeat for central tendency using library or school resources or online at http:// www.mste.uiuc.edu/hill/dstat/dstat.html (which offers fun games that will put mode, mean, and median into a real-life context. Finally, have your child graph the number of each color in a bag of m & ms (or handful of mixed nuts), and then find the mode, mean, and median for this group of data.*

1.2   Understand how additional data added to data sets may affect these computations of measures of central tendency.

1.3   Understand how the inclusion or exclusion of outliers affects measures of central tendency.

1.4   Know why a specific measure of central tendency (mean, median, mode) provides the most useful information in a given context.

2.0 Students use data samples of a population and describe the characteristics and limitations of the samples:

2.1   Compare different samples of a population with the data from the entire population and identify a situation in which it makes sense to use a sample.

2.2 Identify different ways of selecting a sample (e.g., convenience sampling, responses to a survey, random sampling) and which method makes a sample more representative for a population.

2.3 Analyze data displays and explain why the way in which the question was asked might have influenced the results obtained and why the way in which the results were displayed might have influenced the conclusions reached.

2.4 Identify data that represent sampling errors and explain why the sample (and the display) might be biased.

2.5 Identify claims based on statistical data and, in simple cases, evaluate the validity of the claims.

Nine-out-of-ten doctors recommend

 Have your child chart the time three children his age believe they should have to go to bed on a school night, as well as what time three parents believe those children should have to go to bed. Ask your child which data he would use—the answers of the parents or children—if he wanted to convince you that three people agreed with his own definition of a reasonable bedtime. Have your child examine why defending his argument with the data using the term "three people"—rather than specifying parents or children—leaves out important information. How might the two sets of respondents be biased? (Children likely will want to stay up late and parents likely will want an earlier bedtime.) If your child says "three people," he is manipulating the information to support his cause. Now, have your child be a validity detective, discussing various TV and magazine advertisements (supported by doctors, dentists, and other "authorities"). For each one, have your child identify the possible problems with the validity of the claim. If nine-out-of-ten doctors recommend a drug, for instance, how many were asked? Were the doctors given free samples? Were the doctors paid for their recommendation? Did the doctors get to test the product against another drug? Finally, have your child write, edit, and revise a letter (with correct spelling, punctuation, grammar, and well-articulated ideas) to one company, listing all his concerns regarding the claims for the product and requesting a response.

3.0 Students determine theoretical and experimental probabilities and use these to make predictions about events:

3.1 Represent all possible outcomes for compound events in an organized way (e.g., tables, grids, tree diagrams) and express the theoretical probability of each outcome.

3.2 Use data to estimate the probability of future events (e.g., batting averages or number of accidents per mile driven).

Probable outcome

DECK OF CARDS, 1 DIE, 1 COIN Help your child understand probability with the following demonstration. Show your child that a deck contains 52 cards. Ask her to think of one card in particular and try to draw it from the deck. The probability of picking her desired card is 1 in 52 or 1:52 or $\frac{1}{52}$ (the number of favorable outcomes divided by the number of possible outcomes) so it is very unlikely that she will pick her card without repeated tries. Next, show her that the die has six sides, and explain that the likelihood of rolling any one number is 1 in 6 or 1:6 or $\frac{1}{6}$. Have your child choose a number between one and six and roll the die a few times to see how often her number comes up. Then explore the probability of a coin landing on heads or tails. There are only two possible outcomes, so the probability is 1 in 2, or 1:2, or $\frac{1}{2}$

3.3 Represent probabilities as ratios, proportions, decimals between 0 and 1, and percentages between 0 and 100 and verify that the probabilities computed are reasonable; know that if P is the probability of an event, 1-P is the probability of an event not occurring.

Batter up II

Have your child review her work with ratios and batting averages for players in "Batter up I." Before the next game, have your child estimate the probability of each player's hits for the upcoming game, expressing them as ratios, proportions, and decimals. After the game, have your child compare her numbers to the actual results. Have your child continue throughout the season, practicing and honing her ratio, average, and probability skills.

3.4   Understand that the probability of either of two disjoint events occurring is the sum of the two individual probabilities and that the probability of one event following another, in independent trials, is the product of the two probabilities.

3.5   Understand the difference between independent and dependent events.

Linked events

 WWW *Explain that a <u>compound event</u> consists of two or more events, such as tossing a coin two or more times. Together, learn about how probability differs in independent versus dependent events at http://www.mathgoodies.com/lessons/vol6/independent_events.html and http://www.mathgoodies.com/lessons/vol6/dependent_events.html. Conduct the experiments and have your child try her hand at the interactive exercises. As reinforcement, help your child to remember the concept of an <u>independent event</u> by thinking of the meaning of the word independent and its use in daily context, such as growing up to become independent. Likewise, help your child associate dependent with ideas from everyday life, such as how playing outdoors is dependent on the weather. In this case, the events affect one another.*

Mathematical Reasoning

1.0 Students make decisions about how to approach problems:

1.1   Analyze problems by identifying relationships, distinguishing relevant from irrelevant information, identifying missing information, sequencing and prioritizing information, and observing patterns.

Solitary sequence

 WWW 📖 *DECK OF CARDS, RULES FOR THE CARD GAME "SOLITAIRE"* Explain to your child that <u>sequence</u> is any set of terms (numbers or algebraic expressions) arranged in a specific order. (For instance, 3, 6, 9 is a sequence as is the algebraic term ar, ar^2, ar^3, ar^4.) Teach your child how to play the card game "Solitaire," which uses numerical and algebraic (the suits) sequences as its basis. The rules can be found in reference books or online at http://www.solitairecentral.com/.

1.2   Formulate and justify mathematical conjectures based on a general description of the mathematical question or problem posed.

1.3   Determine when and how to break a problem into simpler parts.

2.0 Students use strategies, skills, and concepts in finding solutions:

2.1   Use estimation to verify the reasonableness of calculated results.

2.2   Apply strategies and results from simpler problems to more complex problems.

2.3   Estimate unknown quantities graphically and solve for them by using logical reasoning and arithmetic and algebraic techniques.

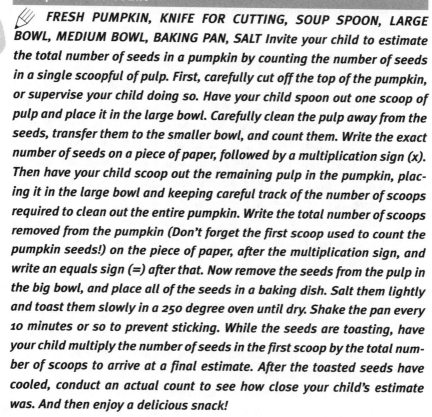

Pumpkin seed count

✍ FRESH PUMPKIN, KNIFE FOR CUTTING, SOUP SPOON, LARGE BOWL, MEDIUM BOWL, BAKING PAN, SALT Invite your child to estimate the total number of seeds in a pumpkin by counting the number of seeds in a single scoopful of pulp. First, carefully cut off the top of the pumpkin, or supervise your child doing so. Have your child spoon out one scoop of pulp and place it in the large bowl. Carefully clean the pulp away from the seeds, transfer them to the smaller bowl, and count them. Write the exact number of seeds on a piece of paper, followed by a multiplication sign (x). Then have your child scoop out the remaining pulp in the pumpkin, placing it in the large bowl and keeping careful track of the number of scoops required to clean out the entire pumpkin. Write the total number of scoops removed from the pumpkin (Don't forget the first scoop used to count the pumpkin seeds!) on the piece of paper, after the multiplication sign, and write an equals sign (=) after that. Now remove the seeds from the pulp in the big bowl, and place all of the seeds in a baking dish. Salt them lightly and toast them slowly in a 250 degree oven until dry. Shake the pan every 10 minutes or so to prevent sticking. While the seeds are toasting, have your child multiply the number of seeds in the first scoop by the total number of scoops to arrive at a final estimate. After the toasted seeds have cooled, conduct an actual count to see how close your child's estimate was. And then enjoy a delicious snack!

2.4   Use a variety of methods, such as words, numbers, symbols, charts, graphs, tables, diagrams, and models, to explain mathematical reasoning.

Mayan math

✍ WWW 📖 Together explore the symbols the ancient Mayans developed to represent numbers by researching the topic using library resources or exploring "Maya Mathematics" online at http://www.michielb.nl/maya/astro.html. Have your child use the symbols to express the individual ages of everyone in your household. Then play a game that requires score keeping, and have your child keep score using Mayan mathematic symbols. 🌐

2.5   Express the solution clearly and logically by using the appropriate mathematical notation and terms and clear language; support solutions with evidence in both verbal and symbolic work.

Cell equations

 Together, learn about cell division by using either an encyclopedia, science reference book, or online at http://www.icnet.uk/kids/cellsrus/cellsrus.html. Then, have your child create both sketches and algebraic equations (using letter variables) to tell the story of cell division. Afterward, have your child narrate—in a clear, engaging, and articulate manner—his drawing of the cell's adventure as it multiplies, using specific references to the researched material.

2.6   Indicate the relative advantages of exact and approximate solutions to problems and give answers to a specified degree of accuracy.

Exact and loose

 Together, make a list of at least five situations where precise measurements are important (for example, when taking medication, when baking bread, when constructing a building, when balancing a checkbook, when air traffic controllers give instructions to pilots) and five situations where approximate measurements are acceptable (when purchasing stretchy mittens, waking up on a weekend morning with no plans). Next, debate whether certain situations need exact or approximate time frames, such as when everyone should eat dinner, what time to arrive at school, and the reasons behind your thinking.

2.7   Make precise calculations and check the validity of the results from the context of the problem.

3.0 Students move beyond a particular problem by generalizing to other situations:

3.1   Evaluate the reasonableness of the solution in the context of the original situation.

3.2   Note the method of deriving the solution and demonstrate a conceptual understanding of the derivation by solving similar problems.

3.3   Develop generalizations of the results obtained and the strategies used and apply them in new problem situations.

GRADE SEVEN

By the end of grade seven, students are adept at manipulating numbers and equations and understand the general principles at work. Students understand and use factoring of numerators and denominators and properties of exponents. They know the Pythagorean theorem and solve problems in which they compute the length of an unknown side. Students know how to compute the surface area and volume of basic three-dimensional objects and understand how area and volume change with a change in scale. Students make conversions between different units of measurement. They know and use different representations of fractional numbers (fractions, decimals, and percents) and are proficient at changing from one to another. They increase their facility with ratio and proportion, compute percents of increase and decrease, and compute simple and compound interest. They graph linear functions and understand the idea of slope and its relation to ratio.

Number Sense

1.0 Students know the properties of, and compute with, rational numbers expressed in a variety of forms:

1.1   Read, write, and compare rational numbers in scientific notation (positive and negative powers of 10) with approximate numbers using scientific notation.

Ask your child to write the number one thousand (1 followed by 3 zeros), one million (1 followed by 6 zeros), and one billion (1 followed 9 zeros). Tired of writing zeros? Explain that <u>scientific notation</u> is an efficient way to express extremely large or small numbers. Scientific notation states a number as a product of a number from 1 to 10, and a power of 10. Thus, 1,000 would be 10 to the 3rd power or 10^3. The 3 here is the <u>exponent,</u> used in an expression to indicate that the same number is multiplied repeatedly. The exponent is written as a small number above and to the right of a symbol or quantity. An exponent of 3 tells us that the equation is 10 x 10 x 10 = 1,000 (or 10^3). Scientists developed this shorthand because some numbers are immensely large (distances between stars or planets for instance). Other numbers are tiny (such as a virus whose diameter measures 10^{-6}, or 10 to the negative 6th power. Have your child write the scientific notation for the expression of the diameter of our galaxy (the Milky Way), which is about 100,000 light years. (10^5). To get a sense of the distance of a light year itself, visit http://school.dis covery.com/schooladventures/universe/itsawesome/lightyears/index.h tml to understand why we use scientific notation when dealing with such overwhelmingly large numbers.

1.2 Add, subtract, multiply, and divide rational numbers (integers, fractions, and terminating decimals) and take positive rational numbers to whole-number powers.

"TREASURE" You and your child should create "treasure hunts" for one another in which the "clues" are an <u>algorithm</u>—a logical sequence of instructions that explains how to accomplish a task. An algorithm must explain exactly how to proceed from one step to the next and have a finite number of steps. First, each of you should hide a "treasure" (small gift, box of raisins, etc.) and then sketch individual floor plans of your home. Mark an X for the starting point (the farthest location possible away from the object) on the floor plan. Then, write out the steps on the floor plan using mathematical equations (add, subtract, multiply, and divide integers) that must be solved in order to uncover the treasure. For instance,

"Step 1: Walk forward 1.5 x 6 steps. Step 2: Turn right and walk 729 ÷ 81 steps. Step 3: Find the square root of the last result and walk backward this amount, turning left at the doorway. Step 4: Kneel down and crawl toward the cabinets 22 steps," etc.) Both you and your child should double-check your algorithms, making sure that the clues are clear and precisely describe the actions to be carried out for each step. Finally, conduct each other's hunts and find the buried treasure!

1.3 Convert fractions to decimals and percents and use these representations in estimations, computations, and applications.

1.4 Differentiate between rational and irrational numbers.

Rational/irrational math

WWW *FOOD AT DINNER Explain to your child that a <u>rational number</u> is any number that can be expressed as an integer (3, 5, 19, etc.) or ratio between two integers (–$\frac{1}{3}$, $\frac{5}{6}$, $\frac{5}{17}$ etc.). Have your child give an example of a rational number using food from her dinner plate. One chicken breast to thirty-five peas would be $\frac{1}{35}$. Seven string beans to 19 French fries would be $\frac{19}{35}$. While munching on your rational numbers, explain that <u>irrational numbers</u> cannot be written as a ratio of a whole number. Give the example of the square root of 2. The <u>square root</u> is the number that multiplied by itself produces the original number. The square root of 4 is 2. (2 x 2 = 4) The square root of 25 is 5. (5 x 5 = 25) It's simple until you try to find the square root of 2. (1 x 1 = 1, not 2.) The square root of 2 is between 1.4142135 and 1.4142136. Because it can't be written as a precise ratio or fraction of a whole number, it's called an irrational number. After dinner, further explore irrational and rational at http://www.cut-the-knot.com/do_you_know/numbers.html#rational.*

1.5 Know that every rational number is either a terminating or repeating decimal and be able to convert terminating decimals into reduced fractions.

1.6 Calculate the percentage of increases and decreases of a quantity.

1.7 Solve problems that involve discounts, markups, commissions, and profit and compute simple and compound interest.

Neither a borrower nor a lender be

Together, explore the difference between compound versus simple interest, explained at http://www.mathleague.com/ help/percent/percent.htm, or in reference books at the library. Next, ask your child to imagine that she is a bank loan officer and you are coming in to request a loan of $1,000 and that you'd like to pay it back over five years. Have your child figure out the simple interest on the loan at 6.5 percent and compound interest on the loan at 5 percent. Your child should then present the two options to you and discuss the benefits and drawbacks of each. (For instance, the compound rate is lower, but it's compounded with the principal, so in the end is it really the better deal?)

2.0 Students use exponents, powers, and roots and use exponents in working with fractions:

Power-walk race

OR SCHOOL MATH TEXTBOOKS, 16 NOTE CARDS, 2 BAGS Together begin by reviewing the definition for <u>exponent</u>—the raised number to the right of the base number that indicates how many times the base number is multiplied by itself; it is also referred to as a "power". (If necessary, review further with library materials and/or school math textbooks or click on "exponents" at http://www.mathleague.com/help /decwholeexp/decwholeexp.htm for a quick review.) Write a simple example, such as 2^3, on a note card and have your child write out and solve for 2 to the third power on the back of the card (2 x 2 x 2 = 8). Continue with more examples on separate note cards until you have written one on each of the 16 note cards, particularly using the power of ten, as described in the standard. (Help your child note that in the power of ten, the exponent indicates the number of zeros that will follow the integer 1. For instance, $10^5 = 10,0000$.) Check to make sure that all the answers on the backs of the cards are correct. Then have your child shuffle the note cards and place 8 in each bag. Move outside to an area where you can walk a long distance. Together, start from the same place and then each of you randomly pick "power cards" from your bags, looking at

the side with the number written with an exponent. Each player com-
putes the power and gets to move forward the resulting number of
steps—if after turning the card over her answer is correct. Whoever gets
the farthest from the starting point at the end of 8 cards wins! For an
extra workout, hop or do jumping jacks the correct number of steps for-
ward.

2.1 Understand negative whole-number exponents. Multiply and divide expressions involving exponents with a common base.

2.2 Add and subtract fractions by using factoring to find common denominators.

2.3 Multiply, divide, and simplify rational numbers by using exponent rules.

2.4 Use the inverse relationship between raising to a power and extracting the root of a perfect square integer; for an integer that is not square, determine without a calculator the two integers between which its square root lies and explain why.

2.5 Understand the meaning of the absolute value of a number; interpret the absolute value as the distance of the number from zero on a number line; and determine the absolute value of real numbers.

Algebra and Functions

1.0 Students express quantitative relationships by using algebraic terminology, expressions, equations, inequalities, and graphs:

1.1 Use variables and appropriate operations to write an expression, an equation, an inequality, or a system of equations or inequalities that represents a verbal description (e.g., three less than a number, half as large as area A).

Tossed salad recipe

SALAD INGREDIENTS, BOWLS FOR INDIVIDUAL SERVINGS Ask your child to be your salad chef. For this activity, you want her to create and write down her own special salad recipe as if it were an algebraic equation. Wash, dry, and slice all the ingredients first. Then place the individual bowls in a row on a counter. Have your child place a handful of lettuce in each bowl and then note this on paper as X. (X = 1 handful of lettuce) Have your child place the desired number of tomato slices in each bowl, marking this down too with a different expression. (For three slices per bowl, your child would write 3Y, for instance.) Continue on, having your child add new ingredients and marking their number and assigned algebraic symbol. Before serving, have your child write out the complete algebraic expression for the salad. It would look something like X + 3Y + 5M (mushrooms) + N (1 onion slice) + 1/2D (1/2 teaspoon of dressing) = 1 mixed salad. Have your child save her recipe to recreate at another dinner.

1.2   Use the correct order of operations to evaluate algebraic expressions.

1.3   Simplify numerical expressions by applying properties of rational numbers (e.g., identity, inverse, distributive, associative, commutative) and justify the process used.

1.4   Use algebraic terminology (e.g., variable, equation, term, coefficient, inequality, expression, constant) correctly.

1.5   Represent quantitative relationships graphically and interpret the meaning of a specific part of a graph in the situation represented by the graph.

Does one thing lead to another?

WWW Together examine local weather maps and graphs in newspapers or online. Discuss some of the different cause-and-effect relationships related to weather, including effects on crops, travel (airport delays caused by rain or snow), nature (forest fires caused by hot, dry seasons), energy use, and so on. Skim articles in the newspaper or on the Weather Channel's website (http://www.weather.com/) and ask you child to identify those that focus on weather's cause-and-effect relationships.

2.0 Students interpret and evaluate expressions involving integer powers and simple roots:

Power root

Explain that a basic concept to remember about both powers and roots of numbers is that they incorporate repeated numbers. Here are other ways to help your child remember how to use these expressions: Have your child make a muscle symbolizing "power" or strength. Which direction is your child's hand pointing in this position, up or down? (Up.) Integer powers are written with the exponent expressed as a small number up and to the right of a symbol or quantity. This <u>exponent</u> indicates that the base number is multiplied repeatedly. So integer <u>powers</u> multiply; they grow bigger, like your child's arm when making a muscle. Have your child practice writing out integer powers such as 10^4 ($10 \times 10 \times 10 \times 10 = 10^4$) 10^6, ($10 \times 10 \times 10 \times 10 \times 10 \times 10 = 10^6$). For square roots, ask your child if roots of trees grow inside or outside the earth (inside). With <u>square roots</u> your child will need to find the number that exists "inside" the given integer that multiplied by itself produces this number. Have your child find the square root of 4. Take each number within the number 4 and multiply it by itself to find the one that equals 4. (1 and 3 are wrong because $1 \times 1 = 1$ and $3 \times 3 = 6$.) Therefore, 2 is the square root of 4 ($2 \times 2 = 4$). Give your child more examples such as finding the square root of 25 (5), 36 (6), 81 (9), and so forth. Have your child rephrase, clearly and articulately, in his own words how to remember the difference between integer powers and square roots.

2.1   Interpret positive whole-number powers as repeated multiplication and negative whole-number powers as repeated division or multiplication by the multiplicative inverse. Simplify and evaluate expressions that include exponents.

2.2   Multiply and divide monomials; extend the process of taking powers and extracting roots to monomials when the latter results in a monomial with an integer exponent.

3.0 Students graph and interpret linear and some non-linear functions:

3.1 Graph functions of the form $y = nx^2$ and $y = nx^3$ and use in solving problems.

3.2 Plot the values from the volumes of three-dimensional shapes for various values of the edge lengths (e.g., cubes with varying edge lengths or a triangle prism with a fixed height and an equilateral triangle base of varying lengths).

3.3 Graph linear functions, noting that the vertical change (change in y-value) per unit of horizontal change (change in x-value) is always the same and know that the ratio ("rise over run") is called the slope of a graph.

3.4 Plot the values of quantities whose ratios are always the same (e.g., cost to the number of an item, feet to inches, circumference to diameter of a circle). Fit a line to the plot and understand that the slope of the line equals the quantities.

4.0 Students solve simple linear equations and inequalities over the rational numbers:

Popped equations

 WWW *LARGE BOWL OF UNBUTTERED POPCORN, SMALL CUP, NOTE CARDS LABELED WITH THE INDIVIDUAL SIGNS FOR =, +, −, x, AND ÷*
Begin by asking your child what clue exists within the word "equation" that provides a hint about this type of mathematical expression. The idea of "equal" is the key here. In a <u>linear equation,</u> the expression on the left side of the equal sign has the same value as the expression on the right side. Start simply. Place 3 popped corn kernels on the table. Place the + sign after them, and then put down 8 popped corn kernels and the = sign. Place the empty cup on the right side of the equal sign, explaining that this represents the unknown variable. Ask your child to solve the equation, putting the correct amount of popped corn into the cup. Together eat the correct "variable" while you create a harder popped-corn equation

(3x — 2 = 7). Remind your child that to keep both sides of the equation equal, you must do exactly the same thing to each side. Here, add 2 popped corn kernels to each side (3x — 2 + 2 = 7 + 2). Have your child simplify the expression, giving you 3x = 9. Finally have your child divide each side by 3 (i.e., $\frac{3x}{3} = \frac{9}{3}$) and then simplify for the final value of the variable (x = 3). Continue snacking on the found "variables" while your child works on increasingly difficult equations. Find further explanations and expressions to solve at http://www.aaamath.com/equ725-equation6.html.

4.1   Solve two-step linear equations and inequalities in one variable over the rational numbers, interpret the solution or solutions in the context from which they arose, and verify the reasonableness of the results.

4.2   Solve multistep problems involving rate, average speed, distance, and time or a direct variation.

Measurement and Geometry

1.0 Students choose appropriate units of measure and use ratios to convert within and between measurement systems to solve problems:

1.1   Compare weights, capacities, geometric measures, times, and temperatures within and between measurement systems (e.g., miles per hour and feet per second, cubic inches to cubic centimeters).

Paper ball toss

 TAPE MEASURE Ask your child to chart how the distance he can throw a crumpled paper ball is affected when additional paper sheets are added to the ball for each toss. First, have your child prepare the chart, dividing a piece of paper into three vertical columns, labeled on top with the terms "# of pieces of paper," "feet," and "meters." Have your child crumple up a single piece of newspaper into a ball; then, either outside or in a room with a lot of space, have him toss

the newspaper ball as far as possible. Tell your child to measure the distance from where he tossed the ball to where it landed using the tape measure. Have him fill in the first two columns on the chart. The number 1 goes under "sheets of paper" and the measured distance under "feet." Leave the third column blank for now. Have your child continue the experiment, adding another piece of paper to the ball with each turn and writing in the resulting numbers for each column. Next, together learn the basics of converting between U.S. length and metric units using library resources or online at http://www.math.com/tables/general/measures/lengths.htm checking your answers with the interactive conversion function at http://www.sciencemadesimple.net/EASYlength.html. Have your child convert the second column into metric units and place the corresponding number for each in the third column. Finally, have your child review his toss chart and draw a conclusion about the relationship between the weight of the paper and the distance he can toss it.

1.2　　Construct and read drawings and models made to scale.

Home archaeology

✎ *2 BLANKETS, 2 TAPE MEASURES, BALL OF STRING, SCISSORS, 4-5 SMALL OBJECTS, GRAPH PAPER Before asking your child to participate in this activity, set up the "dig" on the floor. First place a large blanket flat on the floor. Open both tape measures as far as possible and place them on the blanket so they cross at the center. The horizontal tape measure is the x axis and the vertical tape measure is the y axis. Now place 4–5 items from your home in the different quadrants. Cover the "dig" with another blanket, serving as the top layer of "dirt." Bring your child in and ask her to imagine that she is an archaeologist of the future, who is uncovering this "find" from an ordinary 21st century home. Like all archaeologists, your child must carefully record any finds on paper, which she will do on graph paper, before removing them to for further study. Your child should draw an x and y axis in the center of a piece of graph paper and then carefully "dig" (pull away the blanket) to see what she will uncover. Eureka, your child has found many items in this small plot! Ask your child to carefully mark the items on the graph paper as they appear in the "dig." Have your child use taut string to draw straight lines from the x and y axis to each object to help determine the correct points on which the objects sit. When transferring the information to the graph, your child should use the inch marks on the tape measure as the coordinates on the graph. Hence, if your child "discovers" a coin 5 inches to the left of the central point and 7 inches up, its coordinates on the graph would be (x, y) = (−5, 7). Have your child carefully chart all the objects before removing them. After, have your young archaeologist examine all the objects, and from the point of view of a future scientist, discuss what the materials reveal about this era of human civilization.*

1.3 Use measures expressed as rates (e.g., speed, density) and measures expressed as products (e.g., person-days) to solve problems; check the units of the solutions; and use dimensional analysis to check the reasonableness of the answer.

2.0 Students compute the perimeter, area, and volume of common geometric objects and use the results to find measures of less common objects. They know how perimeter, area, and volume are affected by changes of scale:

Brownie bake

TWO BAKING PANS (ONE SQUARE, ONE RECTANGLE WITH ONE SIDE EQUAL TO THE SIDES OF THE SQUARE PAN) BROWNIE RECIPE AND INGREDIENTS, RULER Have your child help you prepare a brownie recipe (or other bar-type of baking recipe), using the opportunity to practice measuring various volumes (ounces, cups, teaspoons, and so forth). Before baking, have your child pull out the two baking pans mentioned in the materials list. Have your child calculate the <u>perimeter</u> for each pan (2 x height + 2 x width = perimeter). Ask your child to predict the amount (volume) each pan will hold because of the differences in the length of one of the pan's sides. Have your child fill the large pan (9 X 13 inches) up with water and pour it into the smaller square pan. What happens? The extra water spills out, demonstrating why it's important to have the right

size baking pan before pouring in the batter! Have your child prove that changes in perimeter affect <u>volume</u> through math as well, plugging in the numbers from the two pans into the formula lwh = V (length x width x height = volume). Is the volume for the bigger pan larger than the smaller one? Finally, have your child pour the batter into the pan size called for in the recipe, or one with the same or slightly larger volume capacity. (If the recipe calls for a 9 x 13 x 1 inch pan, then you can use any pan that would have a volume capacity of at least 117.)

2.1 Use formulas routinely for finding the perimeter and area of basic two-dimensional figures and the surface area and volume of basic three-dimensional figures, including rectangles, parallelograms, trapezoids, squares, triangles, circles, prisms, and cylinders.

Interior designer

TAPE MEASURE, CARDBOARD, SCISSORS Ask your child to imagine that she is your newly hired interior designer. You will pretend to want to rearrange the furniture in each room at home, but first need to see a floor plan of what it will look like. Have your child/young interior designer use a tape measure to measure the dimensions of each room and then calculate the <u>area</u> for each (width x height). Your child should also note the dimensions and the perimeter for the main pieces of furniture (beds, tables, chairs), measuring the approximate amount of space each piece occupies on the floor. (If necessary, review the formula for rectangle <u>perimeter</u>, which is 2 (l +w), with your child.) Have your young designer draw a floor plan to scale on plain paper, draw each piece of furniture to scale on cardboard, and then cut the cardboard furniture shapes out and label them as "bed," "couch," etc. Have her arrange the cardboard shapes within the floor plan to devise inventive ways of reorganizing your furniture without really having to move it!

2.2 Estimate and compute the area of more complex or irregular two- and three-dimensional figures by breaking the figures down into more basic geometric objects.

2.3 Compute the length of the perimeter, the surface area of the faces, and the volume of a three-dimensional object built from rectangular solids. Understand that when the lengths of all dimensions are multiplied by a scale factor, the surface area is multiplied by the square of the scale factor and the volume is multiplied by the cube of the scale factor.

2.4   Relate the changes in measurement with a change of scale to the units used (e.g., square inches, cubic feet) and to conversions between units (1 square foot = 144 square inches or [1 ft^2] = [144 in^2], 1 cubic inch is approximately 16.38 cubic centimeters or [1 in^3] = [16.38 cm^3]).

3.0 Students know the Pythagorean theorem and deepen their understanding of plane and solid geometric shapes by constructing figures that meet given conditions and by identifying attributes of figures:

Constant right-angle triangles

LONG RULER, TAPE MEASURE The Pythagorean theorem relates to triangles that contain a right angle. Together, learn about the theorem (triangle leg A^2 + triangle leg B^2 = hypotenuse^2, or $a^2 + b^2 = c^2$) using math reference books or an encyclopedia, or online at http://www.harcourtschool.com/glossary/math/glossary8.html. Then get online interactive practice at http://www.gomath.com/algebra/pythagorean.asp. Finally, create right angles with different-length legs against your own walls. Kneel by a wall and place a ruler diagonally from a spot on the floor to a spot on the wall. The wall and floor are the legs and the ruler is the hypotenuse. Have your child use the tape measure to measure two of the variables (either both legs or one leg and the hypotenuse) and then complete the equation for the unknown quantity. Follow up by having your child research Pythagoras himself (using an Internet search engine or library materials). Afterward, ask your child to write a letter to Pythagoras, describing what it is like to learn and use his theory today, more than two thousand years later. Your child should edit and revise his letter for correct spelling, punctuation, and grammar, and clearly communicate his understanding of the theorem.

3.1 Identify and construct basic elements of geometric figures (e.g., altitudes, mid-points, diagonals, angle bisectors, and perpendicular bisectors; central angles, radii, diameters, and chords of circles) by using a compass and straightedge.

3.2 Understand and use coordinate graphs to plot simple figures, determine lengths and areas related to them, and determine their image under translations and reflections.

Flip and turn

GRAPH PAPER, TEE SHIRT, RULER Ask your child to imagine that a world-famous clothing store has just hired him to design a tee shirt for kids and that the client has a very specific request. They want one image on front that is either turned or flipped on the back of the shirt. Have your child sketch a fairly simple design with basic geometric shapes on graph paper. Have him determine the lengths and areas of the figures and write them on the sketch. Your child should use these computations to make sure that the design will actually fit on a tee shirt. Then together, discover all the options of altering the design by watching the animated versions of a translation, rotation, and reflection at http://www.harcourtschool.com/glossary/math/glossary4.html. (Scroll down the alphabetical listing of math topics on the left side of the screen and click on the definition for transformation.) Now, have your young designer make final sketches, flipping and turning (reversing) the image for the back version. Ask your child to present the design to the client (you and other household members), explaining specifically, using mathematical terms, how the image has been manipulated for an intriguing result.

3.3 Know and understand the Pythagorean theorem and its converse and use it to find the length of the missing side of a right triangle and the lengths of other line segments and, in some situations, empirically verify the Pythagorean theorem by direct measurement.

3.4 Demonstrate an understanding of conditions that indicate two geometrical figures are congruent and what congruence means about the relationships between the sides and angles of the two figures.

Congruent-detective race

PROTRACTORS, RULERS, STRING OR YARN, TIMER Explain that players will search for 10 minutes through household cabinets, closets, shelves, and so forth, seeking pairs of geometric-shaped objects that are <u>congruent</u>—have exactly the same shape and size. (e.g., soup can and canned peas, plate and Frisbee, box and book, and so forth.) Players must not only find object pairs, but prove they are congruent, measuring and noting each item's angles and side length, or height and circumference on their answer sheet. (For circumference, wrap a string around the cylinder-shaped object, unfold, and then measure its length with a ruler.) Remind contestants to think big (same-sized window frames or window panes) and small (buttons). After ten minutes, ask all players to return and share their findings and measurements. The one with the most correctly measured congruent examples wins. Play successive rounds to increase your child's and other players' ability to find congruency around the home. Finally, ask your child to consider what he has learned about the word congruent in terms of objects, and apply the concept to another context. What does the word indicate in the sentence, "The mother and father were congruent in their belief that Jose could go to the party"? (The parents agreed.) Have your child devise his own sentence with the word congruent to reinforce for comprehension.

3.5   Construct two-dimensional patterns for three-dimensional models, such as cylinders, prisms, and cones.

3.6   Identify elements of three-dimensional geometric objects (e.g., diagonals of rectangular solids) and describe how two or more objects are related in space (e.g., skew lines, the possible ways three planes might intersect).

Statistics, Data Analysis, and Probability

1.0 Students collect, organize, and represent data sets that have one or more variables and identify relationships among variables within a data set by hand and through the use of an electronic spreadsheet software program:

1.1   Know various forms of display for data sets, including a stem-and-leaf plot or box-and-whisker plot; use the forms to display a single set of data or to compare two sets of data.

m & m graph

 LARGE BAG OF M&Ms OR LARGE PILE OF MIXED NUTS Have your child review the different types of graphs either using a math reference book or online at http://www.mathleague.com/help /data/data.htm. Then, ask your child to examine a large collection of m & ms (or mixed nuts) and decide which graph to use to present data on the quantity of each color m & m (or nut variety). After your child selects one graph type, have her try a different one to represent the same information. Ask your child to compare the two completed graphs. After analyzing them, she should justify her initial graph selection or amend her choice, supporting the argument with specific reference to the activity. Finally, look at different types of graphs in the newspaper (circle, line, bar) and have your child explain why each graph version was used in each particular case.

1.2   Represent two numerical variables on a scatterplot and informally describe how the data points are distributed and any apparent relationship that exists between the two variables (e.g., between time spent on homework and grade level).

Scatterplot sports

WWW **GRAPH PAPER** *Review with your child the definition of a* <u>scatterplot</u>—*a graph made by plotting points on a coordinate plane to illustrate the relationship between two variables in a data set. Reinforce the concept with the online example and definition at http://www.harcourtschool.com/glossary/math/glossary8.html. Then, have your child use the sports pages or watch a live game to plot the relationship between two variables in the sport, such as hits per inning. After plotting for a few units (say, innings of a baseball game), have your child draw conclusions and make predictions based on the information, testing them against the eventual actual results.*

1.3 Understand the meaning of, and be able to compute, the minimum, the lower quartile, the median, the upper quartile, and the maximum of a data set.

All sorts of middles

Together, first review the definitions for the terms listed in the Standard in a math textbook or online at http://www.harcourtschool.com/glossary/math/glossary7.html. Next, have your child list the age of everyone (including pets) in your household horizontally along a piece of paper. Help your child find the median, lower quartile, and upper quartile for this set of data, returning to the website math glossary if necessary. At dinner, your child should be able to share her findings with the household, demonstrating an understanding of the math terms.

Mathematical Reasoning

1.0 Students make decisions about how to approach problems:

1.1 Analyze problems by identifying relationships, distinguishing relevant from irrelevant information, identifying missing information, sequencing and prioritizing information, and observing patterns.

PINE CONES Have your child try his hand at a special type of pattern—Fibonacci patterns. Show your child the following sequence: 1, 1, 2, 3, 5, 8, 13, and have him extend it (21, 34, 55 etc.) Share that this pattern was first described in 1202 by the Italian mathematician Leonardo Fibonacci. Together explore how these patterns are found in nature (flower petals, tree branches, mating patterns of bees, and so forth) at http://www.mcs.surrey.ac.uk/Personal/R.Knott/Fibonacci/fibnat.html. View examples of Fibonacci patterns in a pine cone by clicking on "Pine cones" on the site. Have your child use online or library resources to learn more about Leonardo Fibonacci, and have him create an illustrated biography of this medieval mathematician, with correct spelling, grammar, punctuation, and details to support his main idea.

1.2   Formulate and justify mathematical conjectures based on a general description of the mathematical question or problem posed.

1.3   Determine when and how to break a problem into simpler parts.

2.0 Students use strategies, skills, and concepts in finding solutions:

2.1   Use estimation to verify the reasonableness of calculated results.

2.2   Apply strategies and results from simpler problems to more complex problems here

2.3   Estimate unknown quantities graphically and solve for them by using logical reasoning and arithmetic and algebraic techniques.

ORANGE, STRING, RULER, KNIFE, CARDBOARD Challenge your child to find the approximate <u>circumference</u> (the distance around a circle) of an orange using just string and a ruler. (Wrap the string around the circle once, mark its length, unfold, and then measure it against the ruler.) Now help your child find the orange's circumference using the formula circumference = pi x diameter, to prove whether his

estimated string measurement is correct. (If necessary, review that the <u>*diameter*</u> *is a straight line passing through the center of the circle and meeting the circumference at each end.) Have your child find the diameter of the orange either by cutting the orange in half and measuring its diameter, or placing the cardboard flat across the top of the orange and measuring the distance from the table top to the cardboard. Then ask your child to plug the value of the diameter into the formula. Your child should now solve the formula, using 3.14 for π to test whether his string estimate is correct. As you share the orange, point out to your child that the circumference is always just a bit more than three times the size of the diameter. Together review information about circumference and test yourselves with a few online examples at http://www.ncsa.uiuc.edu/edu /RSE/RSEorange/application.html.*

2.4 Make and test conjectures by using both inductive and deductive reasoning.

2.5 Use a variety of methods, such as words, numbers, symbols, charts, graphs, tables, diagrams, and models, to explain mathematical reasoning.

How far/how long

ROAD MAP WITH DISTANCE NOTATIONS, CALCULATOR Together find your home's location on a road map. Then have your child select a destination on the map for an imaginary trip. Ask your child to figure out how long it will take to drive there. Your child should use the key on the map to figure out the distance to the location. Then, have your child determine how long the trip will take, using an average of 55/miles an hour in her calculations. Help your child check the mathematics with a calculator. Have her consider her final answer and, if the trip appears to be too long for a single car trip, have her add in time for rest stops, meals, and overnight stays. Have your child conduct this activity before you leave on your next actual car trip, so you won't have to answer the inevitable question, "How long until we get there?"

2.6 Express the solution clearly and logically by using the appropriate mathematical notation and terms and clear language; support solutions with evidence in both verbal and symbolic work.

2.7 Indicate the relative advantages of exact and approximate solutions to problems and give answers to a specified degree of accuracy.

2.8 Make precise calculations and check the validity of the results from the context of the problem.

3.0 Students determine a solution is complete and move beyond a particular problem by generalizing to other situations:

3.1 Evaluate the reasonableness of the solution in the context of the original situation.

Brush away I

TOOTHBRUSH AND TOOTHPASTE, VARIOUS TIMING DEVICES Have your child time how long it generally takes to brush his teeth. Share with your child that dentists recommend brushing teeth for a full two minutes, which can feel like a long time. To help everyone in the household keep those pearly whites shining, ask your child to devise a way to accurately and consistently time the two minutes of brushing. Have your child list various methods for timing, such as using a stopwatch himself, having someone else time the tooth brusher, using a timer, setting an alarm clock two minutes ahead, and so forth. Over the next few days, have your child try each of the methods and mark down his opinion of its benefits and drawbacks. Move on to part II.

3.2 Note the method of deriving the solution and demonstrate a conceptual understanding of the derivation by solving similar problems.

Brush away II

After completing and reviewing all the timing options in "Brush away I," have your child propose a solution to gathered household members, stating in an articulate, persuasive manner and clear voice, the process by which he solved the problem and why his recommended method should be unanimously adopted. Move on to "8 glasses every day."

3.3 Develop generalizations of the results obtained and the strategies used and apply them to new problem situations.

Have your child review his problem-solving process in "Brush away I and II." Then pose another challenge. Doctors urge everyone to drink 8 glasses of water a day. (That's water! Juice, soda, milk, tea, and coffee don't count.) What solutions can your child devise to increase everyone's water intake in the household, following similar steps as in "Brush away I and II?"

GRADES EIGHT (THROUGH TWELVE)

Introduction

The standards for grades eight through twelve are organized differently from those for kindergarten through grade seven. In this section strands are not used for organizational purposes as they are in the elementary grades because the mathematics studied in grades eight through twelve falls naturally under discipline headings: algebra, geometry, and so forth. Many schools teach this material in traditional courses; others teach it in an integrated fashion. To allow local educational agencies and teachers flexibility in teaching the material, the standards for grades eight through twelve do not mandate that a particular discipline be initiated and completed in a single grade. The core content of these subjects must be covered; students are expected to achieve the standards however these subjects are sequenced.

Standards are provided for algebra I, geometry, algebra II, trigonometry, math-ematicalanalysis, linear algebra, probability and statistics, Advanced Placement probability and statistics, and calculus. Many of the more advanced subjects are not taught in every middle school or high school. Moreover, schools and districts have different ways of combining the subject matter in these various disciplines. For example, many schools combine some trigonometry, mathematical analysis, and linear algebra to form a precalculus course. Some districts prefer offering trigonometry content with algebra II.

Table 1, "Mathematics Disciplines, by Grade Level," reflects typical grade-level groupings of these disciplines in both integrated and traditional curricula. The lightly shaded region reflects the minimum requirement for mastery by all stu-dents. The dark shaded region depicts content that is typically considered elec-tive but that should also be mastered by students who complete the other disci-plines in the lower grade levels and continue the study of mathematics.

TABLE 1

Mathematics Disciplines, by Grade Level

Grades

Discipline Eight Nine Ten Eleven Twelve

Algebra I (8, 9, 10, 11, 12)

Geometry (8, 9, 10, 11, 12)

Algebra II (8, 9, 10, 11, 12)

Probability and Statistics (8, 9, 10, 11, 12)

Trigonometry (**10, 11, 12**)

Linear Algebra (**10, 11, 12**)

Mathematical Analysis (**10, 11, 12**)

Advanced Placement Probability and Statistics (**11, 12**)

Calculus (**11, 12**)

Many other combinations of these advanced subjects into courses are possible. What is described in this section are standards for the academic content by discipline; this document does not endorse a particular choice of structure for courses or a particular method of teaching the mathematical content.

When students delve deeply into mathematics, they gain not only conceptual understanding of mathematical principles but also knowledge of, and experience with, pure reasoning. One of the most important goals of mathematics is to teach students logical reasoning. The logical reasoning inherent in the study of mathematics allows for applications to a broad range of situations in which answers to practical problems can be found with accuracy.

By grade eight, students' mathematical sensitivity should be sharpened. Students need to start perceiving logical subtleties and appreciate the need for sound mathematical arguments before making conclusions. As students progress in the study of mathematics, they learn to distinguish between inductive and deductive reasoning; understand the meaning of logical implication; test general assertions; realize that one counterexample is enough to show that a general assertion is false; understand conceptually that although a general assertion is true in a few cases, it is not true in all cases; distinguish between something being proven and a mere plausibility argument; and identify logical errors in chains of reasoning. Mathematical reasoning and conceptual understanding are not separate from content; they are intrinsic to the mathematical discipline students master at more advanced levels.

Algebra I

Symbolic reasoning and calculations with symbols are central in algebra. Through the study of algebra, a student develops an understanding of the symbolic language of mathematics and the sciences. In addition, algebraic skills and concepts are developed and used in a wide variety of problem-solving situations.

1.0 Students identify and use the arithmetic properties of subsets of integers and rational, irrational, and real numbers, including closure properties for the four basic arithmetic operations where applicable:

1.1 Students use properties of numbers to demonstrate whether assertions are true or false.

2.0 Students understand and use such operations as taking the opposite, finding the reciprocal, taking a root, and raising to a fractional power. They understand and use the rules of exponents.

3.0 Students solve equations and inequalities involving absolute values.

4.0 Students simplify expressions before solving linear equations and inequalities in one variable, such as $3(2x\text{-}5) + 4(x\text{-}2) = 12$.

5.0 Students solve multistep problems, including word problems, involving linear equations and linear inequalities in one variable and provide justification for each step.

6.0 Students graph a linear equation and compute the x- and y-intercepts (e.g., graph $2x + 6y = 4$). They are also able to sketch the region defined by linear inequality (e.g., they sketch the region defined by $2x + 6y < 4$).

7.0 Students verify that a point lies on a line, given an equation of the line. Students are able to derive linear equations by using the point-slope formula.

8.0 Students understand the concepts of parallel lines and perpendicular lines and how those slopes are related. Students are able to find the equation of a line perpendicular to a given line that passes through a given point.

9.0 Students solve a system of two linear equations in two variables algebraically and are able to interpret the answer graphically. Students are able to solve a system of two linear inequalities in two variables and to sketch the solution sets.

10.0 Students add, subtract, multiply, and divide monomials and polynomials. Students solve multistep problems, including word problems, by using these techniques.

11.0 Students apply basic factoring techniques to second- and simple third-degree polynomials. These techniques include finding a common factor for all terms in a polynomial, recognizing the difference of two squares, and recognizing perfect squares of binomials.

12.0 Students simplify fractions with polynomials in the numerator and denominator by factoring both and reducing them to the lowest terms.

13.0 Students add, subtract, multiply, and divide rational expressions and functions. Students solve both computationally and conceptually challenging problems by using these techniques.

14.0 Students solve a quadratic equation by factoring or completing the square.

15.0 Students apply algebraic techniques to solve rate problems, work problems, and percent mixture problems.

16.0 Students understand the concepts of a relation and a function, determine whether a given relation defines a function, and give pertinent information about given relations and functions.

17.0 Students determine the domain of independent variables and the range of dependent variables defined by a graph, a set of ordered pairs, or a symbolic expression.

18.0 Students determine whether a relation defined by a graph, a set of ordered pairs, or a symbolic expression is a function and justify the conclusion.

19.0 Students know the quadratic formula and are familiar with its proof by completing the square.

20.0 Students use the quadratic formula to find the roots of a second-degree polynomial and to solve quadratic equations.

21.0 Students graph quadratic functions and know that their roots are the x-intercepts.

22.0 Students use the quadratic formula or factoring techniques or both to determine whether the graph of a quadratic function will intersect the x-axis in zero, one, or two points.

23.0 Students apply quadratic equations to physical problems, such as the motion of an object under the force of gravity.

24.0 Students use and know simple aspects of a logical argument:

    24.1 Students explain the difference between inductive and deductive reasoning and identify and provide examples of each.

    24.2 Students identify the hypothesis and conclusion in logical deduction.

    24.3 Students use counterexamples to show that an assertion is false and recognize that a single counterexample is sufficient to refute an assertion.

25.0 Students use properties of the number system to judge the validity of results, to justify each step of a procedure, and to prove or disprove statements:

25.1 Students use properties of numbers to construct simple, valid arguments (direct and indirect) for, or formulate counterexamples to, claimed assertions.

25.2 Students judge the validity of an argument according to whether the properties of the real number system and the order of operations have been applied correctly at each step.

25.3 Given a specific algebraic statement involving linear, quadratic, or absolute value expressions or equations or inequalities, students determine whether the statement is true sometimes, always, or never.

Geometry

The geometry skills and concepts developed in this discipline are useful to all students. Aside from learning these skills and concepts, students will develop their ability to construct formal, logical arguments and proofs in geometric settings and problems.

1.0 Students demonstrate understanding by identifying and giving examples of undefined terms, axioms, theorems, and inductive and deductive reasoning.

2.0 Students write geometric proofs, including proofs by contradiction.

3.0 Students construct and judge the validity of a logical argument and give counterexamples to disprove a statement.

4.0 Students prove basic theorems involving congruence and similarity.

Congruent and similar menu

Begin by reviewing the definitions of <u>congruent</u>—having exactly the same size and shape (e.g., two dimes) and <u>similar figures</u>, those that have the same shape but may not have the same size (dime and a nickel). If necessary, review the "Congruent-detective race" activity. Now explain that your

child is going to design a "menu" for a new restaurant. This eating establishment will not list items according to appetizers, entrées, and dessert, but instead will organize all the food into just two categories—congruent and similar. Have your child fold a large piece of drawing paper in half, writing "congruent" on the left and "similar" on the right side. Now ask your child to list various items for the menu, thinking about different types of foods. A congruent example would be a stack of pancakes. Similar examples would include spaghetti and licorice. See how many congruent and similar food matches your child can come up with to help this new restaurant devise a wide and varied menu. Your child should make quick sketches on the menu for each paired item. Finally, have your child invent a fun but descriptive name for the dining establishment. Later, at dinner, have everyone cut their food into congruent and/or similar shapes before eating with your child making sure everyone understands which ones are congruent and which are similar.

5.0   Students prove that triangles are congruent or similar, and they are able to use the concept of corresponding parts of congruent triangles.

6.0   Students know and are able to use the triangle inequality theorem.

7.0   Students prove and use theorems involving the properties of parallel lines cut by a transversal, the properties of quadrilaterals, and the properties of circles.

8.0   Students know, derive, and solve problems involving the perimeter, circumference, area, volume, lateral area, and surface area of common geometric figures.

Geo-jigsaw puzzle race

 First, both you and your child will create abstract pieces for jigsaw puzzles. Draw lines on construction paper to create straight-edged geometric shapes—squares, triangles, and rectangles of different dimensions so that no space remains. (Your respective pieces of paper should resemble a geometric jigsaw puzzle.) Then cut out the shapes to create your puzzle pieces. Now review the formulas for finding the <u>perimeter</u> (the sum of the lengths of the sides) and <u>area</u> (Area = length × width) for these forms using an encyclopedia or math reference book, or by going online at http://pittsford.monroe.edu/jefferson/cal fieri/geometry/geoframe.html or http://www.math.com/tables/index.

261

html. With pencil and scrap paper for calculations in hand, start the game. Each player must find the perimeter and area for every piece in his or her puzzle. After doing so, the player can put the piece in its correct place to eventually reform the original rectangular puzzle composition. The player whose entire set of calculations is correct and whose puzzle is complete first wins! Play successive rounds with new pieces of cut construction paper to hone your skills.

9.0   Students compute the volumes and surface areas of prisms, pyramids, cylinders, cones, and spheres; and students commit to memory the formulas for prisms, pyramids, and cylinders.

Volume flash game

NOTE CARDS Together, review the math formulas for volume at http://www.math.com/tables/index.html or find them in a math reference book or textbook. Have your child take notes, transferring the formula for each solid onto an individual note card. (Write the name of the corresponding solid on the back of the card.) Also, have your child sketch an image of each solid on a separate card. When complete, play a game by placing all the image cards on the left and all the volume formulas face-up on the right. Time your child as she tries to match up the correct visual image with the right formula card. After making the matches, give your child numbers to plug into the formulas for the length, height, and so forth for each image. Your child gets to keep the card for every correctly calculated volume until all the cards are removed from the table. Play successive rounds to see if your child can beat her time.

10.0   Students compute areas of polygons, including rectangles, scalene triangles, equilateral triangles, rhombi, parallelograms, and trapezoids.

11.0   Students determine how changes in dimensions affect the perimeter, area, and volume of common geometric figures and solids.

Size it down

CUPS AND GLASSES OF DIFFERENT SIZES, WATER, LARGE MEASURING CUP Together, create a physical demonstration that shows how changing the dimensions of a cylinder (cup or glass) affects the volume.

Ask your child to fill the largest cup or glass to the very top with water. Next, have your child pour the water into a measuring cup and write down the measurement next to a quick sketch of the vessel on a piece of paper. Then, have your child pour this water into a smaller cup or glass (over the sink, so the excess runs down the drain). Then, have your child measure its volume by pouring this volume of liquid into the measuring cup, writing down the result next to a corresponding sketch of the cup or glass. Have your child repeat the test, using the same largest glass or cup, and the remaining different-size glasses or cups until you work through the entire group. Afterward, have your child use his scientific notes to describe and support the statement (in a clear, engaging, and articulate manner) that changing the dimensions of cylinders affects their volume.

12.0 Students find and use measures of sides and of interior and exterior angles of triangles and polygons to classify figures and solve problems.

13.0 Students prove relationships between angles in polygons by using properties of complementary, supplementary, vertical, and exterior angles.

14.0 Students prove the Pythagorean theorem.

Prove it!

RULER AND COMPASS Review the Pythagorean theorem—the square of the hypotenuse of a right triangle is equal to the sum of the squares of the other two sides. Now together, see how to prove it by clicking on "Activity 1, Proving the Pythagorean Theorem" at http://www.pbs.org/teachersource/mathline/overview.shtm. Have your child use paper, pencil, ruler, and a compass to recreate the diagrams and test the proofs as described on the site. Afterward, ask your child how proving the Pythagorean theorem affected her understanding of it—instead of just learning it by rote.

15.0 Students use the Pythagorean theorem to determine distance and find missing lengths of sides of right triangles.

16.0 Students perform basic constructions with a straightedge and compass, such as angle bisectors, perpendicular bisectors, and the line parallel to a given line through a point off the line.

17.0 Students prove theorems by using coordinate geometry, including the midpoint of a line segment, the distance formula, and various forms of equations of lines and circles.

18.0 Students know the definitions of the basic trigonometric functions defined by the angles of a right triangle. They also know and are able to use elementary relationships between them. For example, $\tan(x) = \sin(x)/\cos(x)$, $(\sin(x))^2 + (\cos(x))^2 = 1$.

19.0 Students use trigonometric functions to solve for an unknown length of a side of a right triangle, given an angle and a length of a side.

20.0 Students know and are able to use angle and side relationships in problems with special right triangles, such as 30°, 60°, and 90° triangles and 45°, 45°, and 90° triangles.

21.0 Students prove and solve problems regarding relationships among chords, secants, tangents, inscribed angles, and inscribed and circumscribed polygons of circles.

22.0 Students know the effect of rigid motions on figures in the coordinate plane and space, including rotations, translations, and reflections.

Algebra II

This discipline complements and expands the mathematical content and concepts of algebra I and geometry. Students who master algebra II will gain experience with algebraic solutions of problems in various content areas, including the solution of systems of quadratic equations, logarithmic and exponential functions, the binomial theorem, and the complex number system.

1.0   Students solve equations and inequalities involving absolute value.

2.0   Students solve systems of linear equations and inequalities (in two or three variables) by substitution, ith graphs, or with matrices.

3.0   Students are adept at operations on polynomials, including long division.

4.0   Students factor polynomials representing the difference of squares, perfect square trinomials, and the sum and difference of two cubes.

5.0   Students demonstrate knowledge of how real and complex numbers are related both arithmetically and graphically. In particular, they can plot complex numbers as points in the plane.

6.0   Students add, subtract, multiply, and divide complex numbers.

7.0   Students add, subtract, multiply, divide, reduce, and evaluate rational expressions with monomial and polynomial denominators and simplify complicated rational expressions, including those with negative exponents in the denominator.

8.0   Students solve and graph quadratic equations by factoring, completing the square, or using the quadratic formula. Students apply these techniques in solving word problems. They also solve quadratic equations in the complex number system.

9.0   Students demonstrate and explain the effect that changing a coefficient has on the graph of quadratic functions; that is, students can determine how the graph of a parabola changes as a, b, and c vary in the equation $y = a(x-b)^2 + c$.

10.0 Students graph quadratic functions and determine the maxima, minima, and zeros of the function.

11.0 Students prove simple laws of logarithms.

11.1 Students understand the inverse relationship between exponents and logarithms and use this relationship to solve problems involving logarithms and exponents.

11.2 Students judge the validity of an argument according to whether the properties of real numbers, exponents, and logarithms have been applied correctly at each step.

12.0 Students know the laws of fractional exponents, understand exponential functions, and use these functions in problems involving exponential growth and decay.

13.0 Students use the definition of logarithms to translate between logarithms in any base.

14.0 Students understand and use the properties of logarithms to simplify logarithmic numeric expressions and to identify their approximate values.

15.0 Students determine whether a specific algebraic statement involving rational expressions, radical expressions, or logarithmic or exponential functions is sometimes true, always true, or never true.

16.0 Students demonstrate and explain how the geometry of the graph of a conic section (e.g., asymptotes, foci, eccentricity) depends on the coefficients of the quadratic equation representing it.

17.0 Given a quadratic equation of the form $ax^2 + by^2 + cx + dy + e = 0$, students can use the method for completing the square to put the equation into standard form and can recognize whether the graph of the equation is a circle, ellipse, parabola, or hyperbola. Students can then graph the equation.

18.0 Students use fundamental counting principles to compute combinations and permutations.

19.0 Students use combinations and permutations to compute probabilities.

20.0 Students know the binomial theorem and use it to expand binomial expressions that are raised to positive integer powers.

21.0 Students apply the method of mathematical induction to prove general statements about the positive integers.

22.0 Students find the general term and the sums of arithmetic series and of both finite and infinite geometric series.

23.0 Students derive the summation formulas for arithmetic series and for both finite and infinite geometric series.

24.0 Students solve problems involving functional concepts, such as composition, defining the inverse function and performing arithmetic operations on functions.

25.0 Students use properties from number systems to justify steps in combining and simplifying functions.

Probability and Statistics

This discipline is an introduction to the study of probability, interpretation of data, and fundamental statistical problem solving. Mastery of this academic content will provide students with a solid foundation in probability and facility in processing statistical information.

1.0 Students know the definition of the notion of independent events and can use the rules for addition, multiplication, and complementation to solve for probabilities of particular events in finite sample spaces.

Independence

WWW *In <u>independent events</u>, the first action has no effect on the probability of subsequent ones. (For instance, getting heads or tails in a coin toss. The probability of getting the same answer on the second flip is unaffected by the previous result.) Together, learn about and try more activities for independent events at http://www.mathgoodies.com/lessons/vol6/independent_events.html. Try independent event games with friends, such as selecting the right card from a deck, rolling die, flipping coins, and the like.*

2.0   Students know the definition of *conditional probability* and use it to solve for probabilities in finite sample spaces.

3.0   Students demonstrate an understanding of the notion of *discrete random* variables by using them to solve for the probabilities of outcomes, such as the probability of the occurrence of five heads in 14 coin tosses.

4.0   Students are familiar with the standard distributions (normal, binomial, and exponential) and can use them to solve for events in problems in which the distribution belongs to those families.

5.0   Students determine the mean and the standard deviation of a normally distributed random variable.

6.0   Students know the definitions of the *mean*, *median*, and *mode* of a distribution of data and can compute each in particular situations.

7.0   Students compute the variance and the standard deviation of a distribution of data.

8.0   Students organize and describe distributions of data by using a number of different methods, including frequency tables, histograms, standard line and bar graphs, stem-and-leaf displays, scatterplots, and box-and-whisker plots.

Plot away

 GRAPH PAPER Help hone your child's graphing skills. Together, read definitions for the terms listed in the Standard in reference books or at http://www.harcourtschool.com/glossary/math/glossary8.html. Have your child transfer the data from any of the other activities into one of these other graph formats. Then, have your child compare this graph to his original representation of the data. How do the two formats differ? How are they similar? Which one would be most useful if you were seeking answers to specific types of questions?

CALIFORNIA

History-Social Sciences

Grades 6-8
(adopted October 1998, copyright 2000)

Historical and Social Sciences Analysis Skills

The intellectual skills noted below are to be learned through, and applied to, the content standards for grades six through eight. They are to be assessed *only in conjunction with* the content standards in grades six through eight.

In addition to the standards for grades six through eight, students demonstrate the following intellectual reasoning, reflection, and research skills:

Chronological and Spatial Thinking

1. Students explain how major events are related to one another in time.

2. Students construct various time lines of key events, people, and periods of the historical era they are studying.

3. Students use a variety of maps and documents to identify physical and cultural features of neighborhoods, cities, states, and countries and to explain the historical migration of people, expansion and disintegration of empires, and the growth of economic systems.

Research, Evidence, and Point of View

1. Students frame questions that can be answered by historical study and research.

2. Students distinguish fact from opinion in historical narratives and stories.

3. Students distinguish relevant from irrelevant information, essential from incidental information, and verifiable from unverifiable information in historical narratives and stories.

4. Students assess the credibility of primary and secondary sources and draw sound conclusions from them.

5. Students detect the different historical points of view on historical events and determine the context in which the historical statements were made (the questions asked, sources used, author's perspectives).

Historical Interpretation

1. Students explain the central issues and problems from the past, placing people and events in a matrix of time and place.

2. Students understand and distinguish cause, effect, sequence, and correlation in historical events, including the long- and short-term causal relations.

3. Students explain the sources of historical continuity and how the combination of ideas and events explains the emergence of new patterns.

4. Students recognize the role of chance, oversight, and error in history.

5. Students recognize that interpretations of history are subject to change as new information is uncovered.

6. Students interpret basic indicators of economic performance and conduct cost-benefit analyses of economic and political issues.

GRADE SIX

World History and Geography: Ancient Civilizations

Students in grade six expand their understanding of history by studying the people and events that ushered in the dawn of the major Western and non-Western ancient civilizations. Geography is of special significance in the development of the human story. Continued emphasis is placed on the everyday lives, problems, and accomplishments of people, their role in developing social, economic, and political structures, as well as in establishing and spreading ideas that helped transform the world forever. Students develop higher levels of critical thinking by considering why civilizations developed where and when they did, why they became dominant, and why they declined. Students analyze the interactions among the various cultures, emphasizing their enduring contributions and the link, despite time, between the contemporary and ancient worlds.

6.1 Students describe what is known through archaeological studies of the early physical and cultural development of humankind from the Paleolithic era to the agricultural revolution.

Virtual archeology

WWW *Together, take a virtual tour of the cave of Lascaux, one of the most important Paleolithic archeological sites in existence, with more than 1,500 paintings on the walls at http://www.culture.fr/culture/arc nat/lascaux/fr/. First click on "Discover" to explore the find itself and view the images. Then click on "Learn" for fascinating archeological information and techniques. Have your child take notes while visiting the site to discuss what information the archeological site reveals about early human civilization. What do the images indicate about eating and hunting habits? (People hunted bison.) What do the art, and also its location (in a cave), reveal about uses of natural resources? (People would have used fire to illuminate the dark cave when painting. Also, the pigment for the artwork came from plants and animals.) Finally, have your child imagine being an archeologist in the distant future who uncovers your home. Walking around the house, discuss what observations the archeologist could make about contemporary culture—particularly in terms of food, clothing, and work.*

1. Describe the hunter-gatherer societies, including the development of tools and the use of fire.

Flint stone prehistoric survival manual

WWW *Ask your child to travel back in time to the hunter-gatherer societies that lived about 2 1/2 million years ago. Have your child imagine learning to survive by using only natural materials from the environment, and then write a "survival manual" with tips appropriate to the time period. First, help your child create a chart that will serve as an outline for the manual. Tell your child to list "food," "clothing," and "shelter" in separate columns on a sheet of paper and then under each heading write ideas and methods for supplying each the way the hunter-gatherers would have done (e.g., animals and plants for food, animal skins for clothing, wood for shel-*

ter). *Explain that one of the most important implements for survival was sharpened stones. Have your child list how stone tools would help in each of the three categories. For instance, spearheads for hunting would go under food or clothing, axe heads to cut trees under shelter. Next, have your child read more about the Stone Age (lasting until about 8000 B.C.E.), typing the term into a major Internet search engine or using library resources. Your child should search for more information pertaining to the three survival areas. Finally, ask your child to use the research and chart as the basis for an illustrated survival manual that, with correct spelling, punctuation, and grammar, explains how to exist in prehistoric times.*

2. Identify the locations of human communities that populated the major regions of the world and describe how humans adapted to a variety of environments.

3. Discuss the climatic changes and human modifications of the physical environment that gave rise to the domestication of plants and animals and new sources of clothing and shelter.

6.2 Students analyze the geographic, political, economic, religious, and social structures of the early civilizations of Mesopotamia, Egypt, and Kush.

1. Locate and describe the major river systems and discuss the physical settings that supported permanent settlement and early civilizations.

Egyptian cartography

PRINTER Have your child be the cartographer in the ancient world using the online information at http://www.seaworld.org/ Egypt/secrets.html. Then, after studying the map, have your child draw conclusions about how the geography of the area allowed for permanent settlement and the development of civilizations.

2. Trace the development of agricultural techniques that permitted the production of economic surplus and the emergence of cities as centers of culture and power.

California Content Standards with Home Learning Activities

3. Understand the relationship between religion and the social and political order in Mesopotamia and Egypt.

Ancient travel brochure

LONG BLANK PAPER OR A FEW SHEETS TAPED TOGETHER TO CREATE A SCROLL, EXAMPLES OF TRAVEL BROCHURES Ask your child to imagine running a travel agency in ancient times. He needs to put together a new brochure (in the form of an ancient scroll) that will lure potential travelers to Egypt's splendors. You might first examine contemporary travel brochures from local agencies to see what type of information they provide—a region's climate, society, cultural attractions, and the like. Then tour "Ancient Egypt" online at http://library.thinkquest.org/3011/egyptg.htm and http://www.virtual-egypt.com/, or use library reference books to learn about its religion, government, and culture. Have your child use the information as the basis for his travel brochure scroll. Help your child plan the brochure, deciding what text (with correct spelling, punctuation, and grammar) and illustrations will "unfold" as readers unroll the scroll. When complete, have your child share the scroll brochure with someone to see if he or she would have been inspired to visit the ancient land.

4. Know the significance of Hammurabi's Code.

5. Discuss the main features of Egyptian art and architecture.

Egyptian view

Together, find illustrations of figures in Egyptian tomb paintings and carvings in art or travel books, or by typing "Egyptian art" into a major Internet search engine. Share with your child that ancient artists revealed a lot about Egypt through their work. Hunt for the ways artists indicated the most important figure in a scene (typically the largest figure), how they distinguished men from women (males were painted with darker skin because they were out in the sun, whereas women had lighter skin color, indicating their place was indoors). Then, find illustrations of Egyptian architecture (temples, pyramids, sphinxes). Discuss what their size (immense) and material (durable stone) indicate about the rulers who built them. Ask your child to write a travel log (with correct spelling, punctuation, and grammar), imagining that she was the first person to come upon these ancient sites. Looking carefully at the illustrations, what feeling might your child experience before these grand structures? What impression did the rulers wish to make on their people and enemies alike? Finally, have your child draw a picture of your own household in an ancient Egyptian manner, using the same conventions of size, color, shape, and so forth to tell others about your own "dynasty."

6. Describe the role of Egyptian trade in the eastern Mediterranean and Nile valley.

Water access

WWW *Have your child find the Mediterranean Sea, Red Sea, and Nile River on the "Map of Ancient Egypt" at http://www.virtual-egypt.com/newhtml/maps/index.html, or in reference books from the library. Have your child imagine being a trader in ancient Egypt, and identify from which areas potential customers will come. With which countries and cultures would your child be able to conduct business because of Egypt's location and access through its waterways? How would Egypt's location and role in the area's trade impact other civilizations, and vice versa? Have your child use the map to explain why this powerful civilization was a major force in the ancient world.*

7. Understand the significance of Queen Hatshepsut and Ramses the Great.

Egyptian greats

WWW *Together, learn all about the "Queen Hatshepsut" at http://www.bediz.com/hatshep/index.html and "Ramses the Great" at http://home.earthlink.net/~nfrtry/pages/articles/ramses.html, or by researching the two rulers in reference books. Have your child create a celebratory epic poem—a long, narrative poem that describes the life and accomplishments of either Queen Hatshepsut or Ramses the Great. Help your child edit and revise his poem for correct spelling, punctuation, grammar, and use of evocative images and language. Afterward, using the knowledge he has gained, have your child draw a portrait that conveys the personality of the chosen ruler.*

8. Identify the location of the Kush civilization and describe its political, commercial, and cultural relations with Egypt.

9. Trace the evolution of language and its written forms.

6.3 Students analyze the geographic, political, economic, religious, and social structures of the Ancient Hebrews.

1. Describe the origins and significance of Judaism as the first monotheistic religion based on the concept of one God who sets down moral laws for humanity.

Monotheistic mobile

 WWW 📖 *NOTE CARDS, STRING, TAPE, SCISSORS, WIRE HANGER Explain to your child that in ancient times virtually all religions worshipped numerous gods—those of war, love, fertility, protection, and so forth. Judaism, one of the oldest major religions, was the first to teach the belief in one God who prescribes moral laws for people. Help your child visualize Judaism's significance as a monotheistic religion out of which both Christianity and Islam developed. These religions accept the Jewish belief in a single deity and the moral teachings of the Hebrew Bible. Have your child write the word* Monotheism *on a note card and tape it to the center of a wire hanger. Then, have your child write* Judaism, Islam, *and* Christianity *on separate cards and attach short strings to each card. Together, use reference materials or the Internet to research information about all three major monotheistic religions. Have your child add notes to the appropriate card as you gather your research. Hang the* Judaism *card in the middle of the* Monotheism *card, and hang the* Christianity *and* Islam *cards on either side of the* Judaism *card to create a monotheistic mobile.*

2. Identify the sources of the ethical teachings and central beliefs of Judaism (the Hebrew Bible, the Commentaries): belief in God, observance of law, practice of the concepts of righteousness and justice, and importance of study; and describe how the ideas of the Hebrew traditions are reflected in the moral and ethical traditions of Western civilization.

3. Explain the significance of Abraham, Moses, Naomi, Ruth, David, and Yohanan ben Zaccai in the development of the Jewish religion.

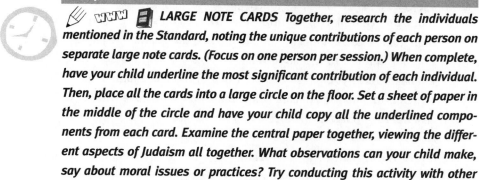

Many contributors

LARGE NOTE CARDS Together, research the individuals mentioned in the Standard, noting the unique contributions of each person on separate large note cards. (Focus on one person per session.) When complete, have your child underline the most significant contribution of each individual. Then, place all the cards into a large circle on the floor. Set a sheet of paper in the middle of the circle and have your child copy all the underlined components from each card. Examine the central paper together, viewing the different aspects of Judaism all together. What observations can your child make, say about moral issues or practices? Try conducting this activity with other major religions to compare and contrast results.

4. Discuss the locations of the settlements and movements of Hebrew peoples, including the Exodus and their movement to and from Egypt, and outline the significance of the Exodus to the Jewish and other people.

5. Discuss how Judaism survived and developed despite the continuing dispersion of much of the Jewish population from Jerusalem and the rest of Israel after the destruction of the second Temple in A.D. 70.

6.4 Students analyze the geographic, political, economic, religious, and social structures of the early civilizations of Ancient Greece.

1. Discuss the connections between geography and the development of city-states in the region of the Aegean Sea, including patterns of trade and commerce among Greek city-states and within the wider Mediterranean region.

Greek poli

Together, explore ancient Greek poli—or city-states (independent states consisting of a city and territories depending upon them). Have your child identify how the city-states came to be and how they functioned using reference books or the information at http://www.mrdowling.com/701greece.html (or by typing the term into any major Internet search engine). Afterward, look at a map of ancient Greece (one can be found online at http://phd.evansville.edu/ tools/greece.htm) to identify how the region's geography of rugged mountains and separate small islands helped isolate one city-state from another and led to the importance of forming leagues against common enemies. Have your child research two of the most famous poli: *Athens and Sparta, and then decide which* poli *she would have wanted to live in. Ask her to support her choice using her research.*

2. Trace the transition from tyranny and oligarchy to early democratic forms of government and back to dictatorship in ancient Greece, including the significance of the invention of the idea of citizenship (e.g., from *Pericles' Funeral Oration*).

3. State the key differences between Athenian, or direct, democracy and representative democracy.

4. Explain the significance of Greek mythology to the everyday life of people in the region and how Greek literature continues to permeate our literature and language today, drawing from Greek mythology and epics, such as Homer's *Iliad* and *Odyssey*, and from *Aesop's Fables*.

Book of myths

 Discover the origins of Greek mythology in library reference books or online at http://www.mrdowling.com/701-mytholo gy.html. To learn more about the Greek Olympian gods, search the wealth of information at http://ancienthistory.about.com/homework/ancien thistory/cs/mytholympians/index.htm. Next, have your child write a story about an exploit of one of the ancient Greek gods, using an engaging, adventurous tone. Then, help your child edit and revise the story for correct punctuation, spelling, and grammar, and have him add illustrations, creating a book to which he can add chapters as he explores the mythology of other cultures.

5. Outline the founding, expansion, and political organization of the Persian Empire.

6. Compare and contrast life in Athens and Sparta, with emphasis on their roles in the Persian and Peloponnesian Wars.

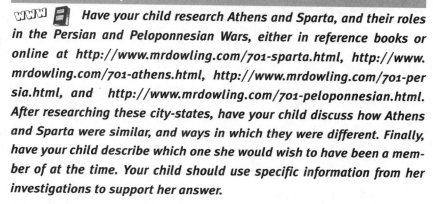

Whose side are you on?

WWW *Have your child research Athens and Sparta, and their roles in the Persian and Peloponnesian Wars, either in reference books or online at http://www.mrdowling.com/701-sparta.html, http://www.mrdowling.com/701-athens.html, http://www.mrdowling.com/701-persia.html, and http://www.mrdowling.com/701-peloponnesian.html. After researching these city-states, have your child discuss how Athens and Sparta were similar, and ways in which they were different. Finally, have your child describe which one she would wish to have been a member of at the time. Your child should use specific information from her investigations to support her answer.*

7. Trace the rise of Alexander the Great and the spread of Greek culture eastward and into Egypt.

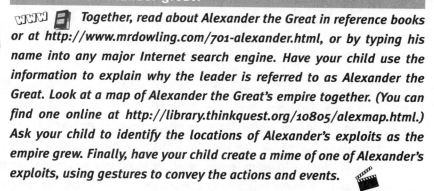

What made Alexander great?

WWW *Together, read about Alexander the Great in reference books or at http://www.mrdowling.com/701-alexander.html, or by typing his name into any major Internet search engine. Have your child use the information to explain why the leader is referred to as Alexander the Great. Look at a map of Alexander the Great's empire together. (You can find one online at http://library.thinkquest.org/10805/alexmap.html.) Ask your child to identify the locations of Alexander's exploits as the empire grew. Finally, have your child create a mime of one of Alexander's exploits, using gestures to convey the actions and events.*

8. Describe the enduring contributions of important Greek figures in the arts and sciences (e.g., Hypatia, Socrates, Plato, Aristotle, Euclid, Thucydides).

California Content Standards with Home Learning Activities

6.5 Students analyze the geographic, political, economic, religious, and social structures of the early civilizations of India.

1. Locate and describe the major river system and discuss the physical setting that supported the rise of this civilization.

2. Discuss the significance of the Aryan invasions.

3. Explain the major beliefs and practices of Brahmanism in India and how they evolved into early Hinduism.

Brahmanism evolves

WWW Together, read about Brahmanism and Hinduism in library resources or online. (Type the words into any major Internet search engine.) Have your child create two columns on a piece of paper, labeling one column "Brahmanism" and the other "Hinduism." Have your child write out the major beliefs and practices of Brahmanism in the appropriate column. Then, have your child show how these beliefs and practices evolved by writing the comparable Hindu beliefs and practices in the "Hinduism" column.

4. Outline the social structure of the caste system.

5. Know the life and moral teachings of Buddha and how Buddhism spread in India, Ceylon, and Central Asia.

Buddha image

WWW Together, read about Buddhism in reference materials or online. (Type "Buddhism" into an Internet search engine.) Then, look at images of Buddha online (at http://www.prs.k12.nj.us/~ewood /World_History/buddha/index.html) or in library materials. Have your child write a poem, using evocative words (correctly spelled and used) to describe Buddha's personality. What makes him appear calm, peaceful, and serene?

6. Describe the growth of the Maurya empire and the political and moral achievements of the emperor Asoka.

7. Discuss important aesthetic and intellectual traditions (e.g., Sanskrit literature, including the *Bhagavad Gita*; medicine; metallurgy; and mathematics, including Hindu-Arabic numerals and the zero).

6.6 Students analyze the geographic, political, economic, religious, and social structures of the early civilizations of China.

1. Locate and describe the origins of Chinese civilization in the Huang-He Valley during the Shang Dynasty.

Dear diary

Together, investigate life during the Shang dynasty (1700–1027 B.C.E.), and its impact on government, daily living, social levels, industry, geography, and culture, online at http://www.penncharter.com/Student/china/index.html and http://www-chaos.umd.edu/history/ancient1.html, and by researching the period in reference books. Have your child take detailed notes during your investigations, and then use them to write a diary entry about what a "typical" day might have been like from the points of view of each person in your household if you all had lived in China at the time. In addition to correct spelling, punctuation, and grammar, your child's writing should reflect an integration and understanding of the information you explored about life in ancient China.

2. Explain the geographic features of China that made governance and the spread of ideas and goods difficult and served to isolate the country from the rest of the world.

3. Know about the life of Confucius and the fundamental teachings of Confucianism and Taoism.

Confucian approach

Together, read about Confucianism in library reference books or online using an Internet search engine. Then, have your child write down the five main virtues of Confucius (kindness, uprightness, decorum, wisdom, and faithfulness). Confucians believed that virtue was

simply the right and proper way of doing things. Ask your child to help you go on a Five Virtue Hunt, during the day, looking for and writing down examples relating to kindness, uprightness, decorum, wisdom, and faithfulness. Have your child discuss what the world might be like if everyone became aware of and attended to these virtues.

4. Identify the political and cultural problems prevalent in the time of Confucius and how he sought to solve them.

5. List the policies and achievements of the emperor Shi Huangdi in unifying northern China under the Qin Dynasty.

6. Detail the political contributions of the Han Dynasty to the development of the imperial bureaucratic state and the expansion of the empire.

7. Cite the significance of the trans-Eurasian "silk roads" in the period of the Han Dynasty and Roman Empire and their locations.

8. Describe the diffusion of Buddhism northward to China during the Han Dynasty.

6.7 Students analyze the geographic, political, economic, religious, and social structures during the development of Rome.

Roman view

 WWW 📺 📕 *Together, use library reference books, or pay a virtual visit to the "Roman Forum" between 100 B.C. and 100 A.D. for an overview of daily life, history, religion, anecdotes, and stories at http://library.thinkquest.org /11402/. Then together, test your knowledge with the fun interactive quiz at http://library.thinkquest.org/11402/homequiz.html. Next, rent and view the 1966 movie version of the highly entertaining, lighthearted Stephen Sondheim musical,* A Funny Thing Happened on the Way to the Forum. *Help your child identify ways Sondheim created humor using ancient Roman history, comparing and contrasting the musical to the historical information you gathered online or at the library.*

1. Identify the location and describe the rise of the Roman Republic, including the importance of such mythical and historical figures as Aeneas, Romulus and Remus, Cincinnatus, Julius Caesar, and Cicero.

Roman icons

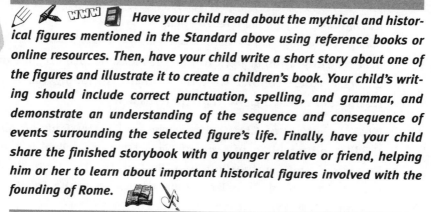 *Have your child read about the mythical and historical figures mentioned in the Standard above using reference books or online resources. Then, have your child write a short story about one of the figures and illustrate it to create a children's book. Your child's writing should include correct punctuation, spelling, and grammar, and demonstrate an understanding of the sequence and consequence of events surrounding the selected figure's life. Finally, have your child share the finished storybook with a younger relative or friend, helping him or her to learn about important historical figures involved with the founding of Rome.*

2. Describe the government of the Roman Republic and its significance (e.g., written constitution and tripartite government, checks and balances, civic duty).

3. Identify the location of and the political and geographic reasons for the growth of Roman territories and expansion of the empire, including how the empire fostered economic growth through the use of currency and trade routes.

4. Discuss the influence of Julius Caesar and Augustus in Rome's transition from republic to empire.

Hail Caesar!

 Ask your child to imagine that a famous man from history has come to him for help writing a resume, which he needs for a job application. The man is Julius Caesar, who changed Greco-Roman history, and whose conquests are summed up in the phrase "Veni, vedi, veci," or "I came, I saw, I conquered!" To help him, your child must learn about Julius Caesar and what made him such a famous historical figure using library materials or information online at http://www.incwell. com/Biographies/Caesar.html or http://ireland.iol.ie/~coolmine/typ/

romans/romans6.html. Your child should write a resume (checked for correct spelling, punctuation, and grammar) that describes in reverse chronological order the "jobs" Caesar held throughout his life, along with his major adventures and experiences. Follow up by renting the 1953 MGM movie, Julius Caesar, and compare the fictional movie to the historical information your child researched.

5. Trace the migration of Jews around the Mediterranean region and the effects of their conflict with the Romans, including the Romans' restrictions on their right to live in Jerusalem.

6. Note the origins of Christianity in the Jewish Messianic prophecies, the life and teachings of Jesus of Nazareth as described in the New Testament, and the contribution of St. Paul the Apostle to the definition and spread of Christian beliefs (e.g., belief in the Trinity, resurrection, salvation).

7. Describe the circumstances that led to the spread of Christianity in Europe and other Roman territories.

8. Discuss the legacies of Roman art and architecture, technology and science, literature, language, and law.

Ancient Roman hunt

Together, examine various images of ancient Roman art and architecture in art books or online at http://harpy.uccs.edu /roman/html/roman.html and also at http://wings.buffalo.edu/AandL/ Maecenas/general_contents.html#Greece. Have your child make special note of the use of columns, arches, and amphitheaters, and then search for traces of these in the civic and public buildings near you. Can your child find columns on the front of banks, libraries, or civic buildings? How about memorial arches, and amphitheaters (which today take the form of arenas and stadiums)? How about wall murals? They appeared on palace walls in ancient Rome. And what about sculptures of prominent figures in the community, as there once were of Roman emperors, gods, goddesses, and common people? Have your child write, revise, illustrate, and distribute a walking tour brochure of the "Roman" influenced art and architecture in your neighborhood. The text

should demonstrate correct grammar, spelling, and punctuation and help visitors understand the Roman "connection" to the art and architecture they are seeing.

World History and Geography: Medieval and Early Modern Times

Students in grade seven study the social, cultural, and technological changes that occurred in Europe, Africa, and Asia in the years A.D. 500–1789. After reviewing the ancient world and the ways in which archaeologists and historians uncover the past, students study the history and geography of great civilizations that were developing concurrently throughout the world during medieval and early modern times. They examine the growing economic interaction among civilizations as well as the exchange of ideas, beliefs, technologies, and commodities. They learn about the resulting growth of Enlightenment philosophy and the new examination of the concepts of reason and authority, the natural rights of human beings and the divine right of kings, experimentalism in science, and the dogma of belief. Finally, students assess the political forces let loose by the Enlightenment, particularly the rise of democratic ideas, and they learn about the continuing influence of these ideas in the world today.

7.1 Students analyze the causes and effects of the vast expansion and ultimate disintegration of the Roman Empire.

Hollywood Rome

Together, watch the 1964 movie, The Fall of the Roman Empire, *starring Sophia Loren, Stephen Boyd, and Alec Guinness. As you move through the related standards, have your child describe which aspects of*

California Content Standards with Home Learning Activities

the film adhered to history and which were modified for entertainment. Have your child build an argument about why commercial films should or should not be viewed as historical records. (Your child should consider the film's primary intent—to entertain viewers and gain audiences—versus the historian's main goal of documenting what actually occurred.)

1. Study the early strengths and lasting contributions of Rome (e.g., significance of Roman citizenship; rights under Roman law; Roman art, architecture, engineering, and philosophy; preservation and transmission of Christianity) and its ultimate internal weaknesses (e.g., rise of autonomous military powers within the empire, undermining of citizenship by the growth of corruption and slavery, lack of education, and distribution of news).

Be the historian

Together, read the outlined version of factors leading to the fall of the Roman Empire at http://www.republic.k12.mo.us/high school/teachers/tstephen/romemp-7.htm. Have your child investigate the social, political, and economic causes further, using the Internet or library materials. Ask your child to "be the historian," deciding from her investigations which two or three conditions were the most important factors in the empire's decline. Have your child present her conclusions to a conference of other historians (household members and friends), supporting her case with specific information presented in a clear, articulate, and persuasive manner.

2. Discuss the geographic borders of the empire at its height and the factors that threatened its territorial cohesion.

3. Describe the establishment by Constantine of the new capital in Constantinople and the development of the Byzantine Empire, with an emphasis on the consequences of the development of two distinct European civilizations, Eastern Orthodox and Roman Catholic, and their two distinct views on church-state relations.

7.2 Students analyze the geographic, political, econo-mic, religious, and social structures of the civi-lizations of Islam in the Middle Ages.

1. Identify the physical features and describe the climate of the Arabian peninsula, its relationship to surrounding bodies of land and water, and nomadic and sedentary ways of life.

2. Trace the origins of Islam and the life and teachings of Muhammad, including Islamic teachings on the connection with Judaism and Christianity.

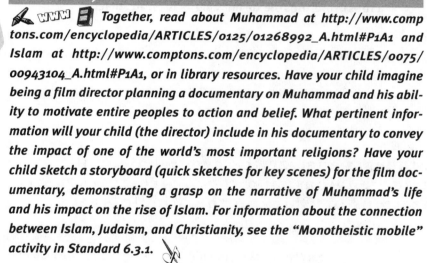

Documentary view

Together, read about Muhammad at http://www.comp tons.com/encyclopedia/ARTICLES/0125/01268992_A.html#P1A1 and Islam at http://www.comptons.com/encyclopedia/ARTICLES/0075/ 00943104_A.html#P1A1, or in library resources. Have your child imagine being a film director planning a documentary on Muhammad and his abil-ity to motivate entire peoples to action and belief. What pertinent infor-mation will your child (the director) include in his documentary to convey the impact of one of the world's most important religions? Have your child sketch a storyboard (quick sketches for key scenes) for the film doc-umentary, demonstrating a grasp on the narrative of Muhammad's life and his impact on the rise of Islam. For information about the connection between Islam, Judaism, and Christianity, see the "Monotheistic mobile" activity in Standard 6.3.1.

3. Explain the significance of the Qur'an and the Sunnah as the prima-ry sources of Islamic beliefs, practice, and law, and their influence in Muslims' daily life.

Islamic basics

Together, explore the basic beliefs of Islam with library resources or online at http://www.ifgstl.org/html/basics/beliefsnf.htm. After reading the related pages, have your child describe in her own words the five pillars of Islamic belief and their importance: Shahada (the oath), Salat (prayers), Siyam (fasting), Zakat (alms), and Hajj (pilgrimage). Are there other religions with which your child is familiar that include any of the same ideas, such as prayer or times of fasting? How do these Islamic pillars influence the daily life of a Muslim?

4. Discuss the expansion of Muslim rule through military conquests and treaties, emphasizing the cultural blending within Muslim civilization and the spread and acceptance of Islam and the Arabic language.

5. Describe the growth of cities and the establishment of trade routes among Asia, Africa, and Europe, the products and inventions that traveled along these routes (e.g., spices, textiles, paper, steel, new crops), and the role of merchants in Arab society.

6. Understand the intellectual exchanges among Muslim scholars of Eurasia and Africa and the contributions Muslim scholars made to later civilizations in the areas of science, geography, mathematics, philosophy, medicine, art, and literature.

7.3 Students analyze the geographic, political, economic, religious, and social structures of the civilizations of China in the Middle Ages.

Mapped dynasties

WWW *Together, click on the different dynasties on the map of China to see their geographic regions at http://emuseum.mankato.msus.edu/ prehistory/china/map/map.html. Have your child use this site as a point of reference when learning about different periods in China's history related to this Standard.*

1. Describe the reunification of China under the Tang Dynasty and reasons for the spread of Buddhism in Tang China, Korea, and Japan.

2. Describe agricultural, technological, and commercial developments during the Tang and Sung periods.

Tang versus Sung hunt

 Have your child compare and contrast the Tang dynasty online at http://emuseum.mankato.msus.edu/prehistory/china/classical_imperial_c hina/tang.html) to the Northern and Southern Sung dynasties at http://emuseum.mankato.msus.edu/prehistory/china/classical_imperial_china/song. html, or using reference books from the library. Ask your child to identify the most significant changes between the two dynasties, supporting his answers with the researched information. Have your child discuss how one of the reproduced images from each period that appears on the Web pages represents an aspect of the dynasty. For example, the horse sculpture from the Tang dynasty relates to the information about the importance of the army, which had some 700,000 horses on record.

3. Analyze the influences of Confucianism and changes in Confucian thought during the Sung and Mongol periods.

4. Understand the importance of both overland trade and maritime expeditions between China and other civilizations in the Mongol Ascendancy and Ming Dynasty.

5. Trace the historic influence of such discoveries as tea, the manufacture of paper, wood-block printing, the compass, and gunpowder.

7.4 Students analyze the geographic, political, economic, religious, and social structures of the sub-Saharan civilizations of Ghana and Mali in Medieval Africa.

1. Study the Niger River and the relationship of vegetation zones of forest, savannah, and desert to trade in gold, salt, food, and slaves; and the growth of the Ghana and Mali empires.

Sub-Saharan medieval Africa

 Begin this Standard with an overview of the importance of "Trade in Medieval Africa" at http://webusers.xula.edu/jrotondo/Kingdoms/Themes/Trade01.html

2. Analyze the importance of family, labor specialization, and regional commerce in the development of states and cities in West Africa.

3. Describe the role of the trans-Saharan caravan trade in the changing religious and cultural characteristics of West Africa and the influence of Islamic beliefs, ethics, and law.

4. Trace the growth of the Arabic language in government, trade, and Islamic scholarship in West Africa.

5. Describe the importance of written and oral traditions in the transmission of African history and culture.

Griot

 WWW *Together, explore the importance of oral history in African cultures using reference books or online at http://www.mrdowling.com/ 609ancafr.html. Learn about the important role griots play in traditional African life at http://artsedge.kennedy-center.org/aoi/events/theater/ griot.html. As historians, praise-singers, and musical entertainers, griots are key to passing on cultural history from one generation to the next. Have your child investigate the evidence of griots in contemporary African society as described on the website. How have their roles changed and what has remained the same? (For instance, the transformation of griot singing to modern, electric music.) Finally, have your child identify who plays the role of the griot in your household—memorizing your family's genealogy and history and relaying it through stories of the "old days." Encourage your child to ask elder relatives to relate family stories so that one day she will be able to also pass on familial history.*

7.5 Students analyze the geographic, political, economic, religious, and social structures of the civilizations of Medieval Japan.

1. Describe the significance of Japan's proximity to China and Korea and the intellectual, linguistic, religious, and philosophical influence of those countries on Japan.

2. Discuss the reign of Prince Shotoku of Japan and the characteristics of Japanese society and family life during his reign.

3. Describe the values, social customs, and traditions prescribed by the lord-vassal system consisting of *shogun*, *daimyo*, and *samurai* and the lasting influence of the warrior code in the twentieth century.

4. Trace the development of distinctive forms of Japanese Buddhism.

Japanese Buddhism tree

Together, read about the three different forms of Japanese Buddhism in medieval Japan: Amida Buddhism, Zen, Nichiren. (Information can be found online at http://www.wsu.edu/~dee/FEU JAPAN/CONTENTS.HTM or in reference books at your library.) Have your child take notes about the similarities and differences between each form. Then help your child sketch a Japanese Buddhism "tree" on paper, delineating the different forms. The tree should be labeled Japanese Buddhism, *with a branch and related information for each form.*

5. Study the ninth and tenth centuries' golden age of literature, art, and drama and its lasting effects on culture today, including Murasaki Shikibu's *Tale of Genji*.

6. Analyze the rise of a military society in the late twelfth century and the role of the samurai in that society.

7.6 Students analyze the geographic, political, economic, religious, and social structures of the civilizations of Medieval Europe.

1. Study the geography of the Europe and the Eurasian land mass, including its location, topography, waterways, vegetation, and climate and their relationship to ways of life in Medieval Europe.

2. Describe the spread of Christianity north of the Alps and the roles played by the early church and by monasteries in its diffusion after the fall of the western half of the Roman Empire.

3. Understand the development of feudalism, its role in the medieval European economy, the way in which it was influenced by physical geography (the role of the manor and the growth of towns), and how feudal relationships provided the foundation of political order.

Feudal basics

WWW *Together, explore the basics of feudalism online at http://www.learner.org/exhibits/middleages/feudal.html, or using reference books from your library, and learn about each person's role in a feudal society. Have your child select the status she would have liked to have had during medieval European times, explaining the choice with information from her research. Have your child consider both the privileges and responsibilities for each person within a feudal society.*

4. Demonstrate an understanding of the conflict and cooperation between the Papacy and European monarchs (e.g., Charlemagne, Gregory VII, Emperor Henry IV).

5. Know the significance of developments in medieval English legal and constitutional practices and their importance in the rise of modern democratic thought and representative institutions (e.g., Magna Carta, parliament, development of habeas corpus, an independent judiciary in England).

6. Discuss the causes and course of the religious Crusades and their effects on the Christian, Muslim, and Jewish populations in Europe, with emphasis on the increasing contact by Europeans with cultures of the Eastern Mediterranean world.

We want you!

WWW *Ask your child to imagine that he is living during the time that the Crusades raged through the medieval world. Together, explore background information either using reference books or online at http://www.mrdowling.com/606islam.html and http://www.mrdowl ing.com/606-latercrusades.html. Discuss with your child the effects of these religious wars on the populations mentioned in the standard. Then, ask your child if he would join up, and ask him to support his answer with*

information from the research. What compelling reasons would your child find to stay or go? Afterward, have your child write and illustrate a "We Want You!" poster for the Crusades, trying to round up soldiers to venture forth into the Holy Land. The poster should reflect a careful consideration of how words and images can be combined for persuasive effect, as well correct grammar, spelling, and punctuation.

7. Map the spread of the bubonic plague from Central Asia to China, the Middle East, and Europe and describe its impact on global population.

8. Understand the importance of the Catholic church as a political, intellectual, and aesthetic institution (e.g., founding of universities, political and spiritual roles of the clergy, creation of monastic and mendicant religious orders, preservation of the Latin language and religious texts, St. Thomas Aquinas's synthesis of classical philosophy with Christian theology, and the concept of "natural law").

9. Know the history of the decline of Muslim rule in the Iberian Peninsula that culminated in the Reconquista and the rise of Spanish and Portuguese kingdoms.

7.7 Students compare and contrast the geographic, political, economic, religious, and social structures of the Meso-American and Andean civilizations.

1. Study the locations, landforms, and climates of Mexico, Central America, and South America and their effects on Mayan, Aztec, and Incan economies, trade, and development of urban societies.

Early Meso-America

WWW *For an overview of the region, start off with the interactive map identifying major archaeological sites at http://www.ancientmexico .com/map/map.html. (Click on the names to see more details.) Then together, explore the art, culture, and history of the ancient Mayans at http://www.penncharter.com/Student/maya/index.html, the Incas at*

*http://www.carmensandiego.com/products/time/incasco9/inca.html,
and the Aztecs at http://www.uwgb.edu/galta/mrr/aztecs/origins.htm.
Also, use any major Internet search engine for additional sites, or use
reference books from the library. Have your child use the research as the
basis for this Standard.*

2.   Study the roles of people in each society, including class structures,
     family life, warfare, religious beliefs and practices, and slavery.

3.   Explain how and where each empire arose and how the Aztec and
     Incan empires were defeated by the Spanish.

4.   Describe the artistic and oral traditions and architecture in the three
     civilizations.

5.   Describe the Meso-American achievements in astronomy and mathe-
     matics, including the development of the calendar and the Meso-
     American knowledge of seasonal changes to the civilizations' agri-
     cultural systems.

7.8 Students analyze the origins, accomplishments, and geographic diffusion of the Renaissance.

Rebirth

WWW *Together, step back in time to the Renaissance at
http://www.twingroves.district96.k12.il.us/Renaissance/GeneralFiles/
Introduction.html and also at http://www.learner.org/exhibits/renais
sance/middleages.html. Both sites provide helpful information for
exploring the Standards in this section.*

1.   Describe the way in which the revival of classical learning and the
     arts fostered a new interest in humanism (i.e., a balance between
     intellect and religious faith).

2.   Explain the importance of Florence in the early stages of the
     Renaissance and the growth of independent trading cities (e.g.,
     Venice), with emphasis on the cities' importance in the spread of
     Renaissance ideas.

3. Understand the effects of the reopening of the ancient "Silk Road" between Europe and China, including Marco Polo's travels and the location of his routes.

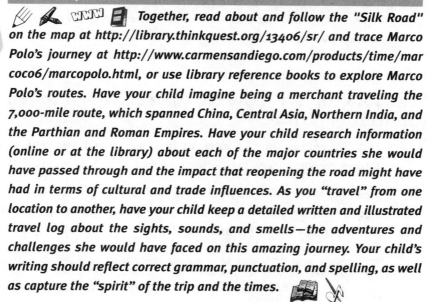

Silk road journal

Together, read about and follow the "Silk Road" on the map at http://library.thinkquest.org/13406/sr/ and trace Marco Polo's journey at http://www.carmensandiego.com/products/time/mar coco6/marcopolo.html, or use library reference books to explore Marco Polo's routes. Have your child imagine being a merchant traveling the 7,000-mile route, which spanned China, Central Asia, Northern India, and the Parthian and Roman Empires. Have your child research information (online or at the library) about each of the major countries she would have passed through and the impact that reopening the road might have had in terms of cultural and trade influences. As you "travel" from one location to another, have your child keep a detailed written and illustrated travel log about the sights, sounds, and smells—the adventures and challenges she would have faced on this amazing journey. Your child's writing should reflect correct grammar, punctuation, and spelling, as well as capture the "spirit" of the trip and the times.

4. Describe the growth and effects of new ways of disseminating information (e.g., the ability to manufacture paper, translation of the Bible into the vernacular, printing).

5. Detail advances made in literature, the arts, science, mathematics, cartography, engineering, and the understanding of human anatomy and astronomy (e.g., by Dante Alighieri, Leonardo da Vinci, Michelangelo di Buonarroti Simoni, Johann Gutenberg, William Shakespeare).

Renaissance man

Explain the term _Renaissance man_—someone who excels in a variety of areas in the arts and sciences. Then have your child research the individuals in the Standard either online or using reference books. After completing the research, have your child select one of the Renaissance men and make a case for why the individual was the quin-

tessential Renaissance man, using information from the research. Afterward, have your child identify a contemporary "Renaissance person"—someone he knows personally or a well-known individual. How do the fields in which this person is accomplished compare to those in which the Renaissance men from the Standard excelled? Is he or she outstanding in science and the arts, or multiple aspects of other areas?

7.9 Students analyze the historical developments of the Reformation.

1. List the causes for the internal turmoil in and weakening of the Catholic church (e.g., tax policies, selling of indulgences).

2. Describe the theological, political, and economic ideas of the major figures during the Reformation (e.g., Desiderius Erasmus, Martin Luther, John Calvin, William Tyndale).

Theological debate

Help your child research information about the individuals mentioned in this section (figures of the Reformation) and in 7.9.5 (leaders of the Counter-Reformation). Have your child write a short script, imagining individuals from both sides trying to persuade people of their particular beliefs. Your child's script should contain correct spelling, grammar, and punctuation, and reflect an understanding of the major differences between the Reformation and Counter-Reformation beliefs. After careful revision, you and your child should rehearse and then perform the script for household members and friends, using clear and articulate voices and appropriate gestures. Afterward, ask the audience to select which way they would have been swayed if they had lived in Western Europe during the time.

3. Explain Protestants' new practices of church self-government and the influence of those practices on the development of democratic practices and ideas of federalism.

4. Identify and locate the European regions that remained Catholic and those that became Protestant and explain how the division affected the distribution of religions in the New World.

5. Analyze how the Counter-Reformation revitalized the Catholic church and the forces that fostered the movement (e.g., St. Ignatius of Loyola and the Jesuits, the Council of Trent).

6. Understand the institution and impact of missionaries on Christianity and the diffusion of Christianity from Europe to other parts of the world in the medieval and early modern periods; locate missions on a world map.

7. Describe the Golden Age of cooperation between Jews and Muslims in medieval Spain that promoted creativity in art, literature, and science, including how that cooperation was terminated by the religious persecution of individuals and groups (e.g., the Spanish Inquisition and the expulsion of Jews and Muslims from Spain in 1492).

7.10 Students analyze the historical developments of the Scientific Revolution and its lasting effect on religious, political, and cultural institutions.

1. Discuss the roots of the Scientific Revolution (e.g., Greek rationalism; Jewish, Christian, and Muslim science; Renaissance humanism; new knowledge from global exploration).

2. Understand the significance of the new scientific theories (e.g., those of Copernicus, Galileo, Kepler, Newton) and the significance of new inventions (e.g., the telescope, microscope, thermometer, barometer).

Early science fair

 Have your child imagine being a news reporter covering a science fair during the 15th and 16th centuries. Ask your child to discover what items would be on display by researching the Scientific Revolution and its leaders, using library reference books or online at http:// www.pbs.org/faithandreason/gengloss/revolution-body.html, and specifics

on Copernicus and Galileo at http://mars.wnec.edu/~grempel/cours es/wc2/lectures/scientificrev.html. Have your child file a news report on the Scientific Invention Fair, using correct grammar, spelling, and punctuation, that reflects an understanding of the items displayed (such as those mentioned in the Standard), who invented them, and their ramifications.

3. Understand the scientific method advanced by Bacon and Descartes, the influence of new scientific rationalism on the growth of democratic ideas, and the coexistence of science with traditional religious beliefs.

7.11 Students analyze political and economic change in the sixteenth, seventeenth, and eighteenth centuries (the Age of Exploration, the Enlightenment, and the Age of Reason).

Enlightening who?

Together, read about the Enlightenment either online or using library materials, and then have your child imagine being a church leader at the time. What ideas about the Enlightenment might this religious leader find threatening to the power of the Church, which had gone virtually unquestioned in Europe until this time?

1. Know the great voyages of discovery, the locations of the routes, and the influence of cartography in the development of a new European worldview.

2. Discuss the exchanges of plants, animals, technology, culture, and ideas among Europe, Africa, Asia, and the Americas in the fifteenth and sixteenth centuries and the major economic and social effects on each continent.

3. Examine the origins of modern capitalism; the influence of mercantilism and cottage industry; the elements and importance of a market economy in seventeenth-century Europe; the changing interna-

298

20-Minute Learning Connection

tional trading and marketing patterns, including their locations on a world map; and the influence of explorers and map makers.

4. Explain how the main ideas of the Enlightenment can be traced back to such movements as the Renaissance, the Reformation, and the Scientific Revolution and to the Greeks, Romans, and Christianity.

5. Describe how democratic thought and institutions were influenced by Enlightenment thinkers (e.g., John Locke, Charles-Louis Montesquieu, American founders).

6. Discuss how the principles in the Magna Carta were embodied in such documents as the English Bill of Rights and the American Declaration of Independence.

Text hunt

Together, using reference books or the Internet, read the original texts of the Magna Carta at http://www.law.ou.edu /hist/magna.html and look for similarities to the Declaration of Independence at http://www.law.ou.edu/hist/decind.html—for instance, the separation of church and state. Have your child translate the texts into her own words to help identify the similarities, being sure to capture the main point of what is being stated and also using correct spelling, grammar, and punctuation. Then, have your child make a list of commonalities between the Magna Carta and the Declaration of Independence she discovered during the writing process. Finally, together reread both original documents to see if there are more similarities you can identify and have your child revise her translations accordingly.

United States History and Geography: Growth and Conflict

Students in grade eight study the ideas, issues, and events from the framing of the Constitution up to World War I, with an emphasis on America's role in the war. After reviewing the development of America's democratic institutions founded on the Judeo-Christian heritage and English parliamentary traditions, particularly the shaping of the Constitution, students trace the development of American politics, society, culture, and economy and relate them to the emergence of major regional differences. They learn about the challenges facing the new nation, with an emphasis on the causes, course, and consequences of the Civil War. They make connections between the rise of industrialization and contemporary social and economic conditions.

8.1 Students understand the major events preceding the founding of the nation and relate their significance to the development of American constitutional democracy.

1. Describe the relationship between the moral and political ideas of the Great Awakening and the development of revolutionary fervor.

Patriotic flick

 Rent the movie of the highly entertaining musical *1776*, based on the proceedings of the Second Continental Congress as it decided whether to declare independence from Britain. Actual statements made in the debates of the Continental Congress, or in the letters and other writings of the historical figures portrayed in the film, have been inserted into the dialogue. (Helpful background information and ideas for how to use the movie as a learning tool appear at http://www.teachwith movies.org/guides/1776.html.) Afterward, have your child identify the moral and political ideas depicted in the movie that contributed to the revolutionary fervor.

2. Analyze the philosophy of government expressed in the Declaration of Independence, with an emphasis on government as a means of securing individual rights (e.g., key phrases such as "all men are created equal, that they are endowed by their Creator with certain unalienable Rights").

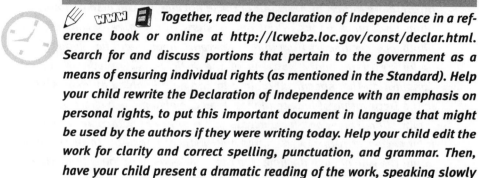

Declaration theater

Together, read the Declaration of Independence in a reference book or online at http://lcweb2.loc.gov/const/declar.html. Search for and discuss portions that pertain to the government as a means of ensuring individual rights (as mentioned in the Standard). Help your child rewrite the Declaration of Independence with an emphasis on personal rights, to put this important document in language that might be used by the authors if they were writing today. Help your child edit the work for clarity and correct spelling, punctuation, and grammar. Then, have your child present a dramatic reading of the work, speaking slowly and clearly, and stressing important words.

3. Analyze how the American Revolution affected other nations, especially France.

4. Describe the nation's blend of civic republicanism, classical liberal principles, and English parliamentary traditions.

8.2 Students analyze the political principles underlying the U.S. Constitution and compare the enumerated and implied powers of the federal government.

1. Discuss the significance of the Magna Carta, the English Bill of Rights, and the Mayflower Compact.

2. Analyze the Articles of Confederation and the Constitution and the success of each in implementing the ideals of the Declaration of Independence.

Together, review the activity, "Declaration theater," related to Standard 8.1.2 Then, take another look at the Declaration of Independence at http://lcweb2.loc.gov/const/declar.html. Read the Articles of Confederation at http://www.ukans.edu/carrie/docs/texts /confeder.htm and the Constitution of the United States of America at http://constitution.by.net/. (All of these documents can also be found in library reference books.) Print out versions of all three documents (or photocopy documents from library reference books) and have your child underline or highlight portions of the Articles of Confederation and Constitution that specifically relate to and help implement ideas stated in the Declaration of Independence. (You can also make a chart with this information if you don't have access to a printer or photocopier.) Use the information at http://www.cr.nps.gov/history/inde5.htm to learn more about the role of each document in the development of the United States government. As an extension, continue with the activity, "Bill of Rights," at 8.1.6. Afterward, have your child explain the ways this document also supports and relates to the Declaration of Independence.

3. Evaluate the major debates that occurred during the development of the Constitution and their ultimate resolutions in such areas as shared power among institutions, divided state-federal power, slavery, the rights of individuals and states (later addressed by the addition of the Bill of Rights), and the status of American Indian nations under the commerce clause.

4. Describe the political philosophy underpinning the Constitution as specified in the *Federalist Papers* (authored by James Madison, Alexander Hamilton, and John Jay) and the role of such leaders as Madison, George Washington, Roger Sherman, Gouverneur Morris, and James Wilson in the writing and ratification of the Constitution.

5. Understand the significance of Jefferson's Statute for Religious Freedom as a forerunner of the First Amendment and the origins, purpose, and differing views of the founding fathers on the issue of the separation of church and state.

6. Enumerate the powers of government set forth in the Constitution and the fundamental liberties ensured by the Bill of Rights.

7. Describe the principles of federalism, dual sovereignty, separation of powers, checks and balances, the nature and purpose of majority rule, and the ways in which the American idea of constitutionalism preserves individual rights.

8.3 Students understand the foundation of the American political system and the ways in which citizens participate in it.

1. Analyze the principles and concepts codified in state constitutions between 1777 and 1781 that created the context out of which American political institutions and ideas developed.

2. Explain how the ordinances of 1785 and 1787 privatized national resources and transferred federally owned lands into private holdings, townships, and states.

3. Enumerate the advantages of a common market among the states as foreseen in and protected by the Constitution's clauses on interstate commerce, common coinage, and full-faith and credit.

4. Understand how the conflicts between Thomas Jefferson and Alexander Hamilton resulted in the emergence of two political parties (e.g., view of foreign policy, Alien and Sedition Acts, economic policy, National Bank, funding and assumption of the revolutionary debt).

Let's party!

Ask your child to name the two major political parties in America today. Explore their origin together by learning about the Federalists led by Alexander Hamilton, and Thomas Jefferson's Democratic-Republicans, using reference books or online at http://gi.grolier.com/presidents/nbk/side/polparty.html. (Scroll down to the section "Parties Begin in the US.") Have your child use the information to identify the differences of opinion and approach to government between the two parties and then design campaign posters, using evocative images and text (with correct spelling, punctuation, and grammar) for both parties, defining and supporting the political stance of each. Finally, have your child imagine trying to throw one fundraiser (at which the posters will be hung) for the Federalists and one for the Democratic-Republicans. Given what your child has learned about the interests of each party, what types of people should your child invite to each party's bash to raise campaign funds? Which party would a big business owner likely support and why? How about a working class citizen?

5. Know the significance of domestic resistance movements and ways in which the central government responded to such movements (e.g., Shays' Rebellion, the Whiskey Rebellion).

6. Describe the basic law-making process and how the Constitution provides numerous opportunities for citizens to participate in the political process and to monitor and influence government (e.g., function of elections, political parties, interest groups).

Citizen influence

WWW **PHONE BOOK** *Ask your child how citizens in the United States can influence government. Most likely, your child will mention elections. But together, explore other ways to make a difference, such as through political parties and special interest groups. Have your child select a topic of concern, such as saving an endangered species, preserving the rain forest, or protecting animal rights. Use the Internet, phone book, and library services to find out more about groups involved with the cause and how they take political action. Ask your child to devise a plan so he can make an impact, even before reaching voting age (e.g., through canvassing, educating those of voting age about the topic, and making contributions to organizations working for the cause). Encourage your child to become involved and to involve other young people in political action.*

7. Understand the functions and responsibilities of a free press.

Free press

 Have your child read a newspaper editorial or magazine article relating a strong opinion about a topic. Discuss that Article I of the Bill of Rights makes it possible to print anything, as long as it's based on truth. Review the wording and meaning of the Article: "Congress shall make no law . . . prohibiting . . . or abridging . . . the freedom of speech, or of the press . . ." declared in force on December 15, 1791. Then learn about the case that brought about its establishment. John Peter Zenger, printer of the New York Weekly Journal, *was arrested in 1734 for publishing articles attacking the policies of colonial governor William Cosby. After reading about the case, have your child write a defense (in persuasive, grammatically correct English) for Zenger, defending his right to freedom of speech and press. Discuss with your child the idea that the press also has responsibilities to the public and define these responsibilities. Over the next week have your child read the newspaper to keep an eye out for articles that further demonstrate the freedom of the press and the ways in which the press fulfills its responsibilities to the public.*

8.4 Students analyze the aspirations and ideals of the people of the new nation.

1. Describe the country's physical landscapes, political divisions, and territorial expansion during the terms of the first four presidents.

2. Explain the policy significance of famous speeches (e.g., Washington's Farewell Address, Jefferson's 1801 Inaugural Address, John Q. Adams's Fourth of July 1821 Address).

3. Analyze the rise of capitalism and the economic problems and conflicts that accompanied it (e.g., Jackson's opposition to the National Bank; early decisions of the U.S. Supreme Court that reinforced the sanctity of contracts and a capitalist economic system of law).

4. Discuss daily life, including traditions in art, music, and literature, of early national America (e.g., through writings by Washington Irving, James Fenimore Cooper).

8.5 Students analyze U.S. foreign policy in the early Republic.

1. Understand the political and economic causes and consequences of the War of 1812 and know the major battles, leaders, and events that led to a final peace.

"Star Spangled Banner"

First sing the "Star Spangled Banner" together (and hear a 19th century version online at http://americanhistory2.si.edu /ssb/6_thestory/6b_osay/fs6b.html). Ask your child to speculate what the words actually mean and what event it describes. Have your child research the causes and consequences of the War of 1812, either online or using reference books. Then, read about the experience of Francis Scott Key, the writer of the "Star Spangled Banner," in the War of 1812 at http://www.icss.com/usflag/francis.scott.key.html and learn how that experience inspired what became the national anthem of the United States. Afterward, ask your child to create a series of related illustrations for the anthem, presenting it as an illustrated songbook to a younger relative or friend.

2. Know the changing boundaries of the United States and describe the relationships the country had with its neighbors (current Mexico and Canada) and Europe, including the influence of the Monroe Doctrine, and how those relationships influenced westward expansion and the Mexican-American War.

3. Outline the major treaties with American Indian nations during the administrations of the first four presidents and the varying outcomes of those treaties.

Native people's rights and treaties

Together, read about the specific rights of Native Americans as both citizens of the United States and of tribal nations, which are sovereign political entities. Discuss the history of these rights, particularly those relating to treaties. (You can find information online at http://www.wld.com/conbus/weal/wnativa1.htm.) Next, read the text of an actual example, the 1795 Treaty of Greenville (http://www. yale.edu/lawweb/avalon/greenvil.htm), or another example that you find in a reference book. Have your child identify in what ways the native peoples, and also the United States government, benefited from the treaty. What was its overall goal? Use the Internet and newspapers to investigate ways in which native peoples today negotiate with the United States government. Have your child identify if/how the issues are similar or different from those of the early peace treaties.

8.6 Students analyze the divergent paths of the American people from 1800 to the mid-1800s and the challenges they faced, with emphasis on the Northeast.

1. Discuss the influence of industrialization and technological developments on the region, including human modification of the landscape and how physical geography shaped human actions (e.g., growth of cities, deforestation, farming, mineral extraction).

2. Outline the physical obstacles to and the economic and political factors involved in building a network of roads, canals, and railroads (e.g., Henry Clay's American System).

3. List the reasons for the wave of immigration from Northern Europe to the United States and describe the growth in the number, size, and spatial arrangements of cities (e.g., Irish immigrants and the Great Irish Famine).

No potatoes

www *Together, view the illustrations and political cartoons of the times related to the infamous Irish potato famine at "Views of the Famine," hosted by Vassar College at http://vassun.vassar.edu/~sttay lor/FAMINE/. Examine how these visual images convey different aspects of the crisis. Discuss how the famine was a major cause of emigration to the United States, as people came in the hopes of finding a better life. Where did they settle? What impact did this have on the culture of the* *existing cities? Were they welcomed, or did they struggle? Afterward, explore the countries of origin for the majority of new immigrants arriving in your own area (using library resources or the United States Census Bureau website at http://www.census.gov/ for information). Together, try to discern the reasons people leave their homes to come to this country today, interviewing immigrants in your community or speaking with community organizations. How do the reasons (political, economic, etc.) compare to those of the Irish in the 19th century?*

4. Study the lives of black Americans who gained freedom in the North and founded schools and churches to advance their rights and communities.

5. Trace the development of the American education system from its earliest roots, including the roles of religious and private schools and Horace Mann's campaign for free public education and its assimilating role in American culture.

6. Examine the women's suffrage movement (e.g., biographies, writings, and speeches of Elizabeth Cady Stanton, Margaret Fuller, Lucretia Mott, Susan B. Anthony).

Women vote!

Together, study the long road to women's suffrage with the timeline from 1776 to 1923 at http://memory.loc.gov/ammem /vfwhtml/vfwtl.html or using library reference books. Have your child research any one event on the timeline, using related biographies, writings, speeches, and so forth. After thoroughly understanding the event, help your child write a short script involving a conversation between a woman involved in the actual event and a contemporary female. Have him discuss the changes in American women's lives. Your child's script should reflect an understanding of the accomplishments of women over the generations and the imagined reaction of the historical female character to such events. Help your child revise his script to clarify points and to correct spelling, grammar, and punctuation. Finally, rehearse and perform the dramatic piece together for the household, using appropriate gestures and clear, articulate speaking voices.

7.	Identify common themes in American art as well as transcendental-ism and individualism (e.g., writings about and by Ralph Waldo Emerson, Henry David Thoreau, Herman Melville, Louisa May Alcott, Nathaniel Hawthorne, Henry Wadsworth Longfellow).

8.7 Students analyze the divergent paths of the American people in the South from 1800 to the mid-1800s and the challenges they faced.

1.	Describe the development of the agrarian economy in the South, identify the locations of the cotton-producing states, and discuss the significance of cotton and the cotton gin.

2.	Trace the origins and development of slavery; its effects on black Americans and on the region's political, social, religious, economic, and cultural development; and identify the strategies that were tried to both overturn and preserve it (e.g., through the writings and his-torical documents on Nat Turner, Denmark Vesey).

Roots

 Together, watch the video version of the 1977 miniseries Roots, *based on Alex Haley's Pulitzer Prize-winning book that details the life of a generation of a black family, starting in Gambia, Africa in 1750 and con-tinuing through emancipation and reconstruction after the Civil War in the United States. Helpful background information and viewing/thinking questions are available online at http://www.teachwithmovies.org/ guides/roots-vol-i.html (with additional questions for each of the six episodes on related pages). Also, visit the online History Channel exhibi-tion with interviews and a wealth of information on African American his-tory at http://www.historychannel.com/exhibits/blackhist/.*

3.	Examine the characteristics of white Southern society and how the physical environment influenced events and conditions prior to the Civil War.

4.	Compare the lives of and opportunities for free blacks in the North with those of free blacks in the South.

8.8 Students analyze the divergent paths of the American people in the West from 1800 to the mid-1800s and the challenges they faced.

1.   Discuss the election of Andrew Jackson as president in 1828, the importance of Jacksonian democracy, and his actions as president (e.g., the spoils system, veto of the National Bank, policy of Indian removal, opposition to the Supreme Court).

2.   Describe the purpose, challenges, and economic incentives associated with westward expansion, including the concept of Manifest Destiny (e.g., the Lewis and Clark expedition, accounts of the removal of Indians, the Cherokees' "Trail of Tears," settlement of the Great Plains) and the territorial acquisitions that spanned numerous decades.

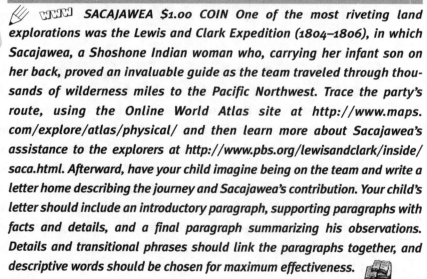

Cross-country trek

SACAJAWEA $1.00 COIN One of the most riveting land explorations was the Lewis and Clark Expedition (1804–1806), in which Sacajawea, a Shoshone Indian woman who, carrying her infant son on her back, proved an invaluable guide as the team traveled through thousands of wilderness miles to the Pacific Northwest. Trace the party's route, using the Online World Atlas site at http://www.maps.com/explore/atlas/physical/ and then learn more about Sacajawea's assistance to the explorers at http://www.pbs.org/lewisandclark/inside/saca.html. Afterward, have your child imagine being on the team and write a letter home describing the journey and Sacajawea's contribution. Your child's letter should include an introductory paragraph, supporting paragraphs with facts and details, and a final paragraph summarizing his observations. Details and transitional phrases should link the paragraphs together, and descriptive words should be chosen for maximum effectiveness.

3.   Describe the role of pioneer women and the new status that western women achieved (e.g., Laura Ingalls Wilder, Annie Bidwell; slave women gaining freedom in the West; Wyoming granting suffrage to women in 1869).

Have your child read about pioneer women online or use reference materials, focusing on Laura Ingalls Wilder and Annie Bidwell as mentioned in the Standard, or on pioneer women in general. From this research, have your child determine what life was like for women of the West during the late 19th century. What were the challenges and rewards? Have your child use the information she found in her research to draw a descriptive portrait that visually conveys the life led by one of these women.

4. Examine the importance of the great rivers and the struggle over water rights.

5. Discuss Mexican settlements and their locations, cultural traditions, attitudes toward slavery, land-grant system, and economies.

6. Describe the Texas War for Independence and the Mexican-American War, including territorial settlements, the aftermath of the wars, and the effects the wars had on the lives of Americans, including Mexican Americans today.

8.9 Students analyze the early and steady attempts to abolish slavery and to realize the ideals of the Declaration of Independence.

1. Describe the leaders of the movement (e.g., John Quincy Adams and his proposed constitutional amendment, John Brown and the armed resistance, Harriet Tubman and the Underground Railroad, Benjamin Franklin, Theodore Weld, William Lloyd Garrison, Frederick Douglass).

Freedom train

Investigate the term "Underground Railroad" with your child and its relationship to the enslavement of blacks in the United States. Ask what the term might mean, picking apart each word and its implications. Does it imply that a train really ran underground? What (and who) made up the actual locomotive for the "railroad"? The National Park Service's "Aboard the Underground Railroad" at http://www.cr.nps.gov/nr/trav el/underground/ is an excellent website that looks at the Underground Railroad, slave trade, and the early abolitionist movement.

2. Discuss the abolition of slavery in early state constitutions.

3. Describe the significance of the Northwest Ordinance in education and in the banning of slavery in new states north of the Ohio River.

4. Discuss the importance of the slavery issue as raised by the annexation of Texas and California's admission to the union as a free state under the Compromise of 1850.

5. Analyze the significance of the States' Rights Doctrine, the Missouri Compromise (1820), the Wilmot Proviso (1846), the Compromise of 1850, Henry Clay's role in the Missouri Compromise and the Compromise of 1850, the Kansas-Nebraska Act (1854), the *Dred Scott v. Sandford* decision (1857), and the Lincoln-Douglas debates (1858).

6. Describe the lives of free blacks and the laws that limited their freedom and economic opportunities.

Early freedom

WWW 📖 *Read about free blacks from revolutionary times to just before the Civil War at http://www.worldbook.com/fun/aajourny/ html/bh113.html, or use reference books from the library. Have your child describe some of the severe challenges most free blacks faced during this time period. What inequities did they experience? Use this activity to introduce the idea of the civil rights movement of the 1960s and the struggle against enduring inequalities.*

8.10 Students analyze the multiple causes, key events, and complex consequences of the Civil War.

1. Compare the conflicting interpretations of state and federal authority as emphasized in the speeches and writings of statesmen such as Daniel Webster and John C. Calhoun.

2. Trace the boundaries constituting the North and the South, the geographical differences between the two regions, and the differences between agrarians and industrialists.

3. Identify the constitutional issues posed by the doctrine of nullification and secession and the earliest origins of that doctrine.

4. Discuss Abraham Lincoln's presidency and his significant writings and speeches and their relationship to the Declaration of Independence, such as his "House Divided" speech (1858), Gettysburg Address (1863), Emancipation Proclamation (1863), and inaugural addresses (1861 and 1865).

Window in time

Have your child read some of Abraham Lincoln's writing and speeches as listed in the Standard, as well as the Declaration of Independence. (Find them using a major Internet search engine or library resources.) Then, have your child imagine being a local newspaper reporter for a southern journal. How will the reporter (your child) respond to Lincoln's words? Make sure your child draws connections between Lincoln's writings and speeches and the Declaration of Independence. Then, have your child take on the role of a northern journalist. Your child's two revised and edited newspaper articles should include correct grammar, spelling, and punctuation as well as convey a keen understanding of how Lincoln's ideas would have been received differently in the North and South.

5. Study the views and lives of leaders (e.g., Ulysses S. Grant, Jefferson Davis, Robert E. Lee) and soldiers on both sides of the war, including those of black soldiers and regiments.

6.   Describe critical developments and events in the war, including the major battles, geographical advantages and obstacles, technological advances, and General Lee's surrender at Appomattox.

7.   Explain how the war affected combatants, civilians, the physical environment, and future warfare.

8.11 Students analyze the character and lasting consequences of Reconstruction.

1.   List the original aims of Reconstruction and describe its effects on the political and social structures of different regions.

Reconstruction I

 www 📖 *Ask your child to devise a definition for the word <u>reconstruction</u>, by breaking the word into its component parts. You can provide a hint: "re" (again) and "construction" (building). Have him apply the definition (rebuilding) to the period in American history just after the Civil War. What events might your child believe would have occurred during Reconstruction, relating to end of slavery and the changes this brought about for the American South? Together, check your child's hypothesis, exploring issues around Reconstruction by using reference books or the Internet. (Information can be found at http://www.worldbook.com/fun/aajourny /html/bho54.html.) Have your child identify some of the gains and serious problems faced by former enslaved black people, as well as the role of the government and people's entrenched attitudes.* 📖

2.   Identify the push-pull factors in the movement of former slaves to the cities in the North and to the West and their differing experiences in those regions (e.g., the experiences of Buffalo Soldiers).

3.   Understand the effects of the Freedmen's Bureau and the restrictions placed on the rights and opportunities of freedmen, including racial segregation and "Jim Crow" laws.

4.   Trace the rise of the Ku Klux Klan and describe the Klan's effects.

5. Understand the Thirteenth, Fourteenth, and Fifteenth Amendments to the Constitution and analyze their connection to Reconstruction.

Reconstruction II

WWW *Have your child review the history of Reconstruction—its advances and problems as outlined in the previous activity. Next, ask your child to read the texts of the 13th, 14th, and 15th Amendments to the Constitution (found online at http://www.ilstu.edu/class/hist136/lectures/13-15amend.html.) After rephrasing them in his own words, have your child describe how these amendments relate to Reconstruction. Discuss how the 14th and 15th Amendments were the basis for minority rights during the 1960s civil rights era.*

8.12 Students analyze the transformation of the American economy and the changing social and political conditions in the United States in response to the Industrial Revolution.

1. Trace patterns of agricultural and industrial development as they relate to climate, use of natural resources, markets, and trade and locate such development on a map.

2. Identify the reasons for the development of federal Indian policy and the wars with American Indians and their relationship to agricultural development and industrialization.

3. Explain how states and the federal government encouraged business expansion through tariffs, banking, land grants, and subsidies.

4. Discuss entrepreneurs, industrialists, and bankers in politics, commerce, and industry (e.g., Andrew Carnegie, John D. Rockefeller, Leland Stanford).

5. Examine the location and effects of urbanization, renewed immigration, and industrialization (e.g., the effects on social fabric of cities, wealth and economic opportunity, the conservation movement).

6. Discuss child labor, working conditions, and laissez-faire policies toward big business and examine the labor movement, including its leaders (e.g., Samuel Gompers), its demand for collective bargaining, and its strikes and protests over labor conditions.

7. Identify the new sources of large-scale immigration and the contributions of immigrants to the building of cities and the economy; explain the ways in which new social and economic patterns encouraged assimilation of newcomers into the mainstream amidst growing cultural diversity; and discuss the new wave of nativism.

8. Identify the characteristics and impact of Grangerism and Populism.

9. Name the significant inventors and their inventions and identify how they improved the quality of life (e.g., Thomas Edison, Alexander Graham Bell, Orville and Wilbur Wright).

New-fangled contraptions

Have your child research the contributions of the inventors mentioned in the Standard. Have your child identify and draw the items each person's invention replaced or improved. For instance, the light bulb replaced oil and gas lamps, and airplanes made long distance travel faster than by horse. Then, ask your child to write a story from the perspective of someone living in the industrial age who experiences one of the inventions for the first time, conveying with correct grammar, spelling, and punctuation, his or her response to this new-fangled contraption and its affect on daily life.